Operating Systems

DeMYSTiFieD®

DeMYSTiFieD® Series

Advanced Statistics Demystified
Algebra Demystified, 2e
Alternative Energy Demystified
ASP.NET 2.0 Demystified
Astronomy Demystified
Biology Demystified
Biophysics Demystified
Biotechnology Demystified
Business Calculus Demystified
Business Math Demystified
Business Statistics Demystified
Calculus Demystified, 2e
Chemistry Demystified
College Algebra Demystified
Data Structures Demystified
Databases Demystified, 2e
Differential Equations Demystified
Digital Electronics Demystified
Earth Science Demystified
Electricity Demystified
Electronics Demystified
Environmental Science Demystified
Everyday Math Demystified
Forensics Demystified
Genetics Demystified
Geometry Demystified
HTML & XHTML Demystified
Java Demystified
JavaScript Demystified
Lean Six Sigma Demystified
Linear Algebra Demystified
Logic Demystified
Macroeconomics Demystified

Math Proofs Demystified
Math Word Problems Demystified
Mathematica Demystified
MATLAB Demystified
Microbiology Demystified
Microeconomics Demystified
Nanotechnology Demystified
OOP Demystified
Operating Systems Demystified
Organic Chemistry Demystified
Pharmacology Demystified
Physics Demystified, 2e
Physiology Demystified
Pre-Algebra Demystified, 2e
Precalculus Demystified
Probability Demystified
Project Management Demystified
Quality Management Demystified
Quantum Mechanics Demystified
Relativity Demystified
Robotics Demystified
Signals and Systems Demystified
SQL Demystified
Statistical Process Control Demystified
Statistics Demystified
Technical Analysis Demystified
Technical Math Demystified
Trigonometry Demystified
UML Demystified
Visual Basic 2005 Demystified
Visual C# 2005 Demystified
Web Design Demystified
XML Demystified

The Demystified Series publishes more than 125 titles in all areas of academic study. For a complete list of titles, please visit www.mhprofessional.com.

Operating Systems
DeMYSTiFieD®

Ann McIver McHoes
Joli Ballew

New York   Chicago   San Francisco   Lisbon   London   Madrid   Mexico City
Milan   New Delhi   San Juan   Seoul   Singapore   Sydney   Toronto

Library of Congress Cataloging-in-Publication Data

McHoes, Ann McIver, 1950-
   Operating systems demystified / Ann McIver McHoes, Joli Ballew.
      p.   cm.
   Includes index.
   ISBN 978-0-07-175226-8 (alk.paper)
1. Operating systems (Computers)   I. Ballew, Joli.   II. Title.
   QA76.76.O63M34   2012
   005.4'3—dc23

                                    2011043863

McGraw-Hill books are available at special quantity discounts to use as premiums and sales
promotions, or for use in corporate training programs. To contact a representative, please
e-mail us at bulksales@mcgraw-hill.com.

Operating Systems DeMYSTiFieD®

1 2 3 4 5 6 7 8 9 0   DOC DOC   1 0 9 8 7 6 5 4 3 2 1

ISBN   978-0-07-175226-8
MHID   0-07-175226-9

Sponsoring Editor Roger Stewart	**Technical Editor** Lisa Kelt	**Composition** Cenveo Publisher Services
Editorial Supervisor Patty Mon	**Copy Editor** Bart Reed	**Illustration** Cenveo Publisher Services
Project Manager Sheena Uprety, Cenveo Publisher Services	**Proofreader** Lisa McCoy **Indexer** Karin Arrigoni	**Art Director, Cover** Jeff Weeks
Acquisitions Coordinator Joya Anthony	**Production Supervisor** Jean Bodeaux	**Cover Illustration** Lance Lekander

Dedicated to Bob Kleinmann, for generously sharing his expertise and love, especially the latter.
—Ann McIver McHoes

For all students, young, old, or in the middle; new, experienced, or simply hobbyists.
May you find this book a welcome addition to whatever goals you're pursuing.
—Joli Ballew

About the Authors

Ann McIver McHoes is author of the award-winning textbook *Understanding Operating Systems*, which has been translated into five languages and adopted at colleges and universities on six continents. She holds a Bachelor of Science in Math and a Master of Science in Information Science, both from the University of Pittsburgh, and currently teaches at Duquesne University. She is a long-time professional technical writer and corporate consultant. Her science advocacy work includes volunteering as a judge for the Pennsylvania Junior Academy of Science (since 1993) and the Pennsylvania Science Bowl. During her free time, Ann enjoys travelling, golfing, and learning about new technology.

Joli Ballew is a best-selling technical author who has written over 40 books, and she has served as a technical editor series editor, and coauthor on countless others. Joli teaches Microsoft certification classes at Brookhaven College in Dallas, Texas, and is the IT Academy Coordinator there as well. Joli also teaches introductory computer classes at other community colleges in the area. In her spare time, Joli enjoys working out at her local gym, spending time with her family and friends, traveling, and serving as butler for her two cats and their pet gerbil, George.

About the Technical Editor

Lisa Kelt is the Information Technology Academic Services Manager at Eastern New Mexico University–Roswell. Additionally, she teaches in the Computer Application Systems and the Computer Information Systems departments. Lisa holds certifications in both Microsoft Windows and Microsoft Office. She has been happily married to her husband James for 28 years, and they have two wonderful grown children, ages 26 and 22.

Contents At A Glance

Contents

Acknowledgments

First and foremost, thanks to Roger Stewart for bringing the authors together, and for bringing this book to our attention. He and his team at McGraw-Hill are terrific, and always seem to find the best talent when it comes to copy editors, technical editors, and layout teams, among others. We both appreciate the opportunity to work with this great group. We'd specifically like to call out Lisa Kelt, our technical editor, who scoured the book for technical accuracy, Joya Anthony, our acquisitions coordinator who kept us on track and on time, and who managed our numerous inquiries and files, and Sheena Uprety, our project manager and final set of eyes from Cenveo Publishing Services, who made sure everything was fit to print.

We'd both like to acknowledge our agent, Neil Salkind, Ph.D., from the Salkind Literary Agency, too. Although he's new to Ann, he has represented Joli for 10 years. He is a great agent and watches out for us both, and he's always around should we need anything from him.

Ann would like to thank Dr. Ida Flynn for her exceptional legacy, and for passing along her love of teaching. Thanks, too, to Bob for his hours of voluntary technical editing and consulting, and to Genevieve and Katherine for their unending encouragement and support. And special thanks to Joli for writing about a third of the book and lending her Windows, networking, and security expertise throughout. It has been a pleasure working with you.

Joli would like to thank various people, too, including her family—Jennifer, Cosmo, Andrew, Dad, and the rest—for well, just being wonderful family members. Joli also thanks her coauthor, Ann McHoes, for patiently and diligently working with her on this project, which took quite a bit of back and forth to complete successfully. Ann has a great deal of knowledge here, and was wonderful to work with.

Introduction

Welcome! Do you want to check under the hood? In these pages you'll learn how operating systems work and how they avoid crashing (most of the time) while juggling many competing requests from their hardware, software, and you.

Would you be surprised to learn that the choices made by operating systems designers, those unsung programmers who labor somewhere in back rooms, have a profound effect on how your computer runs? We'll explore some of those choices, and we believe you'll come to appreciate, as we do, the attempts that designers have made to keep our systems running smoothly in spite of the crushing demands made on them.

Remember that this is a very complex subject and is covered by numerous textbooks. We can't go into much depth in this small space, but our goal is to describe the basics using language that's demystified.

Who Should Read This Book

Whether you're just curious or technically savvy, we invite you to explore the fundamentals of operating system design. For those who are relatively new to the subject, we suggest that you work your way through the book from beginning to end, and if you get to a part that's too complex, move to the next chapter to begin exploring a different aspect of operating systems. Please don't miss the system protection and security chapter—it has tips that everyone can use.

If you're a techie, feel free to target the sections that pique your interest and see how the many parts fit together. If you skip ahead, keep in mind that new terms are defined when they're introduced, often in earlier chapters.

How to Use This Book

The operating system is the computer's chief piece of software, acting as the intermediary between the user and the hardware and software. Remember that the concepts explored in these pages are common to many, if not all, operating systems. For example, every system, no matter how simple or complex, must manage its CPU successfully; therefore, the CPU management concepts explored here apply to many, many operating systems, not just to Microsoft Windows, Mac OS X, or Linux, from which we captured our illustrations and examples.

Chapter Synopsis

Chapter 1 gives an overview of design practices and introduces some of the tradeoffs that programmers take into account when they're creating a new operating system. This chapter also touches on patch management as well as menu-driven and command-driven user interfaces, the part of the operating system that is most likely to be unique.

Chapter 2 studies the boot processes—everything that takes place after you press the power button and before your desktop is loaded and ready to go. It includes the role of boot loaders and firmware (software that's indelibly put on your computer before you buy it).

Chapters 3–5 discuss the critical role of the CPU manager. We begin by exploring the fundamentals of processes and threads, and how the CPU manages them in a simple computing environment. Then we check out several competing CPU allocation schemes and finally look at the challenges of scheduling CPUs without causing system deadlocks or process starvation.

Chapters 6–7 concern the memory manager and how it allows multiple processes and/or threads to share the limited space that's known as main memory or RAM. Chapter 7 explores the concepts of virtual memory and touches on cache memory, as well as two competing page replacement schemes.

Chapter 8 is dedicated to the device manager and its relationship with magnetic, optical, and solid state storage media. Here, we explain the importance of device drivers and buffers. Because computing devices are always swiftly changing, this portion of operating system design is one of the most dynamic.

Chapter 9 explores the role of the file manager and how it stores, retrieves, and modifies data that's held in files of every type—from applications, data files, and even system files. Along the way it explores the requirements for naming files and folders (also known as directories).

Chapter 10 discusses the basics of networking and how operating systems successfully maintain networks of every size. This includes the complications introduced by wireless systems and virtual private networks.

Chapter 11 introduces network routing strategies, conflict resolution, and two Internet protocols. If you're exploring network operating systems, this chapter will provide a helpful primer.

Chapter 12 concludes the book with system protection and security management. In the chapter, you'll learn about intentional and accidental threats and how to protect your system and the data you store on it.

Exercises in each chapter provide hands-on practice using one of several operating systems. Some exercises can be done using Mac OS X (which is based on UNIX) and Linux, though the majority of the exercises require Microsoft Windows. Please let us know which exercises you find most helpful.

The chapter quiz at the conclusion of each chapter is a 10-question test to help reinforce some of the important concepts presented in the preceding pages. For additional practice, we invite you complete the final exam at the back of the book.

How to Contact Us

Please feel free to pass along your comments and suggestions. Your feedback helps us understand your needs and make future editions better. You can reach Ann at mchoesa@duq.edu and Joli at Joli_Ballew@hotmail.com. We look forward to hearing from you.

Part I

Overview

chapter 1

Quick Overview

This chapter introduces the basic concepts that all operating systems share and the many interrelated computer system components that they run. Every operating system must manage its processor, memory, devices, files, networks, and security, and do so in a way that maximizes, if possible, all of its resources. During our tour of the operating system in this chapter, we explore the capabilities and limitations of each part of the computer system and how they all work together—or fail to do so.

CHAPTER OBJECTIVES

In this chapter, you will

- Learn the primary functions of operating systems
- Be able to describe the fundamental differences among the types of operating systems
- Understand how the operating system manages the system's resources
- Learn about patching the operating system to maintaining its integrity

What Is an Operating System?

An operating system is the most important piece of software running on any computer because it manages all of the computer's resources—both hardware (which usually includes, at a minimum, memory, CPU, and storage capacity) and software (including data, applications, and utility programs). An operating system is written by programmers who strive to balance the sometimes-conflicting needs of the computer users and the system's resources that compete for attention.

These conflicts can raise questions, such as the following:

- Which apps should have the highest priority?
- Which files should receive the premium placement on the hard drive to make them the fastest to retrieve?
- What's more important: fast CPU processing or disk access speed?
- Are some users more important than others? Should their waiting time be minimized?
- Who should have authority to make changes to critical databases, files, folders, and even system files?
- Should the computer focus on the installed applications or should it focus on the services running in the background?

These are only a few of the issues that operating systems designers try to balance and the choices they make have lingering effects for all users.

How many operating systems have been written? Thousands. Because this is the chief piece of software, programmers have been writing operating systems for decades. With the mass production of computers, operating systems software became standardized and shipped with each computer product line.

TIP *For an impressive (though usually incomplete) list of operating systems, try an Internet search for "operating systems timeline." Alternatively, narrow your search to a specific system, such as Windows, Linux, Mac OS, UNIX, MS-DOS, BSD, Solaris, Novell, Ubuntu, Minix, HP-UX, Fedora, and so on.*

Types of Operating Systems

Since the early days of computers, operating systems software has been developed in many flavors, depending on the users' needs as well as the resources being managed (CPUs, databases, monitors, laptops, printers, and so on). Some of the most common are mentioned here:

- The *single-user operating systems* date back to the early days of personal computers, and they accommodated only one user (and one task) at a time working on a single computer. Without any access to a network, these operating systems generally managed a single CPU, executed a single process at a time, and worked with a single monitor and only a few peripheral devices that were connected by cables, such as a printer or a modem.

- With the development of *network operating systems* and *distributed operating systems*, computer users could access multiple processes and devices. Access could include multiple CPUs, input/output devices such as printers and scanners (sometimes called *I/O devices*), and wired and wireless connections that even allowed users located in far-off places to perform multiple tasks.

- A *real-time operating system* is one that runs a computing device with urgent time-critical requirements: system performance must be fast and accurate or drastic consequences can occur. An example of a real-time system is the one developed to fly jet aircraft, commonly termed *fly-by-wire* (a 1971 version is shown in Figure 1-1). Within the realm of real-time systems are two subcategories: *hard real-time systems*, which could suffer catastrophic system failure if their strict response deadlines are missed (such as for a jet aircraft), and *soft real-time systems*, which risk substantial performance degradation but not total system failure. Because of their critical nature, real-time operating systems have many fail-safe features.

- *Embedded operating systems* run computers that are housed within other products. Examples of devices that rely on embedded operating systems are too numerous to mention, but they include cars and trucks, remote meters, medical devices, navigators, barcode scanners, ATMs, kiosks, measurement equipment, and handheld games. Traditional operating systems are often too large and might make impossible demands on these devices, which typically have little memory and internal storage capacity. The profound advantage of embedded operating systems is that they can be optimized to match the precise capabilities of the embedded computer and its limited resources.

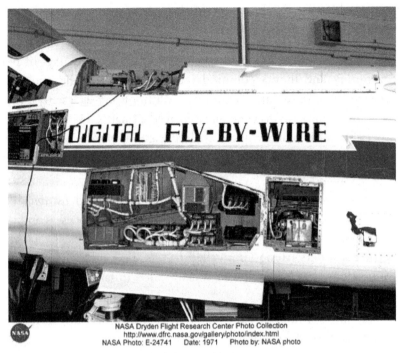

F-8 DFBW on-board electronics

FIGURE 1-1 • NASA digital fly-by-wire system installed in an F-8C aircraft. Credit: NASA, 1971.

TIP   *For details about embedded Linux software, see www.emdebian.org. For information about Microsoft software for embedded devices, visit www .microsoft.com/windowsembedded.*

Manager-in-Chief

The operating system is the chief piece of software and assumes overall responsibility for all of the system's hardware and software. It's the boss. To do its job successfully, the computer system needs to boot up successfully when it's first powered on. To do so, it runs a sequence of instructions, called a *boot sequence*, that's burned onto a chip. These instructions are called *firmware*, and they dictate the proper sequence to get the computer running. The startup sequence often includes self-tests to make sure the computer hardware is working sufficiently, loading device drivers, and initializing specific tasks in turn so that the boot process can proceed. The booting process is critical and complex, as we'll discuss in Chapter 2.

NOTE *Occasionally you may be notified that something has gone wrong and that you can or should restart your system in diagnostic mode (called Safe Mode by Windows or Safe Boot on Macintosh OS X). This is an indication that the booting sequence did not work correctly, causing it to halt prematurely. If you see this message, you have the chance to boot while loading only a limited number of files and drivers, perhaps without access to the Internet. Safe Mode gives you the chance to remove any offending software or hardware. Sometimes, your operating system will repair itself and will reboot successfully thereafter in fully functional mode. Exercise 1-1 details how to Safe Boot a Mac OS X computer and how to start a Windows 7 computer in Safe Mode.*

Exercise 1-1: Start in Safe Mode

To Safe Boot a Mac, follow these steps:

1. If your Mac is powered on, click the Apple logo and click Shut Down.

2. When the computer is completely off, press the power button.

3. Immediately after you hear the startup tone, hold down the SHIFT key until you see the gray Apple icon.

4. To leave Safe Boot mode, restart the computer normally.

To start a Windows 7 computer in Safe Mode, follow these steps:

1. Start with your computer turned off (easiest) or restart it.

2. As the computer starts up, repeatedly tap the F8 key (approximately twice per second, though you might need to try different tapping speeds on your system). Make sure you begin tapping the F8 key well before the Windows logo screen appears. (If you see the logo screen, then Windows has booted normally and you'll need to restart again.)

3. On the screen, use the arrow keys to highlight Safe Mode, and then press ENTER.

4. To leave Safe Mode, restart the computer normally.

One critical part of the boot sequence is loading the *kernel*. As its name implies, this is the most basic part of the operating system, and this is the part that gets the remainder of the operating system loaded into memory so that it can continue the start-up procedures.

Once the operating system is loaded and running correctly, it's ready to take the system's reins and assume its role as boss, with overall responsibility for managing the systems resources: processors, main memory, devices, files and data resources, networks, security, and elements of the user interface.

Management of Processors

With many requests waiting for access to each CPU, the operating system has to decide which processing requests will be honored first, which second, and so on. The smooth allocation of one or more CPUs is essential to the operation of the entire system. The processor manager decides which programs (each program is a collection of *processes*) will run in which order, on each processor, and for how long. Meanwhile, it tracks the status of each process (also called a *task*, or an instance of execution) once it begins running. Some operating systems, such as UNIX, allow *parent processes* to beget *child processes*, all of which must be rigorously managed.

NOTE *Multicore computers are those that have multiple processors, which were once commonly called cores, and now are commonly called CPUs.*

To see how a Windows system manages CPUs and memory, use the Resource Monitor or Task Manager, as shown in Figure 1-2.

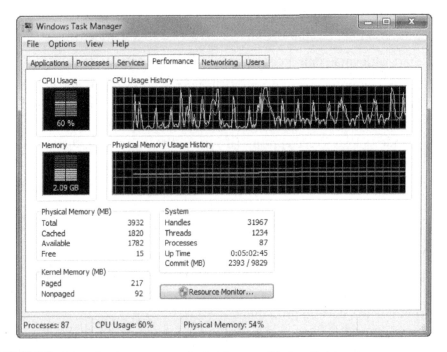

FIGURE 1-2 · CPU and main memory monitoring shown on Windows Task Manager

Process management in a single-user, single-CPU environment is easier; therefore, operating systems dedicated to these simpler systems are much smaller than the large, complex systems that manage multiple users or multiple tasks with access to multiple CPUs. Processor management is the subject of Chapters 3 and 4.

Exercise 1-2: Choose How to Allocate Processor Resources on a Windows 7 Computer

Some decisions that concern computer performance can be made by computer administrators; the operating system doesn't make all the decisions and set all the rules. As an example, it's possible to configure a Windows-based computer to use system resources, such as the CPU, in a specific way—for instance, to focus on background services over installed applications. Follow these steps to see what options are available to a computer administrator on a Windows 7 computer:

1. Left-click the Windows Start button.
2. Right-click Computer.
3. Left-click Properties.
4. Click Advanced System Settings (on the left).
5. Under Performance, click Settings.
6. Click the Advanced tab. As shown in Figure 1-3, you can configure how to allocate the processor's resources (programs vs. background services), as well as how to use the hard drive to manage the temporary data that can't be stored in RAM (random access memory) when RAM is full.
7. From the Visual Effects tab, shown in Figure 1-4, you can also increase performance by disabling specific visual features, although the performance increase is often not noticeable.

Management of Main Memory

Main memory (also called *RAM*) is the place where computing code, data, apps, device instructions, file locations, and many other details are temporarily stored so that the system runs smoothly. However, main memory is limited in size, so everything stored there is stored only temporarily, and as soon as an operation finishes and no longer needs its memory space, it is allocated to the next process. The operating system repeats this cycle over and over again, allocating memory space to incoming processes and later deallocating that space.

FIGURE 1-3 · Choose how the CPU should be prioritized for the best performance possible.

TIP *In computing vernacular, the term virtual refers to something that does not exist physically, but appears to exist. Hence, the virtual machine, virtual memory, virtual world, virtual desktop, and so on, are not tangible things, but they can appear to be.*

Virtual memory is a technique that temporarily uses a portion of the hard drive (or other secondary storage, such as a flash drive) to give the illusion that there is much more memory capacity than there actually is. With this significant innovation, programs that are massive in size can be run, even though tangible main memory may be limited to, say, one gigabyte (1GB) or less. Memory management is discussed in detail in Chapters 6 and 7.

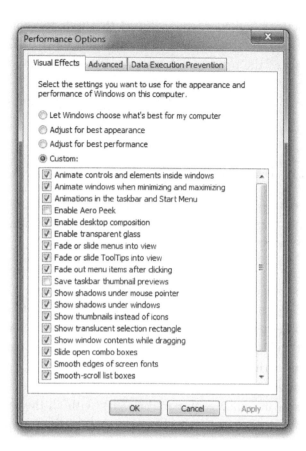

FIGURE 1-4 · You can let Windows choose what's best for your computer, or adjust it manually for best appearance or best performance.

NOTE   *Newer Windows operating systems (including Vista and Windows 7) offer a feature called Ready Boost that enables you to use a compatible USB flash drive to store temporary data, just as if it was a paging file on a hard drive. Ready Boost is a much faster way to access temporary data versus accessing it from the hard drive, and it increases performance noticeably.*

Management of Devices

The constant introduction of new devices in the marketplace makes managing them one of the most dynamic areas of operating systems design. That's because each device connected to the computer (monitor, keyboard, mouse, printer, camera, hard drive, CD/DVD, scanner, port, and so on) has its own specific instructions (called a *device driver*) that tells the computer how to manipulate that piece of hardware. The device manager works closely with every other part of the operating system to allow a user to have access to a device, use it successfully, and then give up access.

Still Struggling

For lots more detail about how specific hardware and software works, visit http://electronics.howstuffworks.com and search for "operating systems" or the computer component of your choice.

The device manager must know the availability (or lack of it) of every piece of hardware that's connected to the system, know its ability to meet incoming requests, and whether or not it can be shared among users. Some devices can be allocated to only one process at a time; these are called *dedicated devices*. One example is a printer, which is allocated to only one user's pages at a time, because if it was shared by several users, it might print pages in a random order (maybe the order in which each page arrived), with all the pages for all the users intermingled. The result would be a substantial amount of sorting as everyone searches through each page in the pile.

NOTE   *Before a device can be used, it must be allocated to that user's process by the device manager. Once allocated, it remains available to that process until the device manager deallocates it. If the process wants to use that device again later, it must wait until it has been allocated to the device.*

To manage these devices—both dedicated and shared—the device manager tracks each device and its status, allocates it when appropriate, and deallocates it later. A device can be deallocated for any number of reasons, including when an operational failure has occurred (such as when a game controller malfunctions), a system interrupts access because someone with higher priority needs the device, or the process has run to completion and no longer needs the device. The complex interaction of system requests, especially in a networked environment with many combinations of devices and user demands, requires constant and tight control by this part of the operating system.

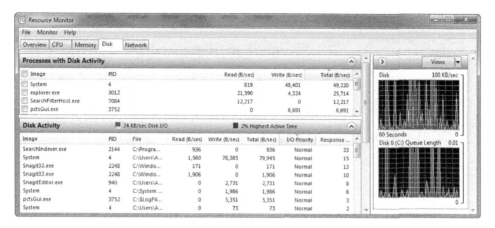

FIGURE 1-5 • Disk management as seen on Windows Resource Monitor

Many operating systems offer device-monitoring tools, such as the one shown in Figure 1-5, so you can see how devices are behaving. Device management is the subject of Chapter 8.

NOTE   *Vaporware is the name given to a device or technology that has been announced, often with much fanfare, yet never released and never canceled. The term is generally used in a derogatory manner. Each year, Wired Magazine announces Vaporware Awards to be given to its "roundup of the tech industry's biggest, brashest and most baffling unfulfilled promises." For the latest award recipients, check out www.wired.com.*

Management of Files

A variety of files populate a computer system, and each one has a unique name and location on a disk, flash drive, or other secondary storage device (as shown in Figure 1-6). The file management portion of the operating system manages the creation, modification, deletion, and access control for every file on the system, including the files that make up the operating system itself. It also manages the formation of directories to hold groups of files and the properties of each directory. And it works in close collaboration with the device manager every time files are written to secondary storage and retrieved.

Briefly, the file manager's job is to monitor the physical disk location of each file, know how each file is broken into fragments (if necessary), track which

FIGURE 1-6 • Typical list of folders and files on a Macintosh running OS X

users have access to each file (and what kind of access they have), and identify which files are ready for deletion. If the hard drive is *compacted* or *defragmented*, the file manager also keeps track of the location where each file now resides.

This is a tall order. And while doing it, the file manager must strictly adhere to the operating system designers' policies, which might dictate properties such as the following:

- The files that are most important or most frequently used
- The files that should be fastest to access
- The files that cannot be changed under any circumstances

We'll discuss the file manager in more detail in Chapter 9.

Management of Networks

With the introduction of networking capabilities (including extensive accessibility offered via the Internet), operating systems assumed the tasks required to manage the sometimes-vast number of resources available to computer users. To do so, the network manager monitors numerous network details

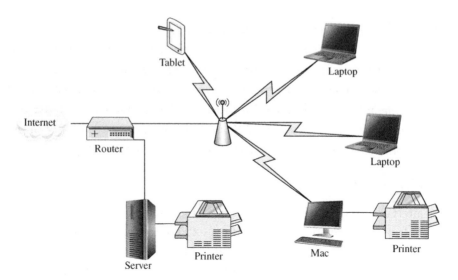

FIGURE 1-7 · Example of a small network with multiple resources

(including its size, makeup, hardware connections, software resources, file inventories, and data transmissions). This complex responsibility is one reason that networking operating systems are often much larger and more complex than those for devices that are not networked.

By directing the actions of each piece of hardware (CPU, devices, monitors, ports) and software (some shared, some not), as demonstrated in its simplest form in Figure 1-7, the network manager performs an intricate balancing act.

How big are networks? They can be small, such as a room where a game console communicates wirelessly to the terminal, or as large as the Internet, which reaches every part of the globe. Chapters 10 and 11 are devoted to network management.

Management of Security

Who gets to access which system resources? Can every user open the database that holds customer credit card numbers? Is the system firewall properly restricting access? Are the files that make up the operating system itself being monitored for unauthorized alterations? These questions offer a small glimpse to the world of system security, which requires careful management of user access to both hardware and software. Details about system protection and security management can be found in Chapters 12 and 13.

TIP   *The group known as hackers has traditionally included everyone who enjoys creatively manipulating software to get it to perform exceptional tricks. Many innovators are proud to be called hackers. In recent years, this group of programmers has been separated into two groups white-hat hackers (those performing their manipulations for the good of society) and black-hat hackers (those with malicious intentions). Keep in mind, though, that one's intentions are not always clear, and sometimes it's difficult to tell who belongs in which group.*

User Interface

The interface is the software that the user manipulates, and the options often vary widely from one operating system to the next. For example, a typical Macintosh interface looks quite different from the screen on the handheld scanner used by a letter carrier to confirm a package delivery. The two primary types of interfaces are the menu-driven window (often termed a *graphical user interface*, or *GUI*), demonstrated in Figure 1-8, and the command-driven terminal screen, shown in Figure 1-9. Some operating systems support both menus and commands.

Each user interface is carefully designed to accommodate the specific needs of the people who are expected to use it. For example, a command-driven system is typically designed for people who are very knowledgeable about the system's capabilities, fluent in the context and spelling of commands (because misspelled commands never work), comfortable typing in precise commands, and patient with the strict requirements of creating and executing them. Remember, the spelling of each command must be exact. Table 1-1 lists four operating systems and their user interface options.

FIGURE 1-8 · Example of a menu-driven interface from Ubuntu Linux

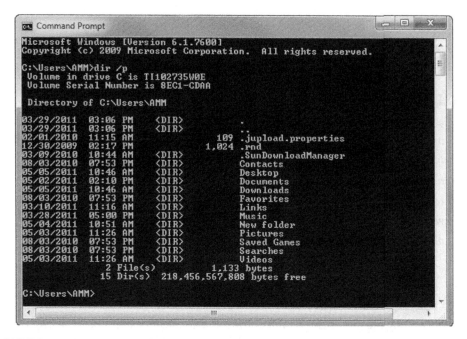

FIGURE 1-9 · Command prompt display available from Windows

These users often have some programming skills and know how to combine commands and/or options into a single command to quickly perform complex tasks, which might take many mouse clicks if they were using only menu commands.

On the other hand, the many computer users who are more comfortable clicking a mouse or touching a screen often prefer menu systems because they are given lists of acceptable options from which to choose. The choices offered are finite, and it's relatively easy to undo any mistakes. Be aware, though, that

TABLE 1-1 Comparison of User Interfaces for Several Operating Systems

Operating System	Default Interface	Optional Interface
Windows	Menu driven	Command Prompt is typically accessible from the Accessories menu.
Ubuntu Linux	Menu driven	Terminal window is accessible from the Accessories menu.
Mac OS X	Menu driven	UNIX command window is accessible from the Terminal application.
BSD UNIX	Command driven	Menu-driven interfaces are available for installation.

menus are usually not comprehensive, so these systems typically do not offer an operating system's full set of features. Instead, menus specialize in making it easy to find the most popular features and execute them quickly and easily.

TIP *Keyboard shortcuts are similar to command lines and allow anyone to quickly issue an order by simply using a quick combination of two keys. For example, in many Windows and Linux applications, the combination of CTRL and C (that is, holding down the CTRL key while pressing the C key, usually written as "CTRL-C") is a shortcut to copy the highlighted item to the clipboard. Similarly, CTRL-V is used to paste, and CTRL-P is used to print. Likewise, these shortcuts on a Macintosh are written as COMMAND-C, COMMAND-V, and COMMAND-P, respectively. These shortcuts, and several others, work consistently in many software packages.*

What's in a Name?

How many meanings can a prefix have? In most science literature, the prefix "kilo-" is an abbreviation that means 1,000; thus, a kilometer is 1,000 meters, and a kilowatt is 1,000 watts. However, in computer science, the industry has assigned a slightly different value to certain terms that begin with the same prefix, depending on the item being described.

For example, when describing the size of a memory chip, disk, DVD, or camera card, one might use the term *kilobyte* (often abbreviated KB) for storage capacity—but this can be misleading because it does not indicate 1,000 bytes. Instead, it represents exactly 1,024 bytes! Likewise, a *gigabyte* (GB) does not indicate 1,000,000,000 bytes of storage but instead signifies precisely 1,073,741,824 bytes, as shown in Table 1-2.

TABLE 1-2 Unit Conversions for Storage Devices

Name	Power of Two	Number of Bytes	Equals
Byte (B)	2^0	1 (8 bits)	1 byte
Kilobyte (KB)	2^{10}	1,024	1,024 bytes
Megabyte (MB)	2^{20}	1,048,576	1,024KB
Gigabyte (GB)	2^{30}	1,073,741,824	1,024MB
Terabyte (TB)	2^{40}	1,099,511,627,776	1,024GB
Petabyte (PB)	2^{50}	1,125,899,906,842,624	1,024TB
Exabyte (EB)	2^{60}	1,152,921,504,606,846,976	1,024PB
Zettabyte (ZB)	2^{70}	1,180,591,620,717,411,303,424	1,024EB

However, this nomenclature does not apply when describing the speed of data communications, which relies instead on the traditional meaning of these prefixes. Therefore, a transmission that is sent at 1,000 bits per second is written as 1 Kbps (kilobits per second). (Remember, a byte is 8 bits.) Likewise, a transmission moving at 1,000,000 bits per second is written as 1 Mbps. For transmission speed, the industry uses the nomenclature found in Table 1-3.

NOTE   *The different uses of these prefixes in Tables 1-2 and 1-3 are due to the former being based on powers of two (such as two to the tenth power, or 2^{10}) and the latter being based on powers of ten (such as ten to the third power, or 10^3).*

TABLE 1-3   Units for Transmission Speed

Name	Power of Ten	Number of Bits
Bit	10^0	1
Kilobits per second (Kbps)	10^3	1,000
Megabits per second (Mbps)	10^6	1,000,000
Gigabits per second (Gbps)	10^9	1,000,000,000
Terabits per second (Tbps)	10^{12}	1,000,000,000,000

Be careful not to confuse *bits per second* with *bytes per second* because 1 byte equals 8 bits. To reduce the chance for error, computer science literature generally describes transmission speeds only using bits per second (bps) with a lowercase *b*.

Historical Glimpse of Operating Systems

The first operating systems were written for individual computers, which often had vacuum tubes and their own locked, air-conditioned rooms. In those days, computing devices were oversized and underpowered. Then-chairman of IBM, Thomas J. Watson (1874–1956) was said to have remarked, "I think there is a world market for maybe five computers."

At the time, user programs and data were submitted one at a time, and the next user's program could not begin until the previous program was finished (either by ending successfully or by being stopped because of a fatal error).

A programmer would write customized programs for each computer to allow it to load data and programs into memory, use each printer, operate each video monitor, and deallocate the resources when a user's program ended. Much has changed since then.

A few operating systems are listed in Table 1-4 with their approximate date of release.

TABLE 1-4 Release Information for Some Key Operating Systems

Operating System	Company	Approximate Date	Remarks
OS/PCP	IBM	1964	A single-task operating system written to run on the IBM 360 computer.
UNIX	—	1969	Original version written by Ken Thompson.
UNIX	AT&T	1971	Written to run on the DEC PDP–11 computer.
VM	Digital Equipment (DEC)	1973	Written to support IBM's Virtual Machine concept and the IBM 370 computer.
MS–DOS	Microsoft	1981	Created to run the first IBM PC computers.
Mac OS 1	Apple	1984	Proprietary OS written for the Macintosh that popularized the GUI and mouse.
Linux	—	1991	Original version written by Linus Torvalds.
Solaris	Sun Microsystems	1994	Based on UNIX and written to operate Sun workstations.
Windows 95	Microsoft	1995	First stand–alone Windows operating system for non–networked computers. (Previous Windows versions required MS–DOS.)
Linux 3.0	Red Hat	1996	Supported the Digital Alpha computing platform.
OpenVMS Alpha 7	Digital Equipment (DEC)	1997	Written for very large memory applications on the Alpha system.
Windows 98	Microsoft	1998	Written for 32–bit home/office computers.
Mac OS X	Apple	2001	Based on UNIX and written for Macintosh computers.
Ubuntu 4	Canonical	2004	The first release of Ubuntu Linux.
Windows Server 2008	Microsoft	2008	Based on Windows NT and written for servers.
Chrome OS	Google	2009	Based on Ubuntu Linux and written for web-accessible devices.
Windows 7	Microsoft	2009	Written for 64–bit home/office computers.

Updates and Patch Management

When should operating systems software be updated? What if a vulnerability has been exposed that needs to be fixed (patched)?

Even if your software was well secured when it was first installed, chances are that in the meantime something has happened that requires you to update it with a *software patch*. In general, there are three reasons why your software may need to be updated: to ensure compliance with constantly evolving legal requirements (perhaps for privacy or data security), to keep it running at the highest efficiency level possible (which includes fixing programming code that isn't working correctly), and to keep the system secure from hackers attempting to exploit a security breach.

Unlike other software, after the operating system is updated, it's not uncommon to receive a message saying that your system needs to be restarted. That's because programming code has to be halted to revise it. Therefore, to revise part of the operating system, the part being repaired must be stopped, and the only way to get it restarted is to reboot the computer with the new and improved operating system software.

Patches are created to address a variety of system problems that often vary in urgency. The most urgent patches are created to correct a critical flaw (such as a known opening for a security breach), while less important updates might repair a portion of a device driver so a printer can work more efficiently. Software companies continuously create patches but instead of issuing them daily, the less urgent updates are combined and released weekly or monthly. However, if the need is urgent, a patch is usually released as soon as it has been written and tested.

When there are numerous updates, they're released as a new a *service pack* or a new *version*, with a new version number. Therefore, Ubuntu Linux version 11.10 is the new and improved software based on version 11.04, both released in 2011.

Updates can range from critical (which should be applied as soon as possible) to recommended or optional, and your system can be updated accordingly. Those who administer systems generally adhere to a regular patching cycle, such as nightly for critical updates (so the system remains available during the business day), weekly for recommended patches, and monthly for optional material. Remember, every time an urgent patch is announced, it's also sent to system attackers who can take advantage of the vulnerability to intrude into systems that have not yet been patched and protected. It's worthwhile to keep your system up to date. In fact, we highly recommend it.

Exercise 1-3: Manually Check for Updates on a Windows 7 Computer

Your Windows computer is likely configured to get critical updates automatically and install them. However, optional updates aren't generally installed automatically. It's best to check for updates manually every now and then to see if anything new should be installed.

To check for updates on a Windows 7 computer, follow these steps:

1. Click the Windows Start button | All Programs | Windows Update, as shown in Figure 1-10.
2. Click Check for Updates.
3. Click the update notifications. In the example shown in Figure 1-11, this would mean clicking "2 important updates are available" and then "19 optional updates are available."
4. Select and install updates, as desired, by clicking the box next to each one.
5. When you have selected all your updates, click OK to install them.

FIGURE 1-10 · Finding Windows Update

FIGURE 1-11 · Checking for updates on any Windows-based computer

What to Expect in This Book

It is impossible to thoroughly describe the vast subject of operating systems in a small book such as this, but we will give you a good introduction to the basics and leave you with a firm background from which you can explore the subject. For more details about any topic mentioned in these pages, we refer you to the many available resources in print and on the Web. And remember, this is a subject that evolves continuously. Computer science has come a long way, but still has a very long way to go.

Still Struggling

Lots of excellent supplemental information and practical research are available from two well-known industry associations: the Association for Computing Machinery (www.acm.org) and the IEEE Computer Society (www.computer.org). Student memberships may be available. Contact each organization for details and resources.

Summary

This chapter introduced the fundamental elements of most operating systems—the way they manage CPUs, main memory, devices, files, networks, and security. We also touched on the fundamentals of the user interface, which is often the most distinctive part of an operating system. Remember, though, that in these few pages we have presented a mere overview of this subject. As you can imagine, there's an enormous level of detail below the surface.

In the next chapter, you'll see what happens when you first turn on the computer and learn about the intricacies involved as the operating system gets itself up and running.

QUIZ

Choose the correct response to each of the multiple-choice questions. Note that there may be more than one correct response to each question.

1. **How many operating systems have been written since 1960?**
   A. 4
   B. 37
   C. Hundreds
   D. Thousands

2. **Of the operating systems discussed in this chapter, which one is most likely to be used to operate a bank's computer system?**
   A. Embedded
   B. Distributed
   C. Real time
   D. Single user

3. **If you're notified that your system is starting in Safe Mode or performing a Safe Boot, which of the following applies?**
   A. The operating system needs to be patched.
   B. The normal boot sequence halted prematurely.
   C. The operating system is operating unsafely.
   D. The operating system is out of date.

4. **Which of these devices might hold an embedded computer system?**
   A. Race car
   B. Parachute
   C. Cable TV receiver
   D. Antique train set

5. **A single-user operating system is typically charged with managing which of these resources?**
   A. User authorization
   B. Hard drives
   C. Applications
   D. Main memory space

6. **GUI stands for what kind of interface?**
   A. Menu-driven user interface
   B. Command-driven user interface
   C. Line-by-line user interface
   D. Interface for a real-time operating system

7. **When you buy an operating system, what is in the box?**
   A. Firmware
   B. Hardware
   C. Software
   D. Vaporware

8. **What is the name given to a system intruder with malicious intentions?**
   A. White-hat hacker
   B. Black-hat hacker
   C. Neither
   D. Can't tell from this description

9. **What is the most important reason for robust system security?**
   A. To protect the job of the security officer
   B. To protect the system's owners
   C. To protect the system's data
   D. To protect the system's hardware

10. **Why might a reboot be required after the operating system is patched?**
    A. The patched file cannot be restarted without the entire system being restarted.
    B. The patched file isn't working.
    C. To aggravate the user.
    D. The patching isn't complete until the system is restarted.

chapter 2

Understanding Boot Processes

This chapter introduces the processes that occur in a computer after you press the power button but before you gain access to any type of welcome or login screen. These processes are called, collectively, the *boot process*. The exact process that occurs differs depending on the operating system, computer manufacturer, and installed peripherals and hardware, but generalized processes, such as initializing firmware and locating and testing required hardware, apply to all of them.

CHAPTER OBJECTIVES

In this chapter, you will

- Understand the basic boot process
- Learn about boot loaders
- Understand how the operating system is loaded for various operating systems

In this chapter you'll learn about the general boot processes that most Windows-based computers go through. You'll learn about what happens when you press the power button, various hardware tests and initiations, and how the Windows operating system is eventually loaded from the hard drive. How the operating system loads is unique to the operating system, just as how hardware initializes is unique to the internal hardware that comprises the computer. Although we'll focus on the latest Windows operating systems, including Windows Server 2008 boot processes here, we'll also take a brief look at the boot processes for earlier Windows, Macintosh (UNIX), and Linux machines.

The Basic Boot Sequence

All computers go through very similar boot processes initially, whether they're Windows based, Macintosh based, or Linux based. For example, all computers have to be powered up, be able to access initial program code to invoke the initial startup tasks, have some sort of self-test that determines whether the hardware inside the computer is working properly, and then load drivers and services, to name a few. In order for any computer to boot up successfully (initialize), each process has to complete enough for the boot process to move forward, and all required hardware must be in good working order.

> A driver *is computer code that enables a specific piece of hardware to communicate with the computer. Every piece of hardware has a driver. You'll learn more about drivers later in this chapter.*

Most of the bootup tasks that occur are hidden behind a logoed or black splash screen. This makes it rather difficult to get a handle on what's actually happening. Some tasks can't be offered up graphically anyway, though (for instance, the transfer of data to and from the various internal computer parts). However, you can enable *boot logging* to review what happens during the process. In Exercise 2-1, you'll enable boot logging on a Windows 7 PC. This will enable you to at least see a little of what happens during the boot process (after the boot process completes).

NOTE *The term "booting" originated from the phrase "pick (or pull) yourself up by your bootstraps." It means to self-start. The phrase was inspired by the story of Baron Munchhausen, who supposedly pulled himself out of a swamp by the straps on his boots (a seemingly impossible task).*

You can also interrupt or modify the boot process by pressing an appropriate key on the keyboard. When you interrupt the boot process (by pressing F8 on a PC, for instance), you gain access to *advanced boot options* such as Safe Mode and Last Known Good, among others. You may have seen these choices before, when troubleshooting a computer that would not boot properly. Figure 2-1 shows this screen for a Windows 7 computer.

A service is an application type that runs in the background and does not offer a user interface. Services provide core operating system features, such as event logging, printing, and error reporting.

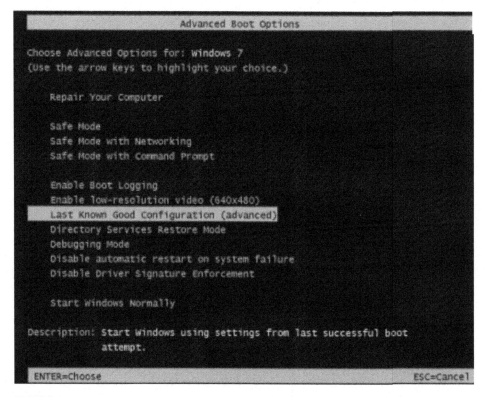

FIGURE 2-1 • Press F8 on a Windows computer to interrupt the boot process. Note the option to enable boot logging.

Exercise 2-1: Enable Boot Logging on a Windows 7 Computer

If you'd like to see more of the boot process, you can enable boot logging on a Windows computer. The boot logging text is recorded in the Ntbtlog.txt file in the %SystemRoot% folder. To enable boot logging, follow these steps:

1. During the boot process, press the F8 key several times.

2. At the Advanced Boot Options screen, use the arrow keys to select Enable Boot Logging. You can see this option in Figure 2-1.

3. Press ENTER to choose this option.

4. After the boot process completes, review the items in C:\Ntbtlog.

NOTE *If you've ever seen an error (after pressing the power button but before you could get to a login screen) that says an operating system or keyboard couldn't be found, you've encountered an error in the boot process.*

Power and BIOS

The boot process begins when you press the power button. The first thing that initializes when you press the power button is the power supply. This is an actual piece of hardware. In a desktop computer, the power supply is fastened to the computer case inside the tower. It's fairly large, perhaps 4- to 5-inches square. With laptops and netbooks, there's an external power adapter to connect, and, of course, you can run the device on a charged battery. Whatever the case, you need something to supply the hardware components with the electricity they need to function. Once the power supply has initiated (and has encountered no errors), it sends a signal to the motherboard and processor (often called the *central processing unit*, or *CPU*) that the power is ready and stable.

Once the power supply is available and ready, the computer must be able to access commands and code that tell it what to do next. This information is often stored on a read-only memory chip (called a *ROM chip*). This means that the data is not stored on the hard drive. Because the bootup instructions are always available (like a tattoo you might have permanently drawn on your skin), the computer can access them even if the hard drive fails.

The information the computer finds in the read-only memory is often called the *BIOS*, or *Basic Input/Output System*. (If computers don't access BIOS, they access something similar.) The BIOS contains instructions for starting the boot process. The instructions stored on these types of computer chips are called *firmware.*

Linux and Mac machines also use BIOS, but they may call it something different. When working with these kinds of computers, keep your eyes open for terms such as BootROM, OpenFirmware, OpenBIOS, and others. Beyond BIOS, the Extensible Firmware Interface (EFI) has established itself as a replacement for older BIOS firmware. EFI was developed in 2005, and has a predecessor, UEFI. You'll see EFI in newer computer models and on Intel-based Macs.

Still Struggling

The instructions on read-only memory chips are referred to generically as *firmware* because the data stored there is fixed (or "firm").

Some of the first things the BIOS does is check the CMOS (complementary metal oxide semiconductor) setup for custom settings, load interrupt handlers and device drivers, and initialize registers and work with power management, all detailed next.

Exercise 2-2: Locate Your Computer's BIOS Manufacturer on a Windows 7 Computer

Reboot a Windows 7 computer. During the boot process, watch the screen and read what appears. Almost all computers offer information about the BIOS. Look for the name of the BIOS manufacturer. After that screen, watch for something that says "Press F12 to Enter the BIOS" or something like it. This describes the keystroke(s) required to enter the BIOS setup screen. Often, this is DEL or F12 (see Figure 2-2).

<DEL>:BIOS Setup

FIGURE 2-2 · When the computer boots, watch for instructions on what to press to enter the BIOS screen and make changes when necessary.

CMOS, Interrupt Handlers, and Device Drivers

There is another chip inside the computer that contains information besides the read-only memory chip. The *CMOS* (complementary metal-oxide semiconductor) *chip* keeps the system time and date as well as information about the hardware installed in the computer, and other information that is dependent on the computer and its manufacturer. Because the CMOS chip is not powered by the power supply (the power supply isn't supplying power when the computer is turned off) and must be powered by something all the time (to keep the time and date), it is kept alive by a CMOS battery. This battery runs even when the computer is turned off, in hibernation, or asleep. If a computer application, website, process, or service can't find the correct time, it may not function properly (if at all). Time is very important—thus the need for the always-on clock found on the CMOS chip.

Interrupt handlers are small pieces of computer code that act as translators between the user or hardware and the OS. The handler is what tells the CPU what the user or hardware wants, and passes the word on to the operating system. Interrupt handlers must be loaded early on so that if, say, the user presses a specific keyboard key during the boot process, the proper signal is sent from the keyboard to the keyboard interrupt handler and appropriate actions are taken. You'll learn more about interrupt handlers in Chapter 7.

Device drivers, mentioned briefly earlier, are small pieces of computer code that act as communicators between the hardware and the OS. It's the device driver that allows the OS to send instructions to the hardware, and the hardware to communicate any messages back to the OS. (You may be familiar with printer drivers already; these drivers enable a computer to send data to a printer and have the printer respond with output.) Drivers are also responsible for transmitting messages from a device back to the computer or user (for instance, to state that a print job is complete or that errors have occurred). Device drivers are required of hardware you may not think about, though. Keyboards, mice, hard drives, and even network, graphics, and video adapters have drivers.

Still Struggling

A hard drive's device driver must be initialized before operating system files can be pulled from it. Thus, device drivers must be loaded near the beginning of the boot process.

In this same general time during the boot process, registers and power management options are initialized. A *register* is a high-speed storage area in the CPU. Data must be displayed in a register before it can be used. The number of registers a CPU has helps determine the CPU type, among other things. A 32-bit CPU has registers that are 32 bits wide. (Each CPU instruction can manipulate 32 bits of data at a time.)

Any *power management* data that is available is also read and initialized at this time. If the computer hardware supports power saving modes or any of the available quick boot methods, the BIOS may be able to bypass part of the standard POST procedure (detailed next). For a cold boot, the entire boot process must be executed; for a soft boot, the BIOS may be able to skip certain processes or load them from a preloaded system device table, if applicable.

POST

BIOS and other firmware options include instructions for starting the *Power-On Self-Test*, or *POST*. Basically, POST is a test to see if the hardware necessary for a successful boot is available and working properly. During POST, the computer is scanned for a working keyboard, random access memory (often referred to as RAM or simply "main memory"), disk drives, and other required hardware. Partitions (sections) on disk drives are also discovered. (Figure 2-3 shows how one of our Windows 7 computer's hard drive is partitioned.) Additionally, file

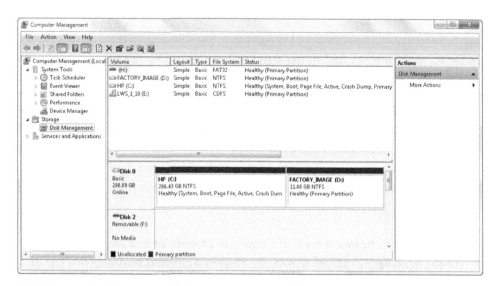

FIGURE 2-3 · You can view the partitions on a Windows 7 computer using the Computer Management tool.

system drivers are set up so that those drives can be accessed. POST checks several additional items, including the integrity of the BIOS, the size of the main memory (RAM), and system buses and devices.

Still Struggling

Partitions are often created to separate data. A computer may store system files on a factory image partition (perhaps D:) while offering a larger partition (perhaps C:) for the user's files. Additionally, some computer hard drives are separated even further, into E:, F:, and more.

POST is responsible for all kinds of tasks, including the following:

- Verifying the integrity of the primary BIOS
- Locating and verifying main memory and determining its size
- Locating and starting system buses and system devices
- Allowing other BIOSes to start, as required (these may be on video or graphics cards, for instance)
- Giving the user the option to access the BIOS's system configuration page
- Locating boot devices and finding one that has boot files
- Completing any additional setup tasks required by the operating system

Although this might seem like a lot for POST to achieve without errors, most of the time the POST goes well. However, if an error is detected during POST, the BIOS instructs the computer to produce an error-coded message regarding it. Error codes come in the form of beeps, but you may also see white text on a black or gray screen. You can research BIOS and POST beep codes in various websites on the Internet; just perform a search for your particular BIOS and the exact beep code or message.

NOTE *Most of the time a successful boot is accompanied by a single beep. More beeps, or no beep at all, could mean that there's a problem. If so, your first line of defense is to find out what those beeps signify, which you can do with a quick*

Internet search (provided you know what BIOS you're using). Often it's a problem with main memory, a missing keyboard, or some other system problem.

After POST

After POST, various other processes occur, many of which involve initializing even more hardware and software. The hardware that's initialized is dependent on the hardware available from the computer manufacturer and the hardware you've attached. After POST, services are loaded as well. An operating system can only run if certain services are initialized. Services you may be familiar with include the Plug and Play Service, the Error Reporting Service, the Networking Service, and the Event Logging Service. Once the boot procedures are complete, you can view running services in Windows under Task Manager, as shown in Figure 2-4.

FIGURE 2-4 · Lots of services run in the background on a Windows computer.

TIP   *You can prevent some services (and device drivers) from loading the next time you boot by using the System Configuration tool. The command is msconfig.exe. There, you can chose Diagnostic Startup or Selective Startup to tell Windows what to load and what not to load. Figure 2-5 shows this tool. (You can also press F8 during the boot process and choose Safe Mode to boot the computer with minimal drivers and services.) To do it yourself, see Exercise 1-3 in Chapter 1.*

During this same time, resources for DMA channels and IRQs are assigned. DMA stands for *direct memory access,* and it's what enables data to be transferred from main memory to a device without passing through the CPU. Computers that use direct memory access can transfer data much more quickly than those that can't. You'll learn more about DMA in Chapter 6. IRQs are interrupt request lines. These lines can be used by devices to send interrupt signals to the CPU. Again, this enables hardware to communicate better with other components and offer better performance. You'll learn more about IRQs in Chapter 8.

After all these tasks have completed, the BIOS looks for a drive to boot from. Finally! The drive can be a floppy drive (yes, floppy drives still exist on older machines), CD/DVD drive, a hard drive, and in some instances, a network drive.

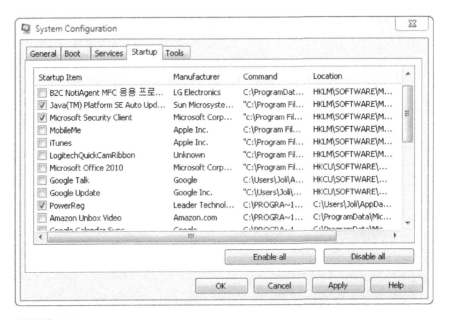

FIGURE 2-5 · Use the System Configuration tool on a Windows-based computer to limit what's loaded during the boot process.

If it finds a drive with boot information on it, the BIOS starts the process of loading the operating system. Once the operating system is loaded and the user can interact with it, the boot process is complete.

NOTE   *If the firmware finds a network drive and is configured to boot from it, it will try. This type of boot is often used to install a computer from a remote location and not generally the way a computer boots every time it's turned on.*

The process of loading the operating system is quite complex, and the rest of this chapter is devoted to it. What's important to know now is everything that has happened so far has happened so that a hard drive can be found and an operating system can be loaded. How the operating system loads from that point on is unique to the operating system.

NOTE   *If no hard drive is found, or if the firmware finds a bootable CD/DVD before it finds the hard drive, the computer may offer the option to boot using it. If you opt for it, the computer can use the boot files it finds on the CD/DVD to start the computer. Most often, the files it finds on an optical disc are used to install or repair the operating system.*

Summary of the Boot Process

Regarding the generic boot process, when broken down broadly, it goes like this:

1. Power to the computer is enabled and the boot loader initializes.
2. Power-On Self-Test (POST) occurs.
3. Other BIOSes are initialized, as applicable.
4. User is prompted to press a specific key to enter the BIOS screen, if desired.
5. A brief memory test is performed and various parameters are set.
6. Plug and Play devices are initialized.
7. Resources for DMA channels and IRQs are assigned.
8. Boot devices are located and initialized.

Figure 2-6 offers a graphical representation of this.

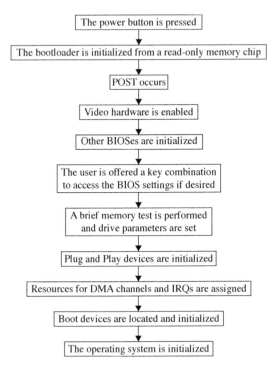

The power button is pressed

The bootloader is initialized from a read-only memory chip

POST occurs

Video hardware is enabled

Other BIOSes are initialized

The user is offered a key combination
to access the BIOS settings if desired

A brief memory test is performed
and drive parameters are set

Plug and Play devices are initialized

Resources for DMA channels and IRQs are assigned

Boot devices are located and initialized

The operating system is initialized

FIGURE 2-6 · The boot process always occurs in a
specific order, although the exact sequence depends on
the computer, BIOS, and hardware manufacturers.

Learn More about Boot Loaders

The boot loader's main function is to load other data and programs into main memory, where they can be read, executed, and swapped out for more information so that, eventually, the operating system can be loaded. Often, multiple-stage boot loaders are used. With multiple boot loaders, several programs and sets of instructions can be loaded one after another, each of increasing complexity, in a process known as *chain loading*, until all the required code is loaded. This is necessary because there are space limitations on read-only memory (also known as RAM or main memory), and everything can't be loaded at once. Therefore, the data needed must be loaded, swapped out to main memory, used from main memory, and then reloaded until all necessary computer code has been processed. Common second-stage boot loaders include BOOTMGR (used on Windows Vista and Windows 7), NTLDR (pre–Windows Vista systems), and LILO (LInux LOader). You'll learn more about these terms later in the chapter.

In order to get the operating system up and running, the boot loader (or loaders) loads the operating system kernel. The computer can't just initiate the entire operating system in one fell swoop; that's why the kernel is so important. It is the kernel that's responsible for managing the communications that occur between the hardware you've learned about so far and the operating system itself. Basically, the computer and its hardware, along with primary and secondary boot loaders, load the kernel, which can then be used to load and initiate the operating system. Figure 2-7 shows the placement of the kernel in the grand scheme of things.

Still Struggling

Hardware inside the computer (such as main memory) can't communicate directly with the software or the operating system. Something has to manage what the hardware is trying to say to the operating system and the applications installed with it. The kernel is that bridge. The kernel manages the data between the data processing that's done at the hardware level and the applications that use that information.

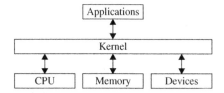

FIGURE 2-7 • The kernel sends data between the CPU, main memory, and hardware devices, and the operating system and applications.

More about First-Stage Boot Loaders

You know that boot loaders are responsible for loading the operating system for the computer. You have also learned that a CPU can only execute program code found on a read-only memory chip or in main memory. Because operating system files for Windows, Mac, Linux, and other machines are stored on hard drives, CDs, DVD, flash memory, and the like, boot loaders are used to load enough information into main memory (and swap it in and out as it's used) so that the computer can eventually pull the files it needs from nonvolatile hardware (such as a hard drive) to offer a user interface.

Because of the sheer amount of code necessary to actually load the OS, often multiple boot loaders are used. The first boot loaders are called first-stage boot loaders. There are various types of first-stage boot loaders that you want to become familiar with.

NOTE   *It's a fact that a computer cannot run without first loading software. However, a computer must be running before any software can be loaded. This apparent paradox is resolved by the information being stored in read-only memory chips and used by boot loaders.*

BIOS

BIOS is the most popular first-stage boot loader, and you've learned quite a bit about it already in this chapter. It's a *de facto standard*. Popular BIOS manufacturers include AMI (American Megatrends), Phoenix Technologies, Award Software International, Inc., and computer manufacturers, including Dell, Gateway, and IBM.

TERM: De Facto Standard

A product or technology that dominates other options and is publicly accepted by just about everyone. HTML is a de facto standard for the code used to create web pages; Microsoft Word file format (.doc) is a de facto standard in word processing; PDF is a de facto standard for printable web documents, e-books, contracts, and invoices that are sent via e-mail and the Web, and is an open format for document exchange.

EFI and UEFI

EFI is also a first-stage boot loader. EFI is firmware that can be used with IBM-compatible computers, just like BIOS can. EFI offers several improvements over BIOS, including but not limited to the following:

- The ability to boot from disks that are very large, over 2 terabytes.
- A faster boot process compared to older firmware options.
- A CPU-independent platform, architecture, and drivers.
- Networking support built right in.
- Enhancements to the existing Advanced Configuration and Power Interface (ACPI).
- The ability to support the existing Master Boot Record disk configuration but a newer partitioning scheme, GPT, or GUID Partition Table. GPT allows for larger disk sizes and does not require you to use a specific file system, such as NTFS (New Technology File System), which was introduced for Windows operating systems.
- Built-in support for 32-bit and 64-bit configurations.
- Its own EFI boot loader, thus removing the need for a dedicated boot loader mechanism.
- The ability to be used with Windows, Mac, Linux, and other software platforms.

Popular EFI manufacturers include Intel, Phoenix, and American Megatrends (Aptio).

UEFI, or Unified Extensible Firmware Interface, is a specification being developed by the Unified EFI Forum. UEFI is not restricted to any specific processor architecture, and can run on top of or instead of traditional BIOS implementations. UEFI offers these advantages:

- The ability to boot from large disks
- Better performance and faster boot processes
- CPU-independent architecture and drivers
- Networking support

Because UEFI is fairly new, you'll want to explore it on your own and keep an eye on the progress. For now, noting that UEFI is an option is enough.

Open Firmware, OpenBoot, and OpenBIOS

Open Firmware, also called OpenBoot, is a standard for computer firmware from Sun Microsystems. Open Firmware is stored on a read-only memory chip and holds the first stored program that needs to be run when the system is powered up (like other boot loaders). It has been used by Apple and IBM as well as various other vendors. In fact, Apple offers the option Open Firmware Password Protection for configuring low-level password protection for your Mac. Some of the Macs that offer this option and firmware include several of the iMacs, eMacs, PowerBooks, and Power Macs. You can find out if you're using Open Firmware on your Mac from the System Profiler, as shown in Figure 2-8, and you can use this information to check for firmware updates.

NOTE   *Open Firmware lets the computer load drivers directly from their PCI card, thus improving compatibility.*

More about Second-Stage Boot Loaders

Although there are various kinds of second-stage boot loaders, only four are widely used: BOOTMGR, NTLDR, GRUB, and LILO. Each of these helps complete the loading of the operating system. They can also be configured to offer the user bootup options, such as booting to a specific OS (if you have more than one on your computer), booting into Safe Mode, and more.

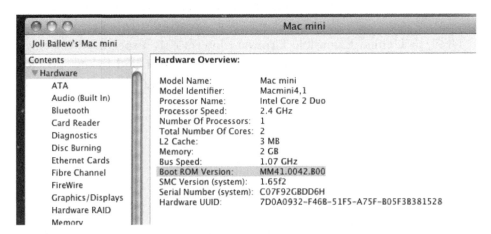

FIGURE 2-8 · Use the System Profiler on a Mac to find system information, including the Boot ROM version.

Although you'll see these terms again and in more depth later in this chapter, it's best to familiarize yourself with them now and recognize them as second-stage boot loaders before continuing.

BOOTMGR (Boot Manager)

This second-stage boot loader is used in Windows-based computers. Specifically, it's used with Windows Vista, Windows 7, Windows Server 2008, and beyond. One of its tasks is to display an operating system menu if more than one OS is installed. You can access BOOTMGR by pressing the SPACEBAR during bootup if this is the case (and if no boot menu delay is already configured).

Although you'll learn more about this later in the chapter, when BIOS is part of a Windows Vista, Windows 7, or Windows 2008 Server system, after the previous bootup tasks have finished, the Master Boot Record is the first thing accessed. This points to and invokes other startup items, including locating the boot sector (which is the part of the hard drive that contains the boot files) and loading BOOTMGR. The BOOTMGR looks for the active partition and also loads (or invokes the loading of) winload.exe, the operating system's boot loader, which is used to load the OS kernel and required device drivers. Thus, the BOOTMGR facilitates the loading of the operating system and is a boot loader.

NTLDR (NT Loader)

This second-stage boot loader is used with pre–Windows Vista computers such as Windows XP, Windows 2000, and Windows Server 2003. As with the newer Boot Manager, one of its tasks is to display an operating system menu if more than one OS is installed, but it requires that the boot.ini file be available also.

GNU GRUB (GNU GRand Unified Boot Loader)

This second-stage boot loader is often used in UNIX-based Linux computers. As with other boot loaders, one of its tasks is to display an operating system menu if more than one OS is installed.

GRUB offers many enhancements compared to other second-stage boot loaders. It is highly configurable, supports file systems including FAT, NTFS, and VFAT, and can be used with various user interfaces. Like other second-stage boot loaders, GRUB loads the kernel for the OS into memory and then passes control to the kernel to initialize the OS.

NOTE *There are many second-stage boot loaders that aren't covered here, including GRUB4DOS, RedBoot, Syslinux, FreeLoader, and Das U-Boot.*

LILO (LInux LOader)

LILO is standard on recent distributions of Linux. Although this second-stage boot loader is used in Linux-based computers, it is not dependent on a single operating system. LILO can be placed in the Master Boot Record or the boot sector of a partition on a hard drive.

Putting It All Together

Figure 2-9 shows how the various parts of the sequence work together. This example is for Windows-based machines, but as you know, the order is basically the same no matter what type of computer is booted.

Exercise 2-3: Configure the Order the Computer Searches for a Boot Device

During booting, the computer looks for a drive to boot from in a specific, pre-set order, as defined in the computer's BIOS or other firmware. Most of the time, the order is to look at the floppy drive first (if one exists), look to the CD/DVD drive next, and then to look for a hard drive. You can shave a little time off the boot process by telling it to look immediately to the hard drive, if desired. You do this in the BIOS of typical Windows-based computers.

CAUTION *You can cause the computer irreparable harm if you make an undesirable change to the BIOS. Be careful! We recommend that you only look at the settings but make no changes unless you're already well versed in the procedures and possible consequences.*

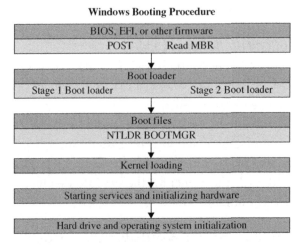

Windows Booting Procedure

FIGURE 2-9 · Booting can be broken down into various sections.

Follow these steps to access the BIOS and reconfigure the boot order on any PC:

1. Reboot the computer.

2. Watch the startup screens for information about accessing the BIOS.

3. Press the appropriate key. Often, this is either DEL or F2, F12, or another Function key.

4. Work through the tabs or category options to locate information about the boot order. Figure 2-10 shows something similar to what you may see.

5. Configure the first boot device, second boot device, and third boot device, as applicable.

6. Save your changes and exit.

NOTE   *When you "flash the BIOS," you update it. This is a dangerous endeavor, though, and can render your computer unusable if done incorrectly. Updating the BIOS, when applicable, is crucial, though, because these updates can enhance your system's capabilities. It can often help to detect devices that were created after the BIOS, improve stability, and fix known problems.*

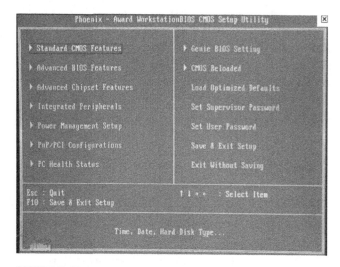

FIGURE 2-10 · The BIOS utility enables you to change the order in which the computer searches for boot files, among other things.

Loading the Windows Vista, Windows 7, or Windows 2008 Server Operating System Kernel

The BIOS has found a hard drive to boot from, so now what happens? For Windows Vista, Windows 7, and Windows Server 2008 (and likely beyond), a few very specific things occur in a specific order. The object is to load the kernel, which in turn loads the operating system and applicable installed applications.

The first things that happens is that the Master Boot Record (MBR) is accessed, as mentioned earlier. This is also called the *partition sector,* which is also called, generically, the *boot sector.* A boot sector is the portion of a disk that is reserved to hold the code for booting the operating system (whose code is located on other parts of the disk). The MBR is stored on the first sector of the hard disk or data storage device that has previously been partitioned.

Note that the MBR is not located on an actual partition. It is located in the area just before the first partition. The structure of the MBR and the partition records is quite complex, and an entire chapter could be dedicated to it. For now, it's important to know that the MBR's job is to hold the partition table, assist in loading the operating system, and identify the types of disks available.

TERM: **Volume Boot Record (VBR)**

The VBR is another type of boot sector. This is the first sector of a drive that has *not* been partitioned, but it can also be the first sector of an individual partition that *has* been partitioned. The VBR can also contain the code required to load operating system files for an OS that is installed on that partition.

The boot sector, once accessed and initiated, now assists in loading the rest of the boot data. This involves loading the Windows Boot Manager (BOOT-MGR). The BOOTMGR locates the active partition, which holds the *Boot Configuration Data (BCD)* store. As you learned earlier, if multiple operating systems are available, it is the Boot Manager's job to keep track of that and offer the user the option to boot from a specific operating system.

The BCD store replaces the older boot.ini file, which was used to manage boot options in earlier versions of Windows, and is a data file located on the system volume. The command-line tool is bcdedit.exe, which can be used to edit the file from a command line (provided you run it with administrator privileges). The BCD store enables the computer to call on winload.exe to load the OS or winresume.exe to resume Windows from hibernation, or boot to a different OS by calling on the appropriate boot files.

The OS loader application (Winload.exe, for example, on a Windows-based computer) once loaded, initializes the kernel. Winload.exe, located in the C:\Windows\System32 folder, is shown in Figure 2-11.

As you learned earlier, the kernel is responsible for managing the communication required between hardware and software. An application must be able to have control of components such as the CPU and main memory to function, and the kernel is what manages that interaction. Once this loader is run, the operating system is ready.

Still Struggling

BOOTMGR reads the boot configuration. The boot configuration is stored in the BootBCD database. The BCD store enables the computer to locate Winload.exe. Winload.exe initializes the kernel. The kernel is the intermediary between the hardware and the applications installed on the computer.

FIGURE 2-11 · Winload.exe is an operating system loader.

The Mac OS X Boot Process

Macs have processes during the initial bootup phase that are similar to those in Windows. Firmware is initiated, hardware is checked, the firmware calls on the required files and initiates them, boot options (if invoked or available) are offered, and the OS is initialized. However, the process, once the hard drive is found by the firmware, is quite different from any Windows- or Linux-based computer.

In a nutshell, here's what happens during the OS X boot process:

1. The BootX boot loader is initialized (or boot.efi on an Intel-based machine).

2. BootX tries to load previously cached device drivers. This, if available, reduces the time it takes for a Mac to boot.

3. Once device drivers are loaded, the kernel initializes and starts the Input/Output Kit (I/O Kit). The I/O Kit links the loaded drivers into the kernel using information it obtained from the device tree created by Open Firmware (or a variation of it).

4. Launchd is invoked by the kernel and runs as the first process on the system. This process loads the rest of the system.

5. After Launchd loads, various scripts and initialization procedures are run and startup items are initialized.

6. Finally, loginwindow is invoked. This is used to authenticate the user by requiring that a password be typed in.

The Linux Boot Process

Linux machines have processes during the initial bootup phase similar to Windows PCs and Macs. Firmware is initiated, hardware is checked, firmware calls on the required files and initiates them, and the operating system is initialized. However, the process, once the hard drive is found by the firmware, is quite different from any Windows- or Apple-based computer. Figure 2-12 shows this, briefly.

In a nutshell, here's what happens during the Linux boot process:

1. In a Linux machine, the second-stage boot loader could more aptly be called a "kernel loader." Once the second-stage boot loader is in memory, the default kernel image is loaded into memory too.

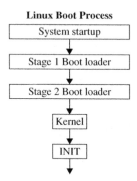

FIGURE 2-12 · The Linux boot process is similar, at least in theory, to other boot processes used with other operating systems.

2. The kernel image is compressed and is thus decompressed before being moved into memory.

3. After the kernel is loaded into memory, it performs various startup tasks, including setting up interrupts, memory management, device and driver initialization, and so forth.

4. The scheduler takes over.

5. The first user-space application is loaded, often /sbin/init.

6. The user is presented with a logon screen.

Summary

A lot happens between the time you press the power button on a computer and when you are greeted by the welcome or login screen, and the entire task is aptly named *the boot process*. Although what happens during this process changes depending on the operating system, computer manufacturer, and installed peripherals and hardware, a generalized process can be outlined. All boot processes go through similar tasks, including initializing firmware, locating and testing required hardware, and initializing the boot device. Once the computer finishes booting and the operating system is loaded, it's ready to begin managing the systems resources, beginning with the CPU, the subject of the next chapter.

QUIZ

Choose the correct response to each of the multiple-choice questions. Note that there may be more than one correct response to each question.

1. **What happens most of the time after the power button is pressed and power has been stabilized by the power supply?**
   A. BIOS or EFI is initiated.
   B. Device drivers are loaded.
   C. CPU registers are initialized.
   D. POST occurs.

2. **Where is the BIOS located?**
   A. In main memory
   B. On the CPU
   C. On the boot sector of a hard disk
   D. In read-only memory

3. **Which of the following are duties of POST?**
   A. To enable the BIOS
   B. To verify the integrity of the BIOS
   C. To verify the size of the main memory
   D. To load the operating system's boot files

4. **What can you do to review the services and drivers that are loaded during any boot process on a Windows computer?**
   A. Enable debugging mode
   B. Enable boot logging
   C. Enable Safe Mode
   D. All of the above

5. **What is an interrupt handler?**
   A. What enables data to be transferred from main memory to a device without passing through the CPU
   B. A small piece of code that acts as the translator between hardware and the operating system
   C. Firmware used to boot the computer
   D. A boot loader

6. **Which of the following are second-stage boot loaders?**
   A. BOOTMGR
   B. NTLDR
   C. EFI
   D. GRUB

7. **What is the first thing accessed from the hard drive when a Windows 7 computer boots?**
   A. Boot.ini file
   B. NTLDR
   C. Master Boot Record
   D. Boot Configuration Data

8. **What is winload.exe?**
   A. A first-stage boot loader
   B. A second-stage boot loader
   C. An operating system loader
   D. The kernel

9. **During the Mac boot process, what is the name of the first file loaded?**
   A. Input/Output Kit
   B. BootX
   C. Launched
   D. Loginwindow

10. **During the Linux boot process, what is the name of the first file often loaded?**
   A. Init
   B. Boot.ini
   C. MBR
   D. BootX

Part II

CPU Management

chapter **3**

Process and Thread Management

Overall system performance can often be tied to efficient management of the CPU. In this chapter, we explore how the operating system attempts to balance the demands made on its processors so that it can maximize the use of these very important resources. We'll explain the role of processes and threads as well as how they are executed in systems with from one to many CPUs.

CHAPTER OBJECTIVES

In this chapter, you will

- Explore the responsibilities of the CPU manager
- Gain an understanding of the interaction between the CPU and other operating system resources
- Learn the fundamentals of processes and threads
- Appreciate the load-balancing issues sought by operating systems designers

Overview

CPU is the most common name given to the *central processing unit*, also known as the *processor*. Its responsibilities, in simplest terms, are to interpret and execute program instructions or requests and perform every calculation for every user. The work that the CPU performs is called *processing*.

The part of the operating system that manages the CPU's activities can have a job ranging from very simple to very complex, depending on the number of users as well as the number of processors. Let's begin by looking at several common configurations and how CPU workload might be managed. Consider these scenarios:

- A single CPU is processing a single request from a single application for a single user. This is easy to manage.
- A single CPU is processing hundreds of requests from several applications for a single user. This is not difficult to manage.
- A single CPU is processing hundreds of requests from many applications for multiple users. This is difficult to manage.
- Multiple CPUs are processing hundreds or thousands of requests from very many applications for multiple users. This is very difficult to manage.

As you can see, CPU scheduling becomes more complex as traffic and users increase. For example, in the first situation, it's easy to choose which request should be serviced first—it's the only one that's in the processing queue. At the opposite extreme is the last example, which requires that the CPU manager keep track of each CPU's workload as well as the allocation scheme that assigns the order or priority of all of the waiting requests so that the proper requests can be serviced first.

When the designers of an operating system are deciding how to manage the available CPU resources, they generally try to allocate them in a way that's fair while balancing the loads of all the other resources, including main memory space, devices, files, and network access. As you can imagine, this is a very challenging assignment.

Let's begin with a few basic definitions. For the purposes of this discussion, the key piece of code that undergoes execution (processing) by the CPU is called a *process*. As we'll explain throughout this chapter, every process is allocated its own set of resources. (These include registers, stacks, and data structures, which we can't fully describe in this small space.) Suffice it to say that a process is a core piece of executable code in the system. It's similar to an atom—a fundamental building block that, although very small, has even smaller components.

TIP *Systems with multiple CPUs are called multicore systems and may have two or more CPUs built on a single chip. The Intel Corporation announced in 2007 that its researchers had built "a single 80-core chip that's not much larger than the size of a fingernail while using less electricity than most of today's home appliances." The term core comes from the early days of computing.*

In some operating systems (called *threading* or *multithreading systems*), processes can have smaller entities called *threads* (just as atoms have electrons). In multithreading systems, a single process can have multiple threads. Each thread shares its process's resources but is allotted its own processor time (and registers and stacks). In these systems, the threads are scheduled for execution and the results are reported back to the process that spun them off.

To understand how a processing system uses threads, consider a mystical wizard who needs to battle an invasion of deadly attackers. Let's say this wizard has the option to either take up weapons himself and go off to defend his land, or to spin off ethereal avatars that will take orders from the wizard, take advantage of the wizard's storehouse of weapons, go off to fight, and report back with results of their success—or lack of it.

In the same way, a system without threading will schedule the process for execution and collect the results itself. This is similar to the scenario when the wizard fights his own battles without avatars.

Alternatively, in a threading system, the process spins off threads, allows *them* to use the process's resources, allows *them* to be executed, and collects the results from each thread. Later, when processing is complete, the threads cease to exist and the process moves forward without them. And just as avatars cannot exist without their wizard, threads cannot exist without their process.

Web browsers take full advantage of threads to perform multiple tasks in (what appears to be) simultaneous moments of time. For example, when you visit a video website, one thread might be retrieving the lyrics of the background song while another streams the video, and a third updates the advertising animation that appears on the site's banner. And while it appears that the system is performing all of these actions simultaneously, it's not physically possible for one CPU to execute more than one thread at any given moment in time.

Although a single browser can spin off many, many threads, a computer system with only a single CPU will require that all the threads take turns being processed (in an order that we'll discuss in the next chapter). The CPU switches from one thread to the next so quickly that it appears to the human eye that all of them are being serviced at the same time. These days, with very fast CPU speeds, a single CPU can allocate processing time to multiple threads in a single second. And if the computer system has multiple CPUs, even more processing time can be shared among the threads. The result? The video on your web browser, along with lyrics and advertisements, are up and running even faster.

CPUs usually have their own dedicated cache memory, which works as a temporary storage area on the CPU chip where recently used data is kept. Cache is based on the assumption that a significant amount of the data that was just removed from memory will be requested again in the very near future. To explain the concept in simplest terms, before data is moved to the hard drive or other secondary storage, it's put into the cache for a brief time to see whether it is requested again soon. If so, the data is moved quickly back into memory (much faster than if it was retrieved from the hard drive, thus speeding up system response time). If the data is not requested, it's moved to the hard drive so that cache can be filled with more recent data. Cache is discussed in more detail in Chapter 7.

NOTE *Throughout this chapter, we refer to threads as the smallest processing entities and to processes as the next smallest. Some books also refer to jobs, a term used to describe a collection of processes that is submitted for processing by the user or application. However, to simplify our discussions in this chapter, we'll usually confine our explanations to processes and threads.*

Process and Thread States

Every item to be processed must move through several *process states* as it proceeds through its execution. (Although these concepts apply to both processes and threads, we'll use the term *process* here to simplify our explanation.) To see how a process cycles from one state to the next, see Figure 3-1.

The four primary processing states are detailed in the following list (note that some operating systems use different names or have additional states than those described here):

- **Ready State** This state is the gathering place for processes that are ready for execution by the CPU. All processes move into the Ready State when they're submitted to the system the first time. Some processes are returned to the Ready State after spending time in the Waiting State. Regardless of

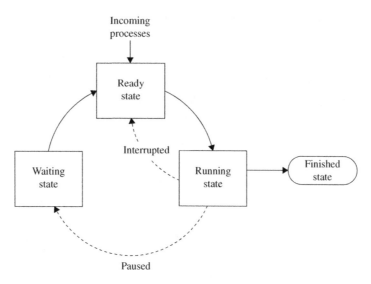

FIGURE 3-1 • Every process moves from Ready to Finished and, sometimes, to the Waiting State.

their history, once a process arrives there, it is generally put into an order of some kind (as we'll describe in detail in the next chapter). For the moment, let's assume that all of them are put into a chronological order with those arriving first at the front of the line for processing.

• **Running State** This state represents the time when execution takes place. If the system has a single CPU, then one process can be in the Running State at one time—systems with seven CPUs can have seven processes in the Running State at once. For each CPU, the process that is in the Running State begins its execution and runs to completion unless one of the following events takes place:

  • If the process finishes its execution, it moves to the Finished State.

  • If the process must stop execution because its allotted processing time (called a *time slice* or *time quantum*) has expired, then it moves back to the Ready State and gets back in line.

  • If the process must pause its execution for some reason, it moves to the Waiting State.

• **Waiting State** Processes move into this state because they are on hold, waiting for some part of the operating system to respond to a request. Examples of these requests include waiting for a printer to print, waiting for an Internet search result, and waiting for input from the human running the computer. (Notice in Figure 3-1 that Waiting is not a mandatory state because while all processes must move into the Ready and Running States, they do not need to move to the Waiting State if all of their requests are fulfilled immediately, or if they make no requests at all.) When the outstanding request is satisfied, the process that's waiting returns to the Ready State and gets back in line so that it can continue processing.

- **Finished State**   This state is the phase when the process releases the system resources (such as files, memory space, and database access) it was allocated, and then the process terminates. Processes go to the Finished State if they successfully complete their execution (even if an error occurs) and processing ends gracefully—meaning that the process can give up its resources properly. This is a critical step because often some of the resources that were allocated to the process may be held exclusively. That is, they cannot be used by any other process until they are deallocated from the process that is finishing. It could well be that some of those resources are required by processes that are now in the Waiting State; without those resources, those processes cannot run to completion.

What happens if a process becomes stranded in the Waiting State as it waits for a resource (such as a printer) that never becomes available? If the CPU manager is working properly, it will check for any stranded processes and send an error message to the user asking for help. If it's a matter of turning on a special printer or refilling it with paper, then the user may be able to make that device available once again and allow the process to print and finish. If the problem cannot be fixed by the user, a message might appear asking for the user to either kill the pages or continue waiting. An example is shown in Figure 3-2.

FIGURE 3-2 · Sample error screen for the Chrome browser asking for user response

Serial vs. Parallel Processing

Serial processing describes a system that can execute only one process (or one thread) at once. This is the common configuration for single-user systems with one CPU, as illustrated in Figure 3-3. With this kind of system, the CPU manager follows a CPU allocation scheme (detailed in the next chapter) to take processes from the Ready State, run them, and move them eventually to the Finished State (although they may spend some time in the Waiting State before reaching the finish line).

In this kind of system, the services of the CPU are allocated to one process at a time. If it switches attention quickly from process to process, the CPU can give the impression that several processes are being executed simultaneously, but this is impossible if the system has only one CPU because it can work on only one thing at a time.

A *parallel processing* system has several CPUs, and all of them can be working simultaneously. In the example shown in Figure 3-4, three CPUs have already finished Processes 1, 2, and 3 (which they executed at the same time), and are now ready to take Processes 4, 5, and 6. Process 7 is waiting for the next available processor.

Several scenarios allow multiple CPUs to work together. Figure 3-4 shows each CPU executing a single process, but another scenario could have each CPU executing a subset of a process (called a *working set* and described in detail in Chapter 5). Yet another could assign a CPU to each incoming job.

In addition to increased processing speed, a huge advantage of multiple CPU systems is increased availability. That's because if a single CPU should fail, there are others that might be able to jump in and do the job, although it might take longer. On the other hand, if the system has only one CPU, there's no backup ready to take over, so everything comes to a halt until a working CPU is installed and the system is back up and running.

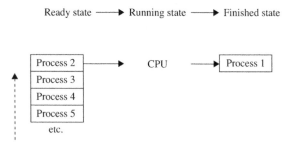

FIGURE 3-3 • Simplified view of serial processing

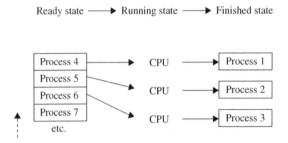

FIGURE 3-4 · One parallel processing scenario

However, a huge complication of parallel processing is the challenge of orchestrating the interaction of running processes, and sometimes their threads, as they move from the Ready State to Finished State, as shown in Table 3-1.

Exercise 3-1: How Many Processors Does Your Computer Have?

Does your computer have one processor, dual processors, or several processors? To find out, you must access the computer's system information page.

Follow these steps on a Windows 7 computer:

1. Left-click the Windows Start button.

2. Right-click Computer.

3. Left-click Properties.

TABLE 3-1 Comparison of Three Levels of Parallelism		
Level of Parallelism	**How Processing Is Done with Multiple CPUs**	**Level of Coordination**
Single process, no threads	Each process has its own dedicated CPU until it reaches the Finished State.	None
Multiple processes, no threads	Each process has its own dedicated CPU until it reaches the Finished State. Processes from different users or jobs must be coordinated.	Moderate
Multiple processes, multiple threads	Each CPU is assigned to the process's threads as required. Threads from different processes, users, or jobs must be coordinated.	Significant

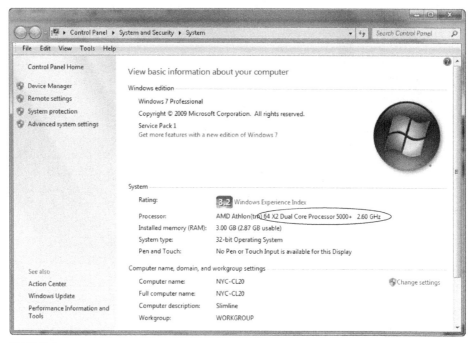

FIGURE 3-5 • This screen indicates that this is dual-core Windows 7 computer.

4. Review the processor information offered. A typical configuration is shown in Figure 3-5. What does this mean? A dual-core processor is a CPU with two separate cores. It's the equivalent of getting two processors on one chip!

On a Mac OS X computer, follow these steps:

1. Click the Apple icon on the menu bar.

2. Click the About This Mac option.

3. Review the processor information offered. A typical configuration is shown in Figure 3-6. (In this example, Core 2 Duo means the Mac has a single chip with two cores.)

On a computer running Ubuntu Linux, follow these steps:

1. Click System.

2. Click Administration.

3. Click System Monitor.

4. Click the System tab.

5. Review the processor information offered. A typical configuration is shown in Figure 3-7. (By clicking the Processes tab, you can see the status of all the processes running on the system.)

FIGURE 3-6 · This is a dual-core Mac OS X machine.

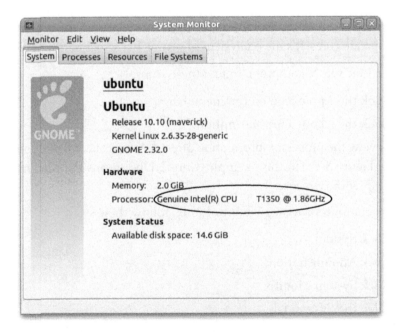

FIGURE 3-7 · Computer running Ubuntu Linux with a single core

Process Control

To carry out certain tasks, a *system call* is used to coordinate activities with the kernel (which was introduced in Chapter 2). You may recall that the kernel is responsible for managing communications that occur between the computer system's hardware and the CPU manager. Specific system calls used by different operating systems can vary enormously (for example, the steps required to open a process is very different in Windows and Linux systems and the number of available calls can range from fewer than 100 to more than 500).

To explain a system call in simplest terms, it conveys instructions from the operating system to the kernel, which is empowered to access the necessary hardware, perform operations there, and then pass control from the kernel back to the operating system. Because the improper use of system calls can easily cause a system-wide crash, each of these control transitions must be carefully managed.

Coordination of process execution can be a complex task. For example, one condition to avoid is called a *race*—a situation where the outcome of a computation can vary depending on some aspect of luck or chance. This concept is best explained with an example. Suppose for a moment that the electric company receives your monthly payment at the same time it receives a notice that your address has changed. Furthermore, suppose that electric company's system has two CPUs to execute the two processes: paying bills and changing addresses. To perform its task, each CPU begins by copying your record from the database (before any changes are made) and prepares to execute its process. CPU #1 marks your record as paid, and prepares to write the finished record to the database so that it can be stored. Meanwhile, CPU #2 changes your address, and prepares to write its version of your finished record to the database for storage. Now consider the following two scenarios:

- If CPU #1 finishes first and modifies the database first, its version will be stored on the disk first—and very soon thereafter, it will be overwritten when CPU #2 stores its version in the same database. The result will be a record with the new change of address, but no indication that you paid the bill.

- If CPU #2 finishes first, it will modify the database first, and soon that version will be replaced when CPU #1 writes its version of your record to the database. The resulting record will show that you paid the bill, but will not have your new address.

Notice that the final record is erroneous in both cases—neither is acceptable. This is called a race because the contents of the resulting record depend on which CPU makes the last modification to the database, enabling its version to prevail.

Process Control Block

Each process has a data structure called a *process control block* (often abbreviated as *PCB*) that keeps track of key information about the process, such as its unique identifier, process state, allocated resources, priority, addresses, and so on. The contents of the PCB are updated as the process moves through its different states; the PCB tracks the process's transition from one state to the next and stores critical information about its progress until it reaches the Finished State.

The PCB plays an important role when processes are put into a certain order, called a *queue*. Whenever that happens, the processes themselves do not move, and neither do their PCBs. Instead, each PCB is linked from one to the next using a pointer, and the order is created through a series of links, as illustrated in Figure 3-8.

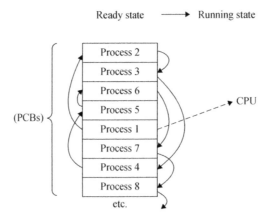

FIGURE 3-8 · Simplified view of a linked list of PCBs for processes in the Ready State

A pointer *is the name given to a piece of data that refers directly to a location in memory where a value (that's stored there) can be found. You can think of it as an arrow, or a link, from one place to another in memory. Pointers are very important in computer systems because they can be used to quickly locate information; in fact, it's often much faster and easier to change pointers than it is to move the data that each pointer targets.*

For example, let's see how pointers make it easy to put queued items in order. Queuing is something that happens routinely and is a critical concept that we'll explore in the next chapter when we describe CPU allocation schemes.

When we say that a process "enters the Ready State," we're actually saying that its PCB is linking to the queue of processes that are already in the Ready State. This makes it easier to change the order of certain processes that are ready for execution. Let's say that the original order shown in Figure 3-8 has no particular process "jumping the line." However, if a certain process (let's say Process 7) is deemed to be more important than all of the others, it must be moved ahead of the others. In that case, the sequence can be changed simply by changing only two links (Process 7 to Process 1, and Process 6 to Process 8), as shown in Figure 3-9.

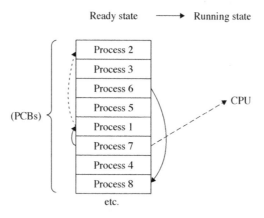

FIGURE 3-9 • Reordered list so Process 7 can go first (new links are shown in solid lines)

Still Struggling

In Figure 3-9, by modifying only two pointers, the list of processes in the Ready State is quickly changed. If the PCBs or the processes themselves had to be physically rearranged, then it would not be nearly as easy to change the order of processing.

Thread Control Block

Just as processes have a PCB, each thread has a *thread control block (TCB)*, which holds data such as its unique thread identifier, thread state, pointer to the process that created it, pointer to any other threads that this thread created, priority, and so on. If you remember, threads have access to the resources that have been allocated to the process that created them, so resource information is not stored in the TCB but remains in the PCB. By using pointers, TCBs are linked in the exact same way as processes were linked in the two previous figures.

Later, when the process finally reaches the Finished State, its PCB and all its threads (and *their* TCBs) are terminated.

Exercise 3-2: View Processes on Your Windows Computer

Do you want to see what processes are currently running on your Windows computer? Here are the steps to follow:

1. Press the CTRL-ALT-DELETE keys together.
2. Click Start Task Manager.
3. Click the Processes tab.
4. Review the list of processes currently running on your computer, as shown in Figure 3-10. You might also want to see what applications are running and which services are using system resources by clicking the respective tabs.
5. Close the window by clicking the red X in the top-right corner.

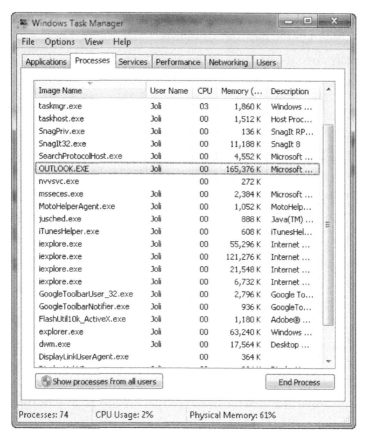

FIGURE 3-10 · Click the Processes tab to see which processes are running.

Parallel Processing in Action

To fully appreciate the power of parallel processing, let's compare it to a common database task. The marketing department at a local electronics store wants to find the names and address for all the people in its database tables who match certain criteria—those who are between 19 and 22 years of age, recently bought a certain popular cell phone, and bought more than $200 in electronics in the past three months.

If the system uses a single CPU to perform this search, it might follow these steps:

1. From the AGE table, select everyone between 19 and 22.
2. From the PRODUCT table, select everyone who purchased the cell phone.

3. From the SALES table, select everyone who bought more than $200 in electronics in the past three months.

4. Identify anyone who appears on all of those lists.

5. Print the results.

However, if we can assign three CPUs instead of only one, the search could be done this way:

1. CPU1 selects everyone between 19 and 22, while CPU2 selects everyone who purchased the cell phone, while CPU3 selects everyone who bought more than $200 in electronics in the past three months.

2. CPU1 compares the three lists to identify anyone who appears on all of them.

3. The results are printed.

As you can see, by assigning two additional CPUs to our searches, we've been able to reduce the number of steps from five to three, and almost certainly the answer will come back faster than if we used a single CPU. However (and this is a big "however"), successful multi-CPU processing is not usually as simple as it appears here because it's not always obvious to the operating system which tasks can be performed simultaneously by different processors.

In this example, it's easy for us to see that we are asking for three unrelated searches in three different places, so we simply assign one CPU to each search and each is carried out at the same time. However, in real life, most requests are much more complex, and although there may be opportunities to perform parallel processing, the operating system may need explicit instructions to do so. One way to do that is to introduce instructions such as COBEGIN and COEND. Let's rewrite our example to introduce those two terms:

```
COBEGIN
CPU select everyone between 19 and 22
CPU select everyone who purchased the cell phone
CPU select everyone who bought more than $200 in electronics
COEND
Compare the three lists to identify anyone on all of them
Print the results
```

With the introduction of these two terms, the instructions still have three steps, but now the operating system is explicitly told to execute the first three instructions at the same time, in parallel. However, notice how much work is involved to add those two instructions. A best-case scenario could include locating the program, opening the instructions for modification, figuring out where to put our new instructions, typing them in, saving the new version, testing the new version to make sure it works, and then replacing the old version with the new one. This is time consuming and gives us a glimpse of one big barrier to parallel processing. Does the time saved by using multiple CPUs compensate for the effort required to revise program instructions? Sometimes it does.

As of this writing, one of the biggest obstacles to large-scale parallel processing is the need to amend millions of program instructions on computers large and small so they can take advantage of systems with multiple CPUs. It's likely that the day will come when a system can be built to do this automatically. Stay tuned.

Order of Operations

When a complex equation is being processed, it's critical that the calculations be performed in the correct order. Known as the *order of operations,* this is a mathematical standard that deciphers the complexities of multipart equations so they will always be solved in the correct order and thus result in only one solution, no matter who or what is doing the solving.

First, let's look only at the four most widely known operations (we'll discuss parentheses and exponents in a minute). Mathematical rules state that *all multiplication and division calculations will be performed before all addition and subtraction calculations.* For equations with multiple multiplications and divisions, they are all grouped together and then each is performed one after the other from left to right. Only then are all additions and subtractions grouped together and calculated, one after the other, from left to right. For example, consider the following equation (note that the asterisk [*] signifies multiplication; the forward slash [/] signifies division).

$$\underbrace{A - 12/C}_{\text{1st}} + \underbrace{3 * B}_{\text{2nd}}$$

Following the standard order of operations, we will always perform our calculations in the following order:

- First, do the division: 12 / C
- Second, do the multiplication: 3 * B

- Third, do the subtraction: A − (result of the 1st step)
- Fourth, do the addition: (result of the 3rd step) + (result of the 2nd step)

If we assume A = 5, B = 8, and C = 4, then the result of this calculation would be as follows:

$$5 - 12 / 4 + 3 * 8 = 26$$

Of course, some equations are more complex. What if the equation has parentheses (sometimes called brackets) or exponents? In that case, the calculations are always performed from left to right in the following order:

- Contents of parentheses are calculated first.
- Exponents and square roots are done second.
- Multiplications and divisions are treated equally and are calculated third.
- Finally, additions and subtractions are at an equal level and are calculated last, from left to right.

As you can see, by using parentheses creatively, one can force an addition to be calculated before a multiplication. For example, if we revise the previous equation to read

$$(A - 12) / (C + 3) * B$$

then the subtraction inside the parentheses would be calculated first (because it's on the left) and the addition second (because it's in the next set of parentheses to the right). Only then would the division and multiplication take place. After we substitute values for the variables (in this case, A = 5, B = 8, and C = 4), the equation looks like this:

$$(5 - 12) / (4 + 3) * 8$$

The steps required to solve the equation are shown in Table 3-2.

In the recent past, some confusion has sprung up regarding the proper way to treat multiplication versus division as well as addition versus subtraction. To be clear, these four operations represent only two levels: All multiplications and divisions are grouped together and each calculation is done, in turn, from the left,

TABLE 3-2 Solution to Equation			
Step	**Calculation**	**Description**	**Result**
1	5 – 12	Contents of the first set of parentheses	= –7
2	4 + 3	Contents of the second set of parentheses	= +7
3	–7 / +7	Results from step 1 divided by results from step 2	= –1
4	–1 * 8	Results from step 3 times 8	= –8

regardless of whether it is multiplication or division. Multiplication does not have a higher priority than division. Likewise, additions and subtractions are grouped together and calculated from the left. In other words, as shown previously, there are only four levels—not six.

Summary

In this chapter, we explored the basics of CPU management, the entities known as processes and threads, and how they move through several process states as they go from Ready to Finished. We also touched very lightly on the concepts of serial and parallel processing and how the latter can become very complex. Finally, we reviewed the mathematical concept called order of operations that ensures complex equations are always performed the same way on every computer.

In the next chapter, we'll continue our exploration of CPU management—specifically, we'll see how a CPU can be allocated fairly to the processes and threads that are awaiting execution.

QUIZ

Choose the correct response to each of the multiple-choice questions. Note that there may be more than one correct response to each question.

1. **When a process is actually being executed, in what state is it?**
   A. Ready
   B. Running
   C. Waiting
   D. Finished

2. **When a process that was halted to print a page is now able to continue, what is its new state?**
   A. Ready
   B. Running
   C. Waiting
   D. Finished

3. **What happens when a process reaches the Finished State?**
   A. All of its PCBs are sent to the Ready queue.
   B. All of its TCBs are terminated.
   C. Its threads are all terminated.
   D. Everything in the Ready queue is terminated.

4. **Why is CPU scheduling important?**
   A. It is a valuable resource that must be shared by many processes.
   B. It is not fair for one process to monopolize the CPU.
   C. It is an important element that contributes to overall system performance.
   D. All of the above.

5. **When a race condition exists, what can we expect of the resulting calculation?**
   A. It's usually correct.
   B. It depends on the order in which competing processes begin executing.
   C. It depends on the order in which competing processes end execution.
   D. It's usually incorrect.

6. **Indicate which of the following statements are true about parallel processing.**
   A. Thread-level parallelism assigns a CPU to each thread during execution.
   B. Process parallelism results in a very significant amount of complexity.
   C. Job parallelism is easily achieved with a single CPU.
   D. All of the above.

7. **Queues can include pointers from which of the following?**
   A. Processes
   B. Process control blocks
   C. Threads
   D. Thread control blocks

8. **What's the role of the commands COBEGIN and COEND?**
   A. They designate when several CPUs can execute a single process.
   B. They designate that there are multiple CPUs in the system.
   C. They designate when several CPUs can execute several processes.
   D. They designate when jobs are ready to begin processing.

9. **If a two-CPU system can execute a job with four processes in 3 seconds, how long would it take a four-CPU system to execute the same job?**
   A. 1.5 seconds.
   B. 3 seconds.
   C. It depends on the processes.
   D. Not enough information is available.

10. **Resolve the following equation following the standard order of operations:**

$$21 / 3 - 31 + 12 * (10 + 10)$$

   A. 720
   B. 255
   C. 216
   D. 264

chapter 4

CPU Management

This chapter introduces several CPU management allocation schemes and the advantages and disadvantages of each. They are presented in chronological order, from oldest to more recent, so that you can see how each one was built on the successes of the one that came before. Keep in mind that in every case, the operating systems designers made critical choices that helped shape the evolution of the CPU-sharing techniques presented here.

CHAPTER OBJECTIVES

In this chapter, you will

- Appreciate the advantages and disadvantages of six CPU management schemes
- Learn about the challenges of internal and external fragmentation
- Understand the role of system design regarding process management

CPU Management Basics

When a computer system has many processes waiting for a turn to run on a single CPU, the operating system has to refer to its built-in policies and procedures to decide which processes will run first and which will be given the chance to finish first. Although these choices may seem inconsequential to the average computer user, the designers of an operating system know that the CPU-scheduling algorithm that they select will have a profound effect on the efficiency of the CPU as well as the rest of the computer system, and therefore they are chosen very carefully. Here are a few of the many things considered when deciding how one CPU will be shared equitably among all the waiting processes:

- Should the waiting processes be rearranged, or should they be run in the same order in which they arrive?
- Should the size and importance of incoming processes be taken into consideration?
- Once a process begins running, should it ever be interrupted? And if so, under what conditions?

The answers to these questions depend on the specific aspect of system performance that the designers are trying to make more efficient, and there are several options:

- If we're going to be absolutely fair, perhaps we might run each process in the same order in which it enters the Ready queue.
- If we want to move many processes from start to finish as quickly as possible, we could consider giving extra attention to the shortest processes and let the longer processes wait.
- If we want to maximize the efficiency of the CPU, we might want to make it easier for those jobs that require lots of processing to get more frequent access to the CPU and make those that are doing a lot of printing wait until later.
- If we want to reduce the chance for one process to monopolize the CPU, we might want to interrupt the execution of long processes.
- If we'd like to move important processes through faster, we could assign them a higher priority and make others that are less urgent wait.

The designers' goal is to take the best advantage of the computer's processing capacity. In this chapter, we'll explore some of the schemes used to allocate a single CPU to many waiting processes and the advantages and disadvantages of each. Before concluding the chapter, we'll talk briefly about allocation schemes for threads and systems with multiple CPUs.

TIP   *A collection of processes is referred to as a job. In a computing environment that supports threads, a process is a collection of threads.*

CPU Allocation Schemes

No single allocation scheme is optimal for every computing environment because each has its own design goals. For example, the operating system that runs the CPUs on a weather satellite would need to have built-in responsiveness 24 hours a day and be maintainable via wireless communications. On the other hand, the goals for the computers that run a university's course registration system would be very different. And the goals for a telephone's operating system would be radically different from both of those.

Allocation schemes come in two primary flavors:

- **Nonpreemptive**   These schemes do not allow process execution to be interrupted.
- **Preemptive**   These schemes allow interruptions.

The earliest allocation schemes were simple and nonpreemptive. The evolution from those to the more complex preemptive system was a major step forward. We'll examine both types in this chapter.

First Come, First Served

The simplest nonpreemptive scheme is *First Come, First Served (FCFS)*, which executes, without interruption, the incoming processes in the exact same order in which they arrive in the Ready queue. Therefore, every process claims 100 percent of the services of the CPU from the time it begins execution until the time it finishes. If the process has to pause from time to time to print a few pages, the CPU remains allocated to this process and sits idle while waiting for the printer to respond; only after printing is completed is the process's execution allowed to continue. Imagine how long it would take a process to finish if it had to wait for the completion of multiple print commands—and it would take even longer if the printer ran out of paper—during which time the CPU would sit idle.

FCFS was one of the first CPU allocation schemes created for computers, and although it might seem like the fairest way to allocate the CPU, throughput can drop dramatically when long processes monopolize the CPU. Because this is a nonpreemptive allocation scheme, interruptions were not allowed.

NOTE   *Throughput is the term for the number of processes that are finished in a given amount of time.*

To illustrate FCFS, let's say that we have five processes (A, B, C, D, E) arriving at virtually the same exact moment, and let's also insist that we know in advance how much CPU time (in milliseconds) each will need to run to completion (4, 7, 18, 3, 1, respectively). The timeline in Figure 4-1 shows when the CPU is allocated to each process (in the order in which it arrives), the time when it begins working on each process, and when each process finishes. Notice that the shortest process (Process E), which requires only 1 ms of processing, waits a very long time (32 ms) before it even begins to run. Notice, too, that none of the processes are interrupted for any reason.

This is certainly a fair allocation scheme because each process is run, in its entirety, as soon as the CPU becomes available and none of the processes is allowed to jump in front of another for any reason. Nothing could be fairer, right? But is this the most efficient use of the CPU, and is system performance predictable when using this scheme?

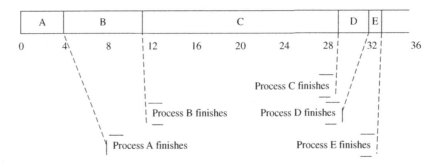

FIGURE 4-1 • Timeline showing FCFS with five processes in the Ready queue when time starts

TABLE 4-1 The Average for All Five Processes Using FCFS				
	Arrival Time	**Processing Time**	**Finish Time**	**Turnaround Time**
Process A	0	4	4	4
Process B	0	7	11	11
Process C	0	18	29	29
Process D	0	3	32	32
Process E	0	1	33	33
Total Turnaround: Average Turnaround:				109 ms 21.8 ms

To find out, check out one statistic that's important to operating systems designers—*turnaround time.* To calculate the turnaround times for each of the processes shown in Table 4-1, we subtract its arrival time (Time 0) from its finish time.

NOTE   *Turnaround time is the length of time it takes a process to move through the execution phase, from the Ready queue to Finished, as illustrated in Figure 3-1 in Chapter 3.*

We then calculate the average by adding all the turnaround times and dividing by the number of processes (in this case, five). For this example, total turnaround time is 109 ms and the average is 21.8 ms.

Let's adjust this example to see what happens if the processes arrive in the Ready queue 4 ms after one another, as shown in Figure 4-2. The resulting turnaround time for the same five processes is shown in Table 4-2.

TABLE 4-2 Processes Arriving over 16 ms, Thus Reducing the Average				
	Arrival Time	**Processing Time**	**Finish Time**	**Turnaround Time**
Process A	0	4	4	4
Process B	4	7	11	7
Process C	8	18	29	21
Process D	12	3	32	20
Process E	16	1	33	17
Total Turnaround: Average Turnaround:				69 ms 13.8 ms

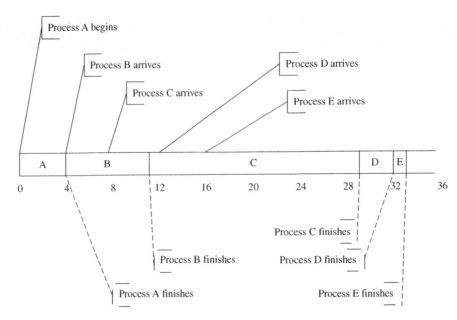

FIGURE 4-2 • Processes arrive every 4 ms, so turnaround decreases.

Notice that while Process C is running, Processes D and E both arrive, so they're both waiting in the Ready queue when the CPU is ready for its next process. But because D arrived before E, Process D is allowed to proceed, even though Process E is shorter, would certainly take less time, and would improve the average turnaround time if it didn't need to wait so long.

Now let's explore another statistic that's important to operating systems designers: consistency of system performance. To do so, let's test the FCFS scheme again, but this time we rearrange the incoming order so that Process C arrives first (and not third), and let's continue to assume that the five processes arrive 4 ms after one another. Remember, the CPU is executing the exact same five processes as before—only the order has changed. The results are shown in Table 4-3.

TIP *To calculate turnaround time, subtract a process's arrival time from the finish time.*

As a result of reordering, the average turnaround time increases dramatically, to 19.6 ms. Notice that when Process C finally completes its execution (at Time 18), all of the remaining jobs have arrived and are awaiting processing. In these examples, even though the exact same five processes were executed and completed

TABLE 4-3	After the Processes Are Rearranged, Average Turnaround Climbs			
	Arrival Time	**Processing Time**	**Finish Time**	**Turnaround Time**
Process C	0	18	18	18
Process A	4	4	22	18
Process B	8	7	29	21
Process D	12	3	32	20
Process E	16	1	33	21
Total Turnaround:				98 ms
Average Turnaround:				19.6 ms

their execution in the same 33 ms, the average turnaround time increased from 13.8 ms to 19.6 ms, which is a 42-percent jump in turnaround time. We can conclude, therefore, that if we performed the same tasks over and over but they appeared in the Ready queue in a different sequence each time, the system's turnaround time could vary significantly (in this case, it increased by a stunning 42 percent).

We can conclude from this example, which yields a wide range of average turnaround times, that FCFS schemes make system performance unpredictable and therefore are unacceptable to systems designers, who strive for consistent system performance. Fortunately, other schemes have more predictable results.

Shortest Job Next

If we consistently reorder incoming processes, can we improve their turnaround times and offer performance that's more predictable than FCFS? *Shortest Job Next (SJN)* is a nonpreemptive scheme that does just that, but it works only if the amount of processing time is known in advance.

To illustrate SJN, look at the same five processes from the previous examples, which are all in the Ready queue at Time 0. Instead of accepting them in their order of arrival, the CPU takes a moment to calculate which processes will likely need the least amount of CPU time and then runs them in ascending order, from shortest to longest. Processes are then executed sequentially, as shown in Figure 4-3.

The data for this sequence of events is shown in Table 4-4. (To make it easy to compare results, the processes in Table 4-4 use the same names as in Table 4-3.

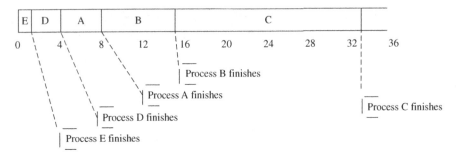

FIGURE 4-3 • Timeline showing the execution of five processes using SJN

Therefore, Process C in this table is the same as Process C from the previous table.)

Because SJN puts these five processes in order from shortest predicted CPU time to longest CPU time, the average for these five processes (12.2 ms) does not change regardless of the order in which they arrive (as long as all five are in the Ready queue at Time 0). Even if the processes arrive in reverse order (from longest to shortest), the CPU will always take a moment before processing begins to put them in order from shortest to longest. For this reason, turnaround times will always be the same. Therefore, this scheme offers the consistent system response that designers want, but it remains vulnerable to backlogs (as was FCFS) if one large process monopolizes the CPU, because it doesn't allow a long process to be interrupted.

What if an urgent process arrives just before Process C begins execution? Shouldn't an important process go before one that's less important even if the latter one arrived first? The next scheme takes into consideration the importance of each process.

TABLE 4-4	Using SJN, Processes Are Arranged in Order from Shortest to Longest			
	Arrival Time	**Processing Time**	**Finish Time**	**Turnaround Time**
Process E	0	1	1	1
Process D	0	3	4	4
Process A	0	4	8	8
Process B	0	7	15	15
Process C	0	18	33	33
Total Turnaround:				61 ms
Average Turnaround:				12.2 ms

Priority Scheduling

The *Priority Scheduling* allocation scheme assigns a priority level to each process in the Ready queue depending on its importance. Then the most important are executed first, without interruption. Only after those are completed are less-important processes allowed to run. With this scheme, processes that can wait the longest are assigned CPU time only when nothing else is in the Ready queue. Here are the key points to keep in mind concerning the Priority Scheduling allocation scheme:

- Urgent processes get the highest priority and the first available CPU time. Some examples of urgent processes could be security scanning of an incoming file or recognition of a new device or printer that you want to use right away.

- Those that are of normal importance but not in the highest category are allowed the usual access to the CPU.

- Low-priority processes are executed when the CPU might otherwise sit idle. In other words, they run only when nothing more pressing needs to be run. Some examples of these processes could be building a current index for a seldom-used database file.

What happens if two processes with the same priority are in the Ready queue? Which goes first? In this case, the process that arrived sooner would be executed first and the other would execute second. In other words, this allocation scheme uses FCFS to break any ties.

But even this allocation scheme is not perfect. What if a very urgent process arrives while a low-priority process is executing and cannot be interrupted? Isn't there a fairer way to assign the CPU? The Shortest Remaining Time scheme addresses this issue by allowing interruptions.

Exercise 4-1: Configure a Priority for an Application in Windows

If you need the CPU to dedicate as much of its resources as possible to a running process, you can increase the program's priority. For instance, you may want to do this if you're rendering a complex edit in a movie-editing program. Here's how to do this on a Windows 7 system:

1. Press CTRL-ALT-DEL on the keyboard.

2. Click Start Task Manager.

3. Left-click the Processes tab, shown in Figure 4-4.

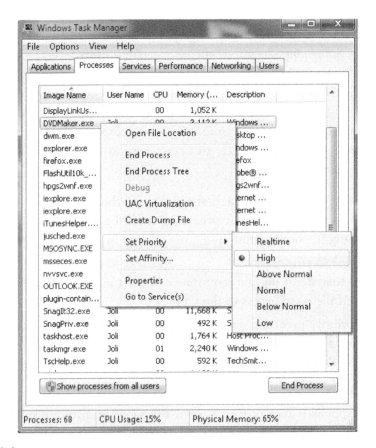

FIGURE 4-4 · As an end user, you can change your process's priority.

4. Right-click the related process.

5. Left-click Set Priority to select a new priority. Be aware that you might slow your system's response by moving a process that's normally low to high.

6. Click OK.

Exercise 4-2: Configure a Priority for an Application in Ubuntu Linux

To increase a program's priority in Linux, follow these steps:

1. Click System.

2. Click Administration.

3. Open System Monitor.

4. Left-click the Processes tab, shown in Figure 4-5.

5. Right-click the related process.

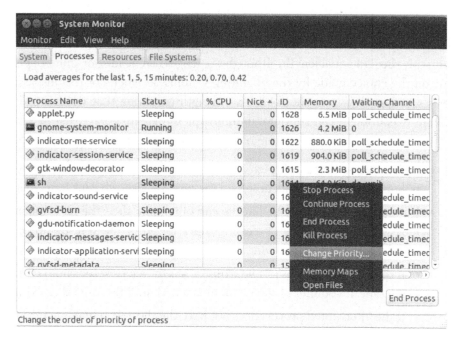

FIGURE 4-5 · Changing the priority of Linux processes

6. Select Change Priority.

7. Select the Nice value. A lower value corresponds to a higher priority.

8. Click Change Priority.

Shortest Remaining Time

The *Shortest Remaining Time (SRT)* scheme is a preemptive version of SJN. Simply stated, it allows processing to be interrupted when a shorter waiting process can finish faster than the process that's currently being executed. For SRT to work, each process must have a prediction of how much CPU time will be needed for the process to move from Ready to Finished.

Still Struggling

There's a lot of unavoidable jargon throughout computer literature. A good source for operating systems terms and definitions can be found at www.whatis .com, as well as at other websites featuring computer science definitions.

SRT introduces *time slices*, which are small units of processing time. It's similar to the way an hour is divided into 60 minutes. Processing time is divided into tiny slices of equal length, although the length can be long or short, depending on the choice made by the operating systems designer. For this discussion, let's say that each time slice is 2 ms in length (meaning that when a process begins execution, it can continue uninterrupted for 2 ms).

When a time slice expires, one of these events takes place:

- If the process that's being executed finishes before a time slice expires, it relinquishes the rest of its time, and the next time slice begins immediately.

- If the process is not finished at the end of its time slice, the CPU manager looks up the remaining processing times for all of the waiting processes and does one of the following:

  - If the process that was just interrupted has the shortest (or same) remaining time, it continues running uninterrupted until this time slice expires.

  - If the interrupted process does not have the shortest remaining time, the process with the shortest remaining time jumps to the front of the line, begins execution, and runs uninterrupted until its time slice expires.

Whenever a time slice expires, this cycle is repeated so that the processes with the shortest remaining execution time are finished faster than those with longer times.

TIP *To calculate the remaining processing time, subtract the processing time already completed from the processing time that was predicted.*

With SRT, the processes that are close to finishing will jump to the front of the line for execution, so they reach the Finished queue soonest. Watch how SRT works when four processes, listed in Table 4-5, arrive for execution.

TABLE 4-5	Results of the Four Processes Illustrated in Figure 4-6			
	Arrival Time	Total Processing Time	Finish Time	Turnaround Time
Process J	0	8	13	13
Process K	1	2	4	3
Process L	5	7	20	15
Process M	6	3	9	3
Total Turnaround:				34 ms
Average Turnaround:				8.5 ms

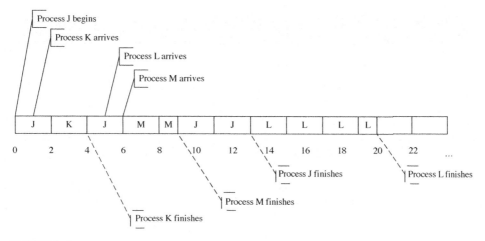

FIGURE 4-6 • With SRT, the CPU interrupts longer processes.

Figure 4-6 illustrates when each process arrives and finishes, using a time slice of 2 ms.

Table 4-6 shows in detail what happens at each instance as each process arrives in the Ready queue, starts or continues its execution, and finishes.

The big advantage to SRT is that it moves the shortest process through execution promptly. But there's a huge disadvantage—it requires that the system know *in advance* how much CPU time will be required by each process. *If* that information is available, this may be the best process scheduling scheme if the system has many important short processes to execute.

However, for computer systems that run programs, applications, or utilities that require varying or unknown execution times, this scheme cannot be used. The next one is better able to deal with waiting processes for which their processing parameters are unknown.

Round Robin

Round Robin is similar to FCFS because it runs each process in the order in which it arrives, but the key difference is that it is preemptive—that is, it allows process execution to be interrupted. And unlike SRT and SJN, it does not need to know the remaining computation time when it chooses which process will go next. Instead, it allows each process in the Ready State to get access to the CPU on a regular basis.

TABLE 4-6 A Step-by-Step Look at the Four Processes Shown in Figure 4-6

Time (ms)	Action
0	Process J, the only process waiting, begins execution for the first time slice of 2 ms.
1	Process K arrives and waits for the first time slice to expire.
2	The first time slice expires. Process J (which needs 6 ms more) is interrupted so Process K (which needs only 2 ms) can begin execution.
4	The time slice expires. Process K ends execution. Because no other process has arrived, Process J resumes execution.
5	Process L arrives.
6	The time slice expires. Process M arrives. Process J (which needs 4 ms more) is interrupted so Process M (which needs only 3 ms) can begin execution. Process L (which needs 7 ms) must wait.
8	The time slice expires. Process M (which needs only 1 ms more) has less remaining time than both Process J (which needs 4 ms) and Process L (which needs 7 ms). Process M continues execution.
9	Process M ends execution. Process J (which needs 4 ms) resumes execution.
11	The time slice expires. Process J (which needs only 2 ms more) has less remaining time than Process L (which needs 7 ms). Process J continues execution.
13	The time slice expires. Process J ends execution. Process L (which needs 7 ms) begins execution. No other processes arrive to interrupt it.
20	The time slice expires and Process L ends execution. If no other processes arrive, the CPU sits idle until one does.

With Round Robin, every time a time slice expires, the CPU checks to see if there are any other processes waiting in the Ready queue. Here is how they are allocated CPU time:

- If no other processes are waiting, the one that is being executed is allowed to continue uninterrupted for the duration of the next time slice.

- If other processes are in line, the currently executing process is interrupted, and it goes to the back of the line in the Ready queue.

- The waiting process (the one that is now first in the Ready queue) is then allowed to execute for the next time slice.
- As other processes arrive, they join the line in the Ready queue and cycle through execution until they eventually finish.

Look what happens when only two processes are in line. If the CPU is idle when two processes arrive in the Ready queue within 1 ms of each other, the one that arrives first begins execution and continues uninterrupted for the length of the time slice (2 ms). If that first process hasn't finished when the time slice expires, it is interrupted and moved back to the Ready queue. The second process takes the next time slice and runs uninterrupted for 2 ms. If the second process hasn't finished when its time slice expires, it is interrupted and moved to the Ready queue so that the first process can resume execution for the next time slice. This cycle (from Ready, to Running, to Ready, to Running, and so on) continues until each process finishes its execution and moves to the Finished state, as shown in Figure 4-7, which is an adaptation of Figure 3-1.

NOTE *In real life, some processes or jobs are stopped prematurely (because of such things as system errors or interruptions issued by the user), and they never successfully reach the Finished state. The examples presented in this chapter are simplified (ignoring these and other legitimate reasons for processes to end prematurely) to illustrate the fundamentals of these complex concepts.*

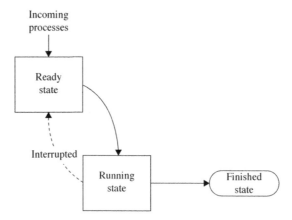

FIGURE 4-7 • With Round Robin, processes can cycle repeatedly from Ready to Running to Ready.

TABLE 4-7	Round Robin Will Service Each Waiting Process in Turn
	Arrival Time
Process J	0
Process K	1
Process L	5
Process M	6

Usually, many processes are waiting in the Ready queue. Each one is cycled through the Running queue, to the Ready queue, and back to the Running queue until each one gets to the Finished State. Let's see how Round Robin works with the four processes shown in Table 4-7. Notice that this table does not list predicted processing time, because that information is not used by this scheme.

The processes shown in Table 4-7 are moved through the Running State as illustrated in Figure 4-8. Notice, in this example, that Process L doesn't arrive until Time 5, midway through the third time slice.

Table 4-8 shows what happens at each moment of time as each process arrives, is executed, and finishes. Remember that if a process is interrupted before it finishes, it returns to the Ready queue and goes to the back of the line behind other processes that are already waiting. After it first arrives in the Ready queue, each process gets its turn to use a time slice no matter how much processing time it eventually requires. In other words, there's no discrimination between short and long processes. Table 4-8 shows in detail when each of the four processes cycles through the Running State.

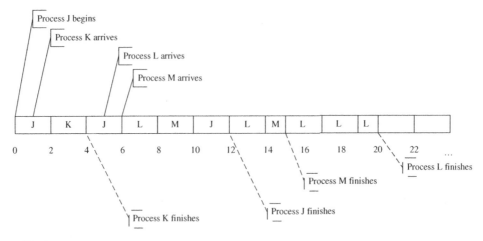

FIGURE 4-8 • Every process gets at least one time slice.

Time (ms)	Action
	TABLE 4-8 A Step-by-Step Look at the Movement of the Four Processes Shown in Figure 4-8
0	Process J, the only process in the Ready queue, begins execution for the first time slice of 2 ms.
1	Process K arrives in the Ready queue and waits for the first time slice to expire.
2	The first time slice expires. Process J is interrupted and returns to the Ready queue. Process K begins execution.
4	The second time slice expires. Process K ends execution and goes to the Finished State. Process J, the only process in the Ready queue, resumes execution for the next time slice.
5	Process L arrives in the Ready queue and waits for the time slice to expire.
6	The time slice expires. Process M arrives in the Ready queue and gets in line behind Process L. Process J is interrupted and rejoins the Ready queue behind Process M. Process L (which is next in line) begins execution.
8	The time slice expires. Process L is interrupted and rejoins the Ready queue behind Process J. Process M (which is next in line) begins execution.
10	The time slice expires. Process M is interrupted and rejoins the Ready queue behind Process L. Process J (which is next in line) continues execution.
12	Process J ends execution and goes to the Finished State. Process L (which is next in line) continues execution.
14	The time slice expires. Process L is interrupted and rejoins the Ready queue. No other processes have arrived, so it is the only one in line. Process M (which is next in line) continues execution.
15	Process M ends execution and goes to the Finished State. Its time slice ends immediately. Process L resumes execution. (No other processes arrive in the Ready queue to interrupt its processing at Time 17 or Time 19.)
20	Process L ends execution and goes to the Finished State.

TABLE 4-9 Total and Average Turnaround Times Using Round Robin			
	Arrival Time	**Used CPU Time**	**Turnaround Time**
Process J	0	8	12
Process K	1	2	3
Process L	5	7	15
Process M	6	3	9
Total Turnaround:			39 ms
Average Turnaround:			9.8 ms

Although we couldn't predict turnaround times before processing took place because the amount of CPU time required by each process was unknown, it can be calculated after execution is complete. The average turnaround time using Round Robin is shown in Table 4-9.

To see how Round Robin stacks up against the previous CPU allocation scheme, compare their average turnaround times. Using SRT, the average for these same processes (8.5 ms) is shorter than the average for Round Robin (9.8 ms, as shown in Table 4-9). Does that make SRT better?

One might conclude from this exercise that if we can have processing information in advance, then SRT would be best, and that if that information is not available, then Round Robin would be best. And for some computing environments, that may be a correct conclusion.

As this example demonstrates, there is *no single best allocation scheme*. The best choice depends on the nature of the computing environment that the allocation scheme is serving.

Multiple Level Queues

Let's look at an allocation scheme that combines several of those already described—it's called *Multiple Level Queues*. As processes arrive for processing, they are assigned to one of several queues, and each queue is managed using one of the previously described schemes and can be either preemptive or nonpreemptive. This allocation scheme selects execution processes from among several queues, moving from queue to queue in a predetermined order, selecting the process that's at the forefront of its respective queue. The scheme might visit some queues more often than others, depending on the overall system goals. For example, it might take two or three processes from Queue 1 for every one process it takes from Queue 4 to make sure that the important processes in Queue 1 can finish faster.

TIP   *To see what priority is assigned to some of the processes running on a Windows computer, open Task Manager, click the Processes tab, and right-click any process to view or change its priority status.*

This scheme offers lots of flexibility for system designers. For example, imagine we might design the system to separate incoming processes into four groups: one is for processes that have pressing deadlines (such as delivering medication to a patient); a second consists of high-but-less-urgent processes (such as responding to a command from the keyboard); a third group includes processes that are expected to need significant CPU time (such as those requiring intensive mathematical calculations); and the fourth includes batch processes that can be executed over several hours (such as those that archive documents overnight).

When designing a Multiple Level Queue scheme for this system, we might designate the first queue to use the SRT scheme; the second queue might use FCFS; the third queue with CPU-intensive processes could use a Round Robin scheme but with time slices that are longer than usual so that they finish faster than they would otherwise; and the fourth queue might be managed using FCFS or SJN. Although this example shows only four groups, actual systems often have from one to hundreds of queues.

There are many versions of Multiple Level Queues. For example, one system might give an extra boost to processes that have already spent a great deal of time in the system without finishing. Another system might move a process from a queue where it is languishing to a higher propriety queue when it starts to demand more processing time. Some systems never move processes from one queue to another; each one stays in the queue where it is originally assigned until it finishes.

Because this allocation scheme offers the system designer the most flexibility, it is the one that's used by many present-day operating systems.

Multicore Systems

Thus far in this chapter, we have limited our discussion to sharing a CPU with only one core among many processes. In every case, this CPU could execute only one process at a time, hence the need to carefully allocate the lone CPU so that its services could be shared most efficiently.

These days, it's not uncommon for a computer to have a CPU with multiple cores (also called *multicore systems*), and the opportunities and challenges for efficient process management are multiplied accordingly.

TIP   *A CPU can have from one to several cores, each of which is a complete processing unit. Therefore, a single-core processor can perform one instruction at a time, and a quad-core system can execute four instructions at once.*

For example, if a computing system has 20 cores, each can execute one process at the same moment, and each core can be assigned using any allocation scheme. However, the successful management of a multicore computer system requires the careful coordination of every queue so that the cores work seamlessly together. Here are some possible techniques that can be used:

- One solution would be for the system designer to assign one core to each queue.
- A more complex solution would be to coordinate several cores to work cooperatively on a single task, such as a database search. For example, each of four cores could be assigned one-fourth of the database to search for the information that's requested. Likewise, the database could be divided into tenths, with 10 cores searching it in parallel.
- Some programs can be written for multiple processors so that the instructions can be performed simultaneously and the final results calculated very quickly (called *parallel programming*). For example, if the program requires that one set of numbers be multiplied by another set of numbers, the programming code can divide the work among several groups, assign one core to each group, and then combine the results in the final stages of execution.

These techniques speed turnaround time significantly, but turnaround is only one part of the system efficiency equation. Other critical system resources also need to be carefully managed, such as memory, data, file storage, network access, and others. Thus, a multicore operating system is more complex than that for a single CPU.

Still Struggling

Additional information on multiple-CPU systems can be found at the Universal Parallel Computing Research Center at the University of Illinois (www.upcrc .illinois.edu).

Multicore system management is a subject that's too intricate to be thoroughly explored in this book. But no matter how complex a computing environment becomes, the basics are the same—making the very best use of the system's processing resources.

Exercise 4-3: Explore Performance Monitor's Processor Options

Performance Monitor is an application that you can use to view how a CPU is performing. It's available in various editions of Windows, including Windows 7 and Windows 2008. Here, you can monitor counters such as %ProcessorTime, %InterruptTime, Interrupts/sec, and more. Figure 4-9 shows three of these counters at the bottom of the screen.

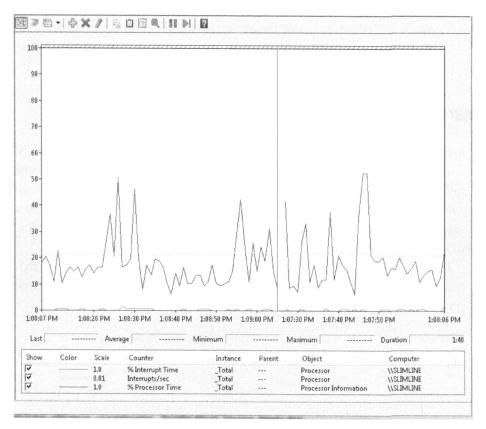

FIGURE 4-9 · Performance Monitor allows you to monitor a CPU's performance.

To access the Performance Monitor and add a counter in Windows 7, follow these steps:

1. Click the Windows Start button, type **Performance Monitor**, and choose it from the list of results.

2. In the panel on the left, click Performance Monitor. (If necessary, enter an administrator password to continue.)

3. Click the green plus (+) sign to see and add available counters.

4. Browse the counter options from the list, and click the down arrow next to one you want to monitor.

5. For each counter you want to track, highlight it and then click Add.

6. When you have finished adding counters, click OK (or click Cancel to close without adding).

7. Watch the counter results. Figure 4-9 shows three counters with check-marks at the bottom of the screen, and the three resulting graphs are shown in color.

Summary

In these pages, we explored six CPU allocation schemes—First Come, First Served (FCFS); Shortest Job Next (SJN); Priority Scheduling; Shortest Remaining Time (SRT); Round Robin; and Multiple Level Queues—and we briefly discussed a few of the strengths and weaknesses of each as it can be implemented on a single-CPU system. Finally, we discussed the implications of allocating multiple CPUs to multiple processes.

In the next chapter, we explore the problems caused by processes that become starved or deadlocked, and we look into a few causes of system-wide crashes.

QUIZ

Choose the correct response to each of the multiple-choice questions. Note that there may be more than one correct response to each question.

1. **What is the primary weakness of First Come, First Served (FCFS)?**
   A. It causes many interrupts.
   B. One large process can delay all the others.
   C. It causes the largest processes to finish last.
   D. It's unfair to the process that arrives first.

2. **A preemptive allocation scheme is important because it does what?**
   A. It allocates the CPU to the most important process.
   B. It is fairer to longer processes.
   C. It can pause the execution of a long process.
   D. It is fairer to short processes.

3. **Which of the following allocation schemes are not preemptive?**
   A. First Come, First Served (FCFS)
   B. Shortest Job Next (SJN)
   C. Shortest Remaining Time (SRT)
   D. Round Robin

4. **The formula to calculate the turnaround time of a process is which of the following?**
   A. Finish time minus processing time
   B. Finish time minus arrival time
   C. Arrival time plus the processing time
   D. Arrival time plus the waiting time

5. **How is the average process turnaround time calculated?**
   A. Finish time minus processing time
   B. Total turnaround time for the processes divided by the number of processes
   C. Number of processes multiplied by their processing times
   D. The total for the processing times of the waiting processes

6. **What is a time slice?**
   A. The time required to execute a very long process
   B. The amount of time it takes a process to go from arrival to finish
   C. The period of time assigned to a process so it can execute
   D. The period of time used by the CPU to rearrange incoming processes

7. **When might you want longer (rather than shorter) time slices?**
   A. When you are running many large processes
   B. When you are running many short processes
   C. When you are using Shortest Job Next (SJN)
   D. When you are using First Come, First Served (FCFS)

8. **If a process begins execution but doesn't need the whole time slice, what happens?**
   A. The rest of the time slice goes unused until the next time slice is scheduled to start.
   B. The remainder of the time slice is allocated to the longest-waiting process.
   C. The process relinquishes the rest of the time slice so the next process can begin at once.
   D. The process finishes faster than expected.

9. **In what way is SJN different from SRT?**
   A. SJN requires that the processing time be known in advance.
   B. SJN allows interruption of long processes.
   C. SRT allows interruption of long processes.
   D. SRT executes processes in the order in which they arrive.

10. **In what way is Round Robin similar to FCFS?**
    A. Both require that the processing time be known in advance.
    B. Both offer consistent turnaround times.
    C. Each one allows interruption of long processes.
    D. Neither one rearranges incoming processes.

chapter **5**

CPU Scheduling and Deadlocks

This chapter introduces the complexities involved when trying to balance a computer system's many resources—including both hardware and software—to keep everything running smoothly, without deadlocks or starved processes. Here, we will examine the conditions for crashes and other deadlocks, how and why they occur, and how system designers try to avoid or resolve them.

CHAPTER OBJECTIVES

In this chapter, you will

- Learn the importance of managing critical resources effectively
- Be able to explain the concepts of deadlock and starvation
- Understand the requirements for a deadlock or livelock to occur
- Learn the role of deadlock prevention and resolution measures

What Is Resource Management?

Good *resource management* requires the allocation of critical system resources in such a way that they do not conflict with each other or allow processes to languish in the system with no hope of running to completion. On a practical level, a common solution to a deadlocked system is to reboot it, thus resetting all the processes so that they can restart their tasks, hopefully with more effective synchronization.

> A deadlock *is a situation in which processes in the Running State are at a standstill and cannot advance. A deadlock can be resolved only with outside intervention.*

But what if the system can't be rebooted? Some systems are mission-critical and can't be paused. If the deadlock occurs on a system that a surgeon is using to manipulate robots while operating on a patient's microscopic blood vessels, then rebooting is not a viable option. Likewise, if the system is managing the timing for the fuel injectors in your car's engine, rebooting could be problematic. Let's look more closely at how deadlocks occur and what can be done about them.

Deadlocks

In the early days of computers, a lack of process synchronization that caused the system to crash was called a *deadly embrace*, a colorful term for what's known today as a *deadlock*. Let's watch how a deadlock can lead to a system crash by slowing down the disintegration of system resource management. A typical series of events looks like this:

1. After a process has been allocated one of the resources that it needs (such as a printer), it tries to claim another critical resource (perhaps a smart card reader) that has already been allocated to another process, which is not planning to release it in the near future.

2. Not knowing that its printer request cannot be satisfied anytime soon, the process pauses, waiting for the tied-up resource (in this example, a smart card reader) to be released. However, while it waits, *it does not release the resource that it has already been allocated.*

3. In a very short time, other processes begin waiting for one or more of the tied-up resources (either the original smart card reader or the printer). These processes also pause and do not release their allocated resources either, so the number of unreleased resources grows.

4. As the system becomes more and more unresponsive, waiting processes join the tangle, each one waiting for a resource that is already held by some other process that will not release it.

5. Finally, the deadlock causes the system to crash because none of the processes in the system can perform any useful processing and none of them can proceed.

6. At this point, the user might notice that the keyboard has stopped responding, the screen has turned blue, or a session-ending message has been displayed.

Deadlocks are only one example of the problem. Other resource management failures are discussed next.

Unresponsive System?

If your computer starts acting strangely or seems to stop running, try these steps, in order:

1. Try to restart the problem application through File | Exit or File | Close, if available. Alternatively, if the Close option is not available (or if the application is frozen), try clicking the X in the corner.

2. Log out of your current session (if applicable).

3. Reboot your computer by holding down the CTRL-ALT-DEL keys together (to open Task Manager on a Windows computer) and choose to restart; click the Apple menu and choose Restart on a Macintosh. If the deadlock is so bad that Task Manager can't open, or if the computer is completely frozen, hold down the power button on the computer for 3–5 seconds to perform a hard reboot.

4. If, after the reboot, problems still exist, disconnect all of your external devices, such as printers, scanners, and so on, and work through these steps again.

Remember, though, that there can be many causes of system freezes, and these steps are just a start. If problems persist, seek expert assistance.

Livelock

Livelock occurs if two processes are alternately requesting and releasing resources, resulting in a kind of dance, with neither process doing any useful work but neither waiting, either. Neither one can run to completion because each is requesting a resource that the other is temporarily holding, and by the time the awaited resource is released, the other is being temporarily held.

It's similar to a familiar event on a narrow walkway. Imagine a hilly path that's wide enough only for two people. As two walkers meet from opposite ends of the path, both step to the hill side, temporarily blocking each other. Then they simultaneously step to the cliff side, again temporarily blocking each other. They both step back to the hill side again. If the choreography continues, the blockage remains, even though both walkers are never technically waiting. The path is clear and yet neither walker can pass the other. That's an example of livelock.

In a computer, this could happen if two processes are requesting different instructions on the same disk. Here's an example of livelock:

1. The first process (Process A) requests data on an inside track of the hard drive, so the request is sent to the mechanism called the disk controller.

2. The disk controller sends the disk's read/write head toward the inside track. Process A temporarily pauses to wait for the requested data, and the disk controller begins taking other requests.

3. Now, Process B requests an instruction on an outside track of the same disk from the controller.

4. With receipt of the new instruction, the disk controller stops the progress of the disk's read/write head and sends it toward the outside track. Instantly, the disk's read/write head changes direction to move toward the outside track. Process B is temporarily paused while it waits for the needed instruction. The disk controller can now take other requests.

5. Now, Process A sends a command reconfirming that it needs the data on the inside track.

6. With receipt of the reconfirmation, the disk controller interrupts the disk's read/write head, sending it back toward the inside track. Instantly, the disk's read/write head reverses direction. Process A pauses while it waits for the needed instruction. The disk controller can now take other requests.

7. Predictably, Process B sends a command reconfirming that it needs the data on the outside track.

8. And so on.

During livelock, neither request is ever granted nor the two processes will move forward. In the flowchart shown in Figure 5-1, these two processes will never finish because the read/write head for the hard drive will never reach either of the two requested tracks shown on the right. (To follow the

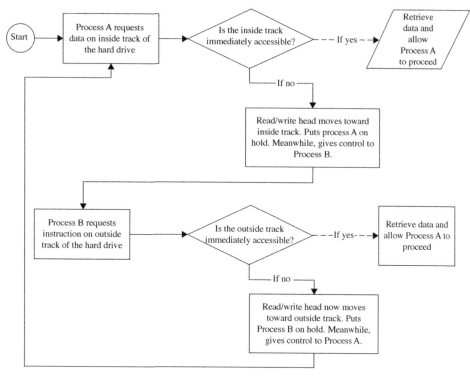

FIGURE 5-1 · During livelock, the desired tracks (on right) will never be reached.

flowchart, start in the upper-left corner and follow the arrows. Decisions are shown inside diamond shapes and processes are shown inside rectangles.)

Livelock is not as serious to the system as deadlock because it affects only a few processes and not the entire system. However, it is serious to the processes that are stuck.

Starvation

Thus far, we've discussed the situation when more than one process fails to finish. What if only a single process stops before completing its processing? Perhaps it is waiting for an event, data, or a resource that will never become available. In any case, this process could sit unnoticed, somewhere between Ready and Finished, but never run to completion. This is an example of process *starvation*.

Let's say that the system has five processes and five resources. Let's further assume that none of these processes can claim a resource unless both resources are available at the same time. (We might make this stipulation to prevent system deadlocks.) Figure 5-2 shows the five processes, each of which needs to claim *both* of the resources located to their right and left before it can proceed.

The sequence might go like this:

- Process A and Process C already hold the two necessary resources and both are executing.
- When Process A finishes, it releases its hold on both resources—the scanner and the smart card reader.
- Now Process B checks to see if it can claim the two resources that it needs, but, alas, the projector on its left is still held by Process C. It is not allowed to claim either resource unless it can claim both of them, so it does not yet claim the smart card reader. Instead, it waits patiently for the projector to be released by Process C.
- Soon Process A wants to restart. It verifies that both resources are available (they are), so it claims them both and starts again.
- Soon Process C completes its execution and releases both resources, including the projector that Process B requires.
- Now Process B checks to see if it can claim both resources that it needs, but although the projector on its left is now available, the smart card reader on the right is now held again by Process A. Because Process B cannot claim both resources at once, it continues to wait.

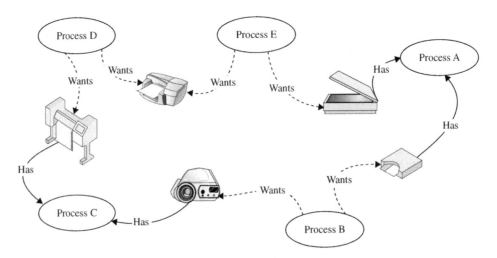

FIGURE 5-2 · Each process needs two resources to proceed.

What happens if Processes A and C alternate their execution and never release their resources at the same time? In that case, Process B will never get the chance to finish and it becomes a victim of starvation, and a failure of good resource management.

To combat starvation, the operating system can track how long a given process has been in the running state; those taking an exceptionally long time could be starving. To rescue those processes, the system can slow the flow of new processes into the system, thus reducing competition for the necessary resources. Alternatively, the languishing processes could be elevated to a higher priority. Remember that checking for starved processes is an overhead process, one that can reduce system efficiency if it's performed too often. On the other hand, if it's not performed often enough, it could cause an increase in starved processes. This is one more example of the delicate balancing act that's performed by operating systems designers.

TIP Overhead *is any task that's required to maintain the system but does not contribute to process execution. Because overhead tasks consume important resources, they reduce overall system efficiency. Designers try to keep overhead to a minimum.*

Exercise 5-1: Use Windows Task Manager to View and End Running Processes

You can use Task Manager on a Windows 7 computer to view running processes and end them. If you know that one process is holding up others, this is where to stop them.

Here's an example: Say you're running the Firefox web browser and it freezes, so you click the X in the top-right corner to close it (because the File | Exit options are not responding), or perhaps the file doesn't close as it should. Perhaps when you try to open the browser again, you receive a message that says something to the effect that Firefox is still running, and you must close it first (before you can open it again—even though you know it is already closed). This is an example of a process gone awry.

To end the process, try these steps:

1. Press the CTRL-ALT-DEL keys together and choose Task Manager from the list.

2. Click the Processes tab.

3. From the list of processes, click the application that appears to be broken (in this case firefox.exe), as shown in Figure 5-3.

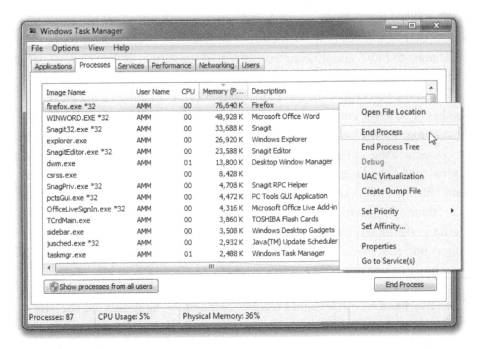

FIGURE 5-3 · The Windows Task Manager allows you to stop processes at will.

4. Right-click the process and choose End Process.

5. You'll receive a warning message that ending the process may cause system instability. Choose either End Process or Cancel.

If the system becomes unstable, we suggest that you reboot it before continuing.

Necessary Conditions for Deadlocks

A variety of external resources have the ability to cause a deadlock. Examples include projectors, scanners, smart card readers, cameras, some distributed databases, plotters, and printers. Notice that these are nonpreemptable devices, files, or other resources—they are not easily shared—so the operating system must take care when allocating them.

Every time a deadlock occurs, four specific conditions are evident:

- **Mutual exclusion**   Only one process is allowed to hold a dedicated (unsharable) resource at one time. Mutual exclusion was described in the preceding example when the smart card reader was claimed by the first process, forcing every other process to wait for its release before proceeding.

- **Resource holding**   This happens when a process refuses to release its resources while it waits for a missing resource that would allow it to run to completion.

- **No preemption**   This means that the operating system does not interrupt (doesn't preempt) the claim of a process on its claimed resource.

- **Circular wait**   This is the condition whereby several processes are waiting for a resource that's held by another. To watch circular wait in action, imagine four processes (Processes A, B, C, and D), each one holding a nonsharable resource on its left (shown with a solid line in Figure 5-4) and waiting for a nonsharable resource on its right (shown with a dotted line in Figure 5-4). Because none of the claims that have already been granted can be preempted, none of the needed resources will ever be released.

Although these four are present with every deadlock, the opposite is not true: a deadlock does not occur every time these four conditions coexist in the system.

So, you might ask, if we build an operating system without one of these conditions, could we make it deadlock-proof? Sadly no, because, as you'll see in the remainder of this chapter, each of these conditions is required for an operating system to run smoothly. However, by adopting a proactive strategy to watch for the symptoms of deadlocks, the system can take the first step toward preventing or resolving them.

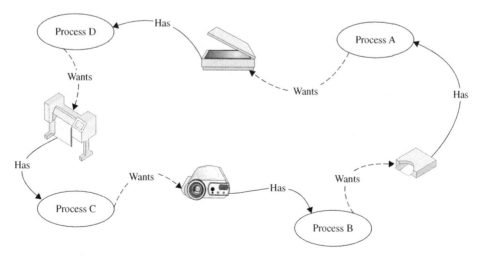

FIGURE 5-4 · An example of circular wait

Deadlock Strategies

Strategies to deal with deadlocks generally fall into several categories: prevention, avoidance, detection, and recovery. Remember, during processing, once a resource is allocated to a process, there isn't an easy way for the system to deallocate the resource unless the process gives it up voluntarily or processing ends prematurely due to an error or an unanticipated event.

NOTE   *One deadlock strategy that's mentioned in computer science research is the ostrich algorithm, which assumes that too much overhead is required to prevent, avoid, or recover from a deadlock. Therefore, as its name implies, this algorithm calls on the operating system to assume that a deadlock will not occur (and, if and when it does, the user receives a message to reboot).*

Prevention

Because all four conditions are necessary for a deadlock to occur (mutual exclusion, resource holding, no preemption, and circular wait), the operating system could simply remove one of the conditions and thereby prevent deadlocks, right? In theory, this sounds like an acceptable prevention strategy, but this is much more difficult than it sounds because each of these four conditions is required for some part of the operating system:

- Mutual exclusion is required for some of the system's devices, especially for those that are assigned exclusively (such as projectors, scanners, printers, plotters, and so on). If we suspend mutual exclusion and allow the conference room projector to be shared equally at the same time among several presenters, imagine the ensuing chaos. The interwoven presentations would lack the cohesion that one would obviously desire. Therefore, this device requires mutual exclusion so that each presenter, in turn, is granted total control of the projector for the duration of the presentation.
- Resource holding, which allows a process to hold on to critical resources throughout processing, causes deadlocks when several processes that are already holding one critical resource request another resource that is already being held by another process, which will never release it. If the operating system disallowed resource holding, and instead mandated that each incoming process request, in advance, all of the resources it will need, then deadlocks might be prevented because each process would be

allowed to begin only when 100 percent of its resources were being held by that process. However, in interactive computing environments, resources are routinely requested and released on the fly. Imagine how slow processes would move through the system if each incoming process that required a certain printer could not begin until the previous process released that printer, and then held on to the printer for the duration of its processing, even if it needed to print only a single page at the conclusion of the job? The result would be a lot of wasted CPU time and the printer would become a huge bottleneck.

- No preemption could be eliminated if the operating system is given permission to preempt the allocation of a resource to a process. This might be beneficial if an urgent process needed to take control of a resource already allocated to another. However, if it is a large-format printer that's half way through a big banner, and it's taken over by a competing process that intends to print a campaign poster, the result would undoubtedly be unusable. In fact, the interruption of any process's access to a dedicated device is often problematic.

- Circular wait could be removed if the operating system kept constant watch for any circular pattern of resource holding and requests, as was shown in Figure 5-4. By preventing any of these four resources from holding one of the nonsharable resources (shown with solid lines), a deadlock could be prevented. The operating system could remove this possibility by requiring each incoming process to request in advance its needed resources. However, this is not feasible in interactive computing environments where resources are allocated and deallocated on the fly.

Exercise 5-2: Practicing Real-World Avoidance and Prevention Techniques

In some instances, you can avoid or prevent deadlocks by limiting what runs in the background on the computers you use. To see what's running in the background on a Windows-based computer, search for a program called msconfig.exe (you can search for this file or open a box to type in its name by pressing the WINDOWS-R keys). When you open this program, you'll see a window similar to the one shown in Figure 5-5. Click the Startup tab. Deselect items you don't use every day (the changes will take effect after you restart your computer). By limiting what runs in the background, you are limiting calls to resources, and in doing so, may prevent problems that result in a deadlock.

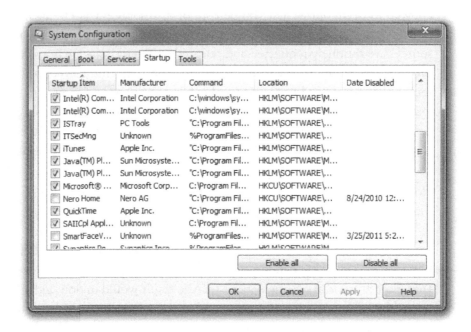

FIGURE 5-5 · The System Configuration window shows your startup programs.

As you can see, deadlocks are extremely difficult to prevent, but can they be avoided? That's been the subject of much operating systems research, which we'll explore next.

Avoidance

If we can't prevent deadlocks, perhaps we can avoid them. Published research explored several options that operating systems can use to avoid deadlocks. One of the most famous problems in operating systems theory was proposed in 1965 by a computer scientist from the Netherlands, Edsger Dijkstra. Named the Banker's Algorithm, Dijkstra's problem proposed to regulate the allocation of resources to avoid deadlocks.

Dijkstra suggested that a computer system's collection of critical resources is analogous to a bank with a fixed amount of available cash to make customer loans. All customers request a credit limit, against which they can request smaller loans. The bank has four operating principles:

- Each customer will be granted a maximum credit limit when the account is opened.

- No customer will be granted a credit limit that exceeds the total amount of cash in the bank.

- No customer will be allowed to borrow more than the credit limit.
- The sum total of all the bank's loans will never exceed the total cash in the bank.

Notice that the bank is not required to have enough cash to fulfill the maximum credit limit of *all its borrowers at the same time*. Rather, it requires the bank to carefully manage its cash assets so that it can grant loans to all its borrowers over time, as long as the four operating principles are not violated.

For example, if the bank has $10,000 and four customers with credit limits of $1,000, $3,000, $4,000, and $7,000, then the bank cannot grant maximum loans to all four borrowers at the same time, because together they would require $15,000, which is more than the total amount available for loans ($10,000). However, the bank can grant maximum loans to each borrower by choosing them carefully. Notice that the bank can grant maximum loans to the first three customers at the same time ($1,000 + $3,000 + $4,000 = $8,000) without any risk, and then grant the last loan ($7,000) as soon as a minimum of $7,000 in loans has been repaid by some combination of the first three borrowers. (For this discussion, we are ignoring any additional interest that would accrue on the loans and be paid to the bank, thus increasing its total cash.)

The Banker's Algorithm identifies two states for the bank: a safe state and an unsafe state. A *safe state* is one in which the bank has enough available funds, after making loans, to satisfy *at least one of the borrower's maximum requests*. An *unsafe state* occurs when all of the borrowers' maximum remaining credit totals more than the bank's available cash.

Let's watch what happens when each of the four borrowers requests a loan that is smaller than the borrowers' collective maximum credit limit. Table 5-1 shows an example of a safe state because the bank's maximum amount of

TABLE 5-1   A Safe State—Remaining Cash ($1,100) Exceeds at Least One Maximum Credit Limit

Customer	Credit Limit	Loan Amount	Remaining Credit
Customer W	1,000	200	800
Customer X	3,000	2,300	700
Customer Y	4,000	700	3,300
Customer Z	7,000	5,500	1,500
Total	15,000	8,900	6,100

cash ($10,000) minus the total of amount of loans already granted ($8,900) is $1,100, which is *greater than the remaining credit for at least one customer.* In fact, $1,100 is greater than the maximum remaining loans that could be requested by both Customer W ($800) and Customer X ($700), assuming that they make their maximum requests sequentially. (However, if they were to make their loan requests at the same time, both loans could not be fulfilled because together they need $1,500.)

Table 5-2 shows how a safe state can degenerate into an unsafe state with a single additional loan of $700 to Customer Z, because the bank's maximum cash minus the total of loans already granted (10,000 – 9,400 = $600) *is less than the remaining credit for any customer.* With that single $700 loan, the bank has become vulnerable. Now, if *any* customer uses the remainder of its credit limit, then the bank, with only $600 in its coffers, will *not* be able to accommodate the loan. This is an unstable state.

By avoiding an unsafe state, we can avoid deadlocks, but the opposite is not true. As you can see, an unsafe state opens the door for a deadlock to occur, but it does not guarantee that it will occur. If all the customers take out loans that are less than their limits, the system might continue in an unsafe state without peril. An unsafe state is one that presents the opportunity for a deadlock.

When we apply the Banker's Algorithm to a computer system, the cash is represented by the total number and type of resources available on the system, and the credit limit is the maximum number and type of resources that each customer (process) may need.

For this system to work, each process must declare its resource needs in advance. Using the concepts proposed here, the operating system has to guard against satisfying any resource request that moves it from a safe state to an unsafe state.

TABLE 5-2 An Unsafe State—Remaining Cash ($600) Is Less Than All Remaining Credit Lines

Customer	Credit Limit	Loan Amount	Remaining Credit
Customer W	1,000	200	800
Customer X	3,000	2,300	700
Customer Y	4,000	700	3,300
Customer Z	7,000	6,200	800
Total	$15,000	$9,400	$5,600

The Banker's Algorithm can work if there are few resources, but becomes problematic when systems grow in size, or if the incoming processes are not prepared to announce, in advance, their resource requirements.

Detection

Before a system can recover from a deadlock, the deadlock first has to be detected. One way to do so is to look for interrelationships, such as a circle of requested and held resources, as illustrated previously in Figure 5-4. However, in a complex network or a computing system with many resources to be shared among many processes, it may be difficult to identify the specific processes and resources that are locked up.

Often, network administrators incorporate system tools to monitor processes. Figure 5-6 shows the Resource Monitor on a computer running Windows 7.

One way to try to identify processes causing a deadlock is to follow this sequence of steps:

1. Identify all processes that are using their resources and are not waiting for one. Because these processes are not waiting, we can assume that they are not part of the deadlock and therefore eliminate them from our investigation.

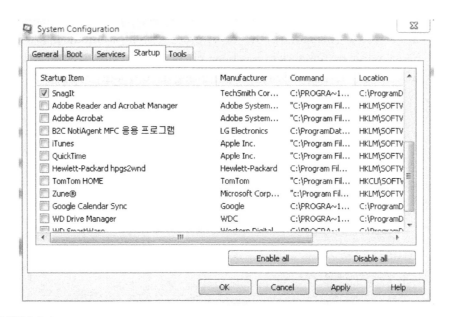

FIGURE 5-6 · The Resource Monitor reveals details of the system's performance.

2. Identify all processes that are waiting for resources that are still sufficiently available. Because they will eventually run to completion, these processes are not part of the deadlock.

3. If there are any processes left that are awaiting resources that are not, or will not, become available, this indicates that these processes are deadlocked.

After identifying the processes that are causing the deadlock, we can explore options for recovery.

Recovery

If a system stops, it's time to pick up the pieces. An early indication of a possible impending deadlock is a message that at least one program has stopped prematurely, as shown in Figure 5-7. Let's explore a few ways to recover from a deadlock as elegantly as possible.

When a deadlock is detected, the operating system ideally attempts to recover gracefully, with minimal disruption and without crashing. Most recovery solutions require that at least one process (called a *victim*) be halted and restarted. Several recovery options, some more attractive than others, are listed here:

- The first solution is to ignore the detection information and simply declare that *every process* is deadlocked. All become a victim, all are terminated, and the system is restarted, thereby forcing every process to begin again from scratch. This requires that every process keep careful track of what it has done so far, what data has been changed and saved, and how it can successfully start again without corrupting its instructions and data.

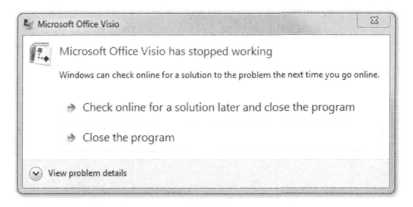

FIGURE 5-7 · Sample warning that a program has stopped working

- The second solution is to identify the exact processes that are deadlocked, make them the only victims, and force them to restart.

- The third solution also identifies the exact processes that are deadlocked, but kills them off one at a time so that the remaining deadlocked processes have a chance to become untangled and move forward without restarting. With this scenario, only one victim at a time must restart. For example, notice in Figure 5-4 that if any one of these four processes is killed, the remaining processes would all be able to run to completion successfully.

- The fourth solution merely pauses one deadlocked victim at a time, and does so temporarily. In this scheme, the victim is merely halted long enough for the deadlock to be resolved, and then it is allowed to resume its operation from where it stopped. Notice that this option works only if the process keeps careful track of its progress, and only if the operating system is built to save that information so the victim can resume without disturbing its operation, no matter how complex that may be.

- The fifth solution identifies one or more *nondeadlocked processes that are holding critical resources* and preempts them, allocating the critical resources to any waiting deadlocked processes so that they can run to completion. Only then are the resources returned to the nondeadlocked processes so that they can finish.

- The sixth solution halts all of the processes in the Ready queue waiting to enter the system. It then allows the processes that are in the Running State to finish and thereby release their resources as they routinely do upon completion of their processing. With the release of more and more resources, the deadlock may resolve itself, but that's not guaranteed. This option works only if the required resource is among those that will be released with the finishing processes. Otherwise, the nondeadlocked processes will run to completion, but the deadlock will remain.

Only the last option does not require a victim. This raises an interesting question: are certain processes more likely to be chosen as a victim? Yes, most operating systems consider a process's priority, criticality, and remaining processing time when choosing which ones will be stopped or paused. If the process is urgent or one that affects many other processes, it is less likely to be interrupted.

TIP *When a computer system crashes and tells you to reboot, the likely cause is a system deadlock, and the solution that many operating systems offer is the first option listed here: to kill off all processes and restart the computer.*

Summary

In this chapter, we explored the need to thoughtfully allocate system resources to avoid conflicts that can result in deadlocks, process starvation, or races. We also examined the conditions that can lead to system-wide crashes and other inconveniences, as well as some techniques commonly used to prevent, avoid, detect, and recover from deadlocks. Finally, we explored the thinking behind a common deadlock solution—rebooting the entire system.

In the next chapter, we describe several ways the memory manager can regulate the allocation of its main memory (commonly known as RAM) as well as the advantages and disadvantages of each method.

QUIZ

Choose the correct response to each of the multiple-choice questions. Note that there may be more than one correct response to each question.

1. **Which of these are conditions for deadlock to occur?**
   A. Starvation
   B. Mutual exclusion
   C. Circular wait
   D. Avoidance

2. **Which resources typically cause deadlocks?**
   A. Hardware but not software
   B. Software but not hardware
   C. Dedicated resources, hardware or software
   D. Sharable resources, hardware or software

3. **Which system conflict involves two processes that remain busy but never move forward?**
   A. Deadlock
   B. Starvation
   C. Circular wait
   D. Livelock

4. **What are the four necessary conditions for deadlock to occur?**
   A. Mutual exclusion, circular wait, no preemption, resource holding
   B. Resource holding, avoidance, prevention, circular wait
   C. No preemption, starvation, dedicated resources, mutual exclusion
   D. Circular wait, starvation, livelock, resource holding

5. **The Banker's Algorithm offers which of the following?**
   A. A concept to avoid deadlocks
   B. A way to manage sharable resources
   C. A theory on cash control for banks
   D. A strategy to avoid livelocks

6. **Deadlocks can be prevented by which of these actions?**
   A. Make sure the four conditions for deadlock can coexist at the same time.
   B. Eliminate all sharable resources.
   C. Use the Banker's Algorithm.
   D. Remove one of the necessary conditions for deadlock.

7. **Which of these actions might help a deadlocked system to recover?**
   A. Force all processes to stop and then reboot the system.
   B. Pause one deadlocked process and let it resume after the deadlock is resolved.
   C. Kill off one process at a time until the deadlock is broken.
   D. Pause a nondeadlocked process and release its resource so the deadlock can be resolved, and then allow it to finish.

8. **What is the role of the victim in deadlock resolution?**
   A. The victim is the first process allowed to finish.
   B. The victim is killed off so the other processes can finish.
   C. The victim is never allowed to restart its processing.
   D. The victim must release its resources so other processes can finish.

9. **What is the goal of an operating system's designer regarding deadlock, livelock, and starvation?**
   A. All three should be minimized.
   B. All should be detectable so the system can recover gracefully.
   C. Each one happens very rarely and therefore can be ignored.
   D. System crashes occur every now and then, so users need to live with them.

10. **Choose which of the following statements are true.**
    A. A Windows system cannot become deadlocked.
    B. A Macintosh system cannot become deadlocked.
    C. An Ubuntu Linux system cannot become deadlocked.
    D. None of the above.

Part III

Memory and Disk Management

chapter **6**

Managing Main Memory

In this chapter, we introduce several memory allocation schemes that have been developed to help the operating system manage its main memory efficiently. Effective management of this critical system resource can improve the throughput of the overall system. Conversely, if it's done inefficiently, throughput can suffer. Systems designers hoping to optimize memory use begin by identifying their priorities (speed vs. efficiency) before choosing memory allocation policies for their operating system. We'll explore some of these options in this chapter.

CHAPTER OBJECTIVES

In this chapter, you will

- Be able to describe the advantages and disadvantages of several memory allocation schemes

- Learn the differences between first-fit and best-fit allocation

- Understand how memory defragmentation is performed and the advantages it offers

- Learn about memory upgrades that might help system efficiency

Main Memory—A Critical Resource

Main memory is the system's scratch pad—a virtual clipboard if you will. It's a place where things are temporarily stored, such as the code currently being used to run the operating system's programs and any data you only need for a minute or two—perhaps data you need to cut and paste, such as a street address or an image. It's also the place where the system stores the instructions, file names, and details about, say, a printer that it needs to perform the work you're asking it to do (to print a letter, perhaps).

Main memory can only hold so much data, though, so after you've finished cutting and pasting and begin to write and print that letter, the operating system writes over the data it has stored during the cut-and-paste process, as well as any instructions in memory that it doesn't need any longer. It then replaces that data with the word processing instructions that allow letter writing. The operating system repeats the process again and again to load into memory the files and other data it needs to perform subsequent tasks.

Many people confuse main memory and the storage capacity of hard drives, optical discs, and other secondary storage devices, which are discussed in Chapter 8. Think of the difference this way: The contents of main memory are *temporary* and disappear when the power is turned off. On the other hand, the contents of a storage device can be retrieved *after a power disruption*.

NOTE Flash memory *is different from main memory and comes in many forms: smart media, compact flash, memory sticks, thumb drives, photo cards, and so on. Although some operating systems take advantage of flash memory to extend usable memory (to temporarily serve as additional main memory or virtual memory), these devices are actually examples of permanent storage. Therefore, in this book we will discuss them in Chapter 8 with other secondary storage devices.*

There are several names for main memory, including RAM (random access memory) and primary storage. Figure 6-1 shows what main memory, or RAM, typically looks like.

FIGURE 6-1 • Typical memory board for a desktop computer

To understand the complexities involved with managing main memory, consider all the types of data stored there, each of which must be safeguarded from being inadvertently overwritten. Here are a few:

- The instructions and data required by the operating system to run. (If this data is accidently altered, it can cause the entire computer system to crash.)
- Instructions and data for every open application.
- The instructions and data for each user's program.
- Data related to calculations the system must perform to provide a result, perhaps to render a photo, paste data, or send data to a printer.

TIP *The total amount of memory minus the "usable memory" equals the size of memory reserved by the operating system for its own use. In Windows 7, this calculation can be found in the Computer window.*

Exercise 6-1: Find Out How Much Usable Memory Your Computer Has

To find out how much usable memory a computer running Windows 7 has, follow these steps:

1. Left-click Start.
2. Right-click Computer.
3. Left-click Properties.

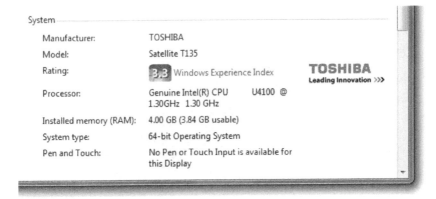

FIGURE 6-2 • Viewing the amount of available memory

4. A typical System display is shown in Figure 6-2 (yours will likely be different). In this example, the installed memory is 4GB and the available memory is 3.84GB (RAM).

How Main Memory Works

How does memory work? Its management has evolved over the years. The earliest computers allowed each person running a job to reserve the computer's entire available memory and run a single job in that space, but those days are long gone. Now memory space is shared among multiple jobs, each running multiple processes and multiple threads, and they do this without (ideally) bringing the system to a crashing halt.

NOTE *Throughout this chapter, the term* **job** *indicates a collection of processes you send to the processor for execution. Remember that a single job often consists of multiple processes, and a process can have from one to many threads.*

To see how memory is allocated, let's assume that the system has been powered on, the boot procedures have been run, and the computer is ready to do your bidding (to simplify our explanation, we will ignore network activity).

Main memory is divided into two sections. During booting, the operating system claimed a reserved section to hold its most important jobs, and this portion of memory stays protected so that no other jobs are allowed to overwrite the code in that section. Your apps and data are allowed to use the available

Operating system	Unused memory

| Lowest addresses | | Highest addresses |

FIGURE 6-3 · The operating system is loaded into the lowest memory addresses.

memory as they like, but they are not permitted to intrude on the operating system's memory space.

Therefore, after bootup and before any apps or other jobs are running, main memory consists of the two sections shown in Figure 6-3.

The lowest addresses of main memory are reserved for the operating system, and the remainder is available for incoming jobs. Unused memory is available for incoming processes according to the memory allocation scheme chosen by the designers of the operating system. The earliest scheme is explained next.

Single-User Allocation

In the simplest systems (such as those developed for the first computers), each job is loaded into main memory as a unit (complete with every instruction and all data) and it claims all of the available memory, even if it uses only a fraction of it, as illustrated by Job A in Figure 6-4.

If an incoming job is too big to fit in the available memory space, then it is rejected by the system. If this job can be rewritten as a smaller unit, it could run in the available space. If not, it will never be executable on this system.

After Job A is loaded, no other job is allowed to enter until Job A finishes. Even if there is unused memory space (as is the case here), this space is never allocated to another job because only one job is allowed to inhabit memory at a time. When the first job terminates, the entire amount of available memory is allocated to the next one in line.

The *single-user memory allocation scheme* offers obvious disadvantages to operating systems designers, but it was quite appropriate for the oldest computer systems because in those days, users sometimes stood in line to run their jobs—one at a time. Although this scheme is rarely used now, it was the precursor for all the others that followed.

Operating system	Job A	Unused memory

FIGURE 6-4 · Only one job can be processed at a time.

Fixed Partitions

To allow several jobs to occupy main memory at one time, memory space is divided into sections, the size of which is unchangeable until rebooting. Only at startup or after rebooting can the computer operator dictate new partition sizes. This *fixed-partition allocation scheme* requires that each job be loaded in its entirety in memory before any instructions can be executed, but it allows several jobs to be loaded into main memory at the same time. For example, if the computer divides available memory into seven partitions and eight jobs are waiting to be executed, the operating system tries to load each of the jobs (in their entirety) into a partition that is big enough to hold it. Each job that is successfully loaded into a partition stays there until it finishes. At that time, it gives up its partition and makes it available to the next waiting job *that can fit into that space*. This continues until each waiting job has its chance to be loaded and executed.

For each job, according to its order of arrival (from first to last), the memory manager tries to fit it into an available space. Here are some points to keep in mind concerning this scheme:

- If the first job fits into the first available partition, it is loaded and the memory manager moves to the second job in line.
- If the first job doesn't fit into the first available partition, the memory manager tries to load it into the next available partition. It repeats this cycle until it finds a partition that is large enough to accommodate the job.
- If the memory manager cannot find an available partition that's large enough, that job is put on hold and the memory manager moves to the next job in line and starts again.

The sizes of both the partition and the job are critical to the success of this scheme. To illustrate, let's watch as four jobs (Jobs A, B, C, and D) wait in turn to be loaded into seven partitions of fixed size, as shown in Figure 6-5:

1. Notice that Job A is too big to fit into Partition 1, but it does fit into Partition 2, so it's loaded there.

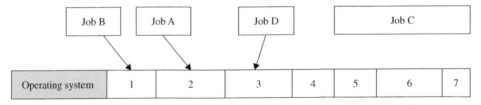

FIGURE 6-5 · Job C is too big to fit into any memory partition.

2. The memory manager then fits Job B into Partition 1.

3. When the memory manager tries to load Job C into memory, it turns out that it's too big to fit into any of the seven partitions, so it is put on hold until a partition large enough is set free.

4. The memory manager then tries and succeeds in loading Job D into Partition 3 (because Partitions 1 and 2 are already occupied).

But what happens to Job C? It is too big to fit into any of the partitions, so even if they were all available, Job C would never be loaded until a partition of sufficient size is created—and that can happen only if the computer is restarted and the computer operator creates a partition that is large enough for the largest waiting job. This scheme's inability to accommodate occasional large jobs without rebooting is a huge disadvantage.

Another disadvantage is that in the vast majority of cases, each of the incoming jobs fills only a portion of the partition that it occupies. For example, if a job of 490KB is loaded into a partition that is 512KB, the surplus memory of 22KB goes unused. In fact, if the incoming job is not exactly 512KB (and the chance of that is very small), there will again be memory space that's not used within the boundaries of that partition. This unused memory space *within a partition* signifies valuable memory resources that are going to waste and is called *internal fragmentation*. The next memory allocation scheme eliminated internal fragmentation.

Dynamic Partitions

The development of *dynamic partitions* still required that the entire job reside in memory before execution could begin, but it allowed main memory to be partitioned on the fly, without the system being rebooted. Here's how it works: If we have eight jobs ready for execution, the system loads the first job (in its entirety) at the beginning of the available space and erects a partition immediately after it. Because each job completely fills up its partition space, there is no internal fragmentation. If memory space is left after a job is loaded, the memory manager tries to load each of the following jobs, in turn, erecting a partition after each one until there's either not enough available memory left to accommodate another job or not another job in line, as shown in Figure 6-6, where only four jobs were waiting.

Operating system	Job A	Job B	Job C	Job D	Unused memory

FIGURE 6-6 · After initial loading, there's no wasted memory space between jobs.

The remaining jobs wait until a resident job is completed and vacates its memory space, and then the system finds a job waiting that can fit into the newly available space in memory. If the next job is too large to fit into an available partition, the memory manager puts it on hold and tries the next waiting job, and then the next, and so on.

Although this scheme offers a flexibility that's not offered by the fixed-partitions scheme, it does introduce a new complication: wasted memory space *between the partitions*, which is called *external fragmentation*.

To see how this works, check out what happens after Jobs A, B, and C all finish and their spaces are reallocated to the next incoming Jobs: E, F, and G, as illustrated in Figure 6-7.

- Job A finishes first, so the memory manager tries to fit Job E into that space, but it's too big to fit into any available spaces, so it's set aside. Next it tries, and succeeds, in fitting Job F into the space left by Job A and erects a new partition at the end of Job F (thus creating a slice of unused memory between the end of Job F and the partition that remains where Job A ended.

- Job B finishes next, so the memory manager tries to fit Job E into that space, but it's too big to fit, so it's set aside. Next, it tries, and succeeds, in fitting Job G into the space left by Job B and erects a new partition at the end of Job G (creating a slice of unused memory between the end of Job G and the partition that remains where Job B ended).

- Job C finishes next, so the memory manager fits Job E into that space. It then erects a new partition at the end of Job E (creating a sliver of unused memory between the end of Job E and the partition that remains where Job C ended).

As you can see, external fragmentation is caused by repeatedly partitioning and repartitioning the memory space. For example, let's watch what happens to one partition as Job A (which is 490KB in size) is loaded; it claims 490KB of

| Before | Operating system | Job A | Job B | Job C | Job D | Unused memory |

| After | Operating system | Job F | Job G | Job E | Job D | Unused memory |

FIGURE 6-7 · As new memory spaces are allocated, they naturally become smaller and smaller.

memory space and a partition is placed right after it. When Job A finishes, its memory space is allocated to the job that fits in its space, Job F, which is 466KB, so a partition is placed after Job B. As you can see, this causes the creation of a tiny partition of 24KB (490KB − 466KB = 24KB), which is available to an incoming job that's 24KB or less. As memory is allocated to more and more incoming jobs (and more and more partitions are created), the result is a stunning fragmentation of main memory and the creation of many tiny unused slivers of memory.

Like the preceding allocation scheme, the dynamic partitions can be erased by letting all the resident jobs finish and rebooting the system. Because this is not always a convenient solution, other schemes were developed. The next one addresses this problem with more elegance.

Two Ways to Allocate Partitions

Before moving to the next memory allocation scheme, let's examine how partitions are allocated to incoming jobs. The exact amount of memory fragmentation resulting from the dynamic partitions memory allocation scheme depends on the specific instructions given by the operating system designers to allocate space to incoming jobs. Two are described here: first-fit and best-fit.

First-Fit Memory Allocation

As its name implies, this scheme allocates memory to each job based solely on the availability of the first available partition that's large enough to accommodate it. The exact size of the partition is inconsequential; the only factor that matters is whether or not it's big enough to hold the incoming job. To see how this works in practice, watch how the memory manager assigns the first of several jobs to partitions in memory:

- Determine if the job fits into the first partition. If so, put it there and go to the next waiting job.
- If the job does not fit in the first partition, the following steps occur:
    1. Try the second partition. If the job fits, put it there. If not…
    2. Try the third partition. If the job fits, put it there. If not…
    3. Try the fourth partition. This continues until all the partitions are tried.
- If the job fits in *none* of the partitions, put it in the Waiting queue for later. Then perform the same series of actions with the next waiting job.

Because this is a simple set of instructions, first-fit is faster to execute than the one we'll discuss next, but it causes more memory to be wasted because it's not trying to keep internal fragmentation to a minimum.

Best-Fit Memory Allocation

This scheme allocates memory to each job based on two factors: the partition's availability and its size. The goal of best-fit is to match as closely as possible the size of the incoming job with the size of the partition where it is placed, with the goal of minimizing the amount of wasted space. To see how this works in practice, watch how the memory manager assigns a job using the best-fit scheme:

- Determine the size of the job.
- For every available partition in memory, subtract the job size from the partition size to calculate the potential wasted memory space for every partition.
- Choose the partition that offers the least waste (the one that is both larger than the job and closest in size) and put the job there. Then repeat with the next waiting job.
- If *none* of the partitions fits the job, put it in the Waiting queue for later (with the intent of trying it again when a large-enough partition becomes available). Then repeat the same series of actions with the next waiting job.

Obviously, the CPU has more work to do with best-fit, because it must subtract the size of the incoming job from the sizes of every available partition. Therefore, it has less time to execute processes that are currently residing in memory. This illustrates one of the classic tradeoffs of operating system design: speed versus optimization of resources.

First-fit is faster by far, but it wastes valuable memory space, whereas best-fit saves space but takes more time. Which is better? It depends on which one the system has in excess: memory space or CPU speed. The answer is not the same for every system.

Relocatable Dynamic Partitions

The relocatable dynamic partitions memory allocation scheme still requires the entire job to reside in memory before execution can begin, but it allows the operating system to place and then move the contents of a partition from one area in memory to another (without rebooting). In this way, it can

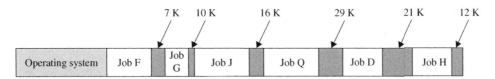

FIGURE 6-8 · There are many tiny slivers of available memory before compaction.

consolidate all available memory into a single large block—which can then be allocated to an incoming job. This movement of jobs in memory is called *compaction*. The resulting section of free memory can be used to accommodate the next waiting job that can fit in that space.

When it first starts up, this scheme is identical to the dynamic partition scheme. For example, with eight jobs in the Ready queue, the system loads the first job at the beginning of the available memory space and erects a partition immediately after it—there is no internal fragmentation. Then, the memory manager loads each of the following jobs and erects a partition after each one until there's either not enough available memory left to accommodate another job or no other jobs are waiting in line. Later, as jobs are moved into and out of memory, the available space becomes slivered, just as it did with dynamic partitions, but here's the crucial difference—whenever it's time to collect those slivers into a useable whole, the memory manager compacts the jobs by moving them next to each other at the lowest memory addresses. And it does so without rebooting the system.

Figure 6-8 shows what memory looks like before compaction, after several jobs have finished, leaving lots of external fragmentation.

At this moment, there is no room for the smallest job waiting in line, which is 30KB (notice that it's larger than 29KB, the size of the largest available block of memory). By compacting these jobs (moving each one immediately after the job in lower addresses of memory), the memory manager causes a big block of unused memory to become available (95KB), as shown in Figure 6-9, so that the waiting jobs can be accommodated. This improvement in memory use is dramatic indeed.

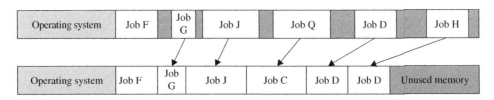

FIGURE 6-9 · Unused memory consolidation before and after compaction

For this memory allocation scheme to be most productive, compaction must be performed on a regular basis. The disadvantage here is that compaction is an overhead task, meaning that it is considered system maintenance. (While the CPU is moving jobs and adjusting addresses, it is unavailable to process any job instructions. This diversion of the CPU necessarily reduces system efficiency and throughput.)

NOTE *An* overhead task *is one that is required to maintain the system, but takes time away from job and process execution. Therefore, it reduces overall system efficiency. Designers try to keep overhead tasks to a minimum.*

Although this scheme was a big improvement over those described thus far, it gave way to a new one that did away with partitions of varying sizes.

Paged Allocation

The *paged memory allocation scheme* allows a job to be divided into equally sized sections called a *page*, and each page is loaded into a section of memory, called a *page frame*. Unlike the other schemes discussed so far, these page frames can be located anywhere in main memory—they do not need to be located next to each other.

The page frames' uniformity of size allows memory space to be allocated much more efficiently. Generally, paging works most efficiently when the size of the page frame equals the size of each page of the program, which also equals the size of a sector in secondary storage (such as a hard disk or CD/DVD disc), as shown in Figure 6-10.

For many years, the size of these sectors/pages/page frames was 512 bytes. Now, disk manufacturers are making secondary storage devices (including disk drives and solid state drives) with sectors that are 4,090 bytes (4KB) to improve efficiency. As a result, newer configurations have increased the sizes of pages and page frames. We discuss drives and sectors in Chapter 8.

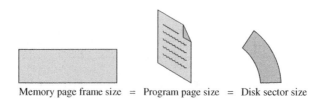

Memory page frame size = Program page size = Disk sector size

FIGURE 6-10 · Comparative sizes of page frame, page, and disk sector

To successfully load a job into main memory, the operating system must do three things:

- Determine the number of available page frames.
- Determine the number of pages in the incoming job.
- Load each of the job's pages into an available page frame *somewhere in main memory.*

NOTE *The status of every page frame (free or busy) in main memory is listed in the Memory Map Table, which is updated constantly by the operating system.*

To determine the number of pages a job has, some arithmetic is required:

- Every job that is smaller than the page frame size is loaded in its entirety into a single page frame.
- Any job that is larger than a page frame is divided into pages, which are then loaded into individual page frames.

For example, if we assume that the entire job is 1,280 bytes, as shown in Figure 6-11, the job is divided accordingly.

When the page size is 512 bytes and the entire job is 1,280 bytes, then the job is divided into three equally sized pages. Page 1 holds the job's first 512 bytes, Page 2 holds the second 512 bytes, and Page 3 holds the program's last 256 bytes. The remaining half of Page 3 is wasted memory space, as another example of *internal fragmentation.* Page 3 is not smaller than Pages 1 and 2.

After the job has been divided into pages, it's time to load the job, so the system looks for three available page frames anywhere in memory. These page frames do not need to be located adjacently or even near each other, but all three pages must reside in memory before execution can begin.

512 bytes   512 bytes   256 bytes

FIGURE 6-11 · A single program of 1,280 bytes divided into three pages of equal size.

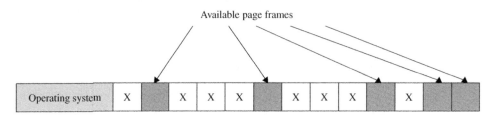

FIGURE 6-12 · Page frames marked with an X are already allocated to other jobs.

To demonstrate, Figure 6-12 shows main memory before the new job, which needs three page frames, is loaded. The system has 5 of 13 page frames available (8 of them are occupied).

Figure 6-13 shows how the three pages are loaded into memory. Notice that any page frames located anywhere in main memory can be used by any page of any job. But, because they are scattered in memory, the system must have a way to track the locations of each page and their order of execution.

To do this, it uses a Page Map Table (PMT) that lists each page number and its corresponding page frame number. (For the purposes of this discussion, we have over simplified the contents of the PMT, which actually holds additional critical details about each page of a job.)

NOTE *Typically, operating systems start numbering pages and page frames with zero (that is, the first page is Page 0). However, to keep our explanations as simple as possible, we start with one (that is, the first page is called Page 1).*

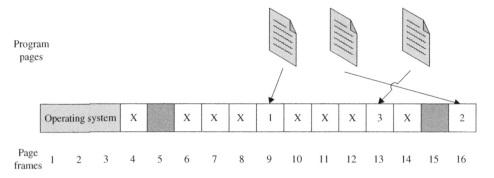

FIGURE 6-13 · Each page is loaded into an available page frame somewhere in memory.

TABLE 6-1 A Job's Page Map Table Correlates Each Page and Its Page Frame

Page Number	Page Frame Number
1	9
2	16
3	13

The simplified PMT for the job shown in Figure 6-13 is shown in Table 6-1.

By referring to the job's PMT, the operating system can quickly find the location of each of its pages. What if there are multiple jobs in memory at the same time? To keep track of them, the operating system uses a Job Table, which shows the address of the Page Map Table for each job currently in main memory. A simplified Job Table is shown in Table 6-2. Notice that Jobs 3 and 5 are already finished executing, so they are no longer listed in the Job Table.

This raises an interesting question: what's the maximum size that an incoming job can be? The answer is, the total number of all of the page frames available in memory. The system shown in Figure 6-13, with 13 page frames (not including those occupied by the operating system) can accommodate a job with a maximum of 13 pages, but only when *all* the page frames are available at the same time, because the *entire job* has to be loaded before the first instruction can be executed by the CPU.

Therefore, a job with 14 pages will never fit in this system using this memory allocation scheme. This restriction was lifted with the development of virtual memory and the next scheme: demand paged, which is one of the virtual memory allocation schemes discussed in Chapter 7.

TABLE 6-2 The System Has One Job Table to Track Each Job in Memory

Job Number	Job Size (KB)	Address of PMT
1	1,280	960
2	690	4096
4	3,974	7420
6	8,231	3150

Adding More Memory?

To add memory to your computing device, you'll need to find out how much your computer already has, how much more can be added, if any, and in what format. Here are the most critical pieces of information:

- Type of memory that your computer system can accommodate
- The maximum amount of memory that your computer system can use
- The maximum amount of memory that can be supported by your operating system
- The number of memory slots that are available

Computers are sometimes designed to use pairs of equal-sized memory modules. For example, if your computer has two memory slots and each holds a memory module of 500MB, it currently has a total of 1GB of RAM. If the maximum amount of memory supported by your computer hardware is 4GB, you may be able to replace each currently installed module with a 2GB module, for a total of 4GB—resulting in a 400-percent increase in processing power.

TIP   *When buying a computer, look for the size of main memory (commonly called RAM). A computer with 2GB of memory can store 2^{30} bytes of data; 4GB can store twice as much. More memory may improve performance if the cause of your system's slowdown is a lack of available main memory. But if another resource (such as processing power) is the limiting factor, then increasing the size of memory might not increase throughput significantly.*

As you might expect, adding memory requires some computer disassembly, which is actually fairly easy to do with many desktop computers. However, you may need professional assistance to upgrade memory for a difficult-to-disassemble desktop, laptop, netbook, or other small computing device.

The precise procedures for evaluating system potential and adding more memory are different for each computing device and too complex to fully explain here. For details, ask the manufacturer or visit the website of a memory supplier, some of which offer scanning tools to evaluate the options for your particular device, as you can see in Exercise 6-2.

Exercise 6-2: Let Crucial.com Figure It Out for You

Crucial.com is a website that sells computer memory. On its home page, find the option called "System Scanner," or just go to www.crucial.com/systemscanner.

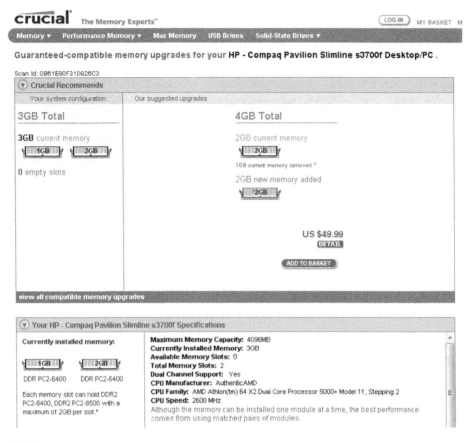

FIGURE 6-14 • Sample RAM scan analysis

This scanning tool, once downloaded and run, scans your system for the type of RAM installed and figures out how much more RAM you can add. It will then recommend the RAM you need. In our experience, you can get detailed information in less than three minutes. Figure 6-14 shows the results on one of our systems.

How Direct Memory Access Works

A standard feature of the hardware for most computers and microprocessors is *direct memory access* (commonly known as *DMA)*, which allows certain hardware to communicate directly with main memory, using special DMA channels. DMA reduces CPU overhead because it can perform other functions during routine data transfer.

DMA spans the disciplines of processor management and memory management and has been built into many computing systems since the days of the first IBM personal computers. By allowing incoming data from the device to be read and stored in memory (where the CPU can retrieve it later) without requiring that the CPU monitor the transfer of each byte, DMA enables data transfer and computation to take place at the same time—even on a single core computer.

DMA allows devices such as disk drive controllers, graphics cards, network cards, and sound cards to send and receive streams of data at a high rate of speed. To get the data stream started, the CPU initiates the transfer and goes off to perform other computations while the data stream continues under the supervision of the DMA controller. When the data stream ends, the CPU is notified so that it can return to this process and move to the next phase of its work.

Computers with multiple cores routinely use DMA to transfer data between each core's local memory and system devices without requiring the attention of the processor, thereby freeing it to perform other tasks.

Summary

In these pages, we introduced several memory management schemes: single user, fixed partition, dynamic partitions, relocatable dynamic partitions, and paged allocation. When we compared the strengths and weaknesses of each, we found that all of them presented some benefits as well as some problems. We also demonstrated two competing methods to allocate available memory space: first-fit and best-fit. Finally, we introduced the concept of direct memory access and briefly described its importance.

The concepts described in this chapter laid the groundwork for the development of virtual memory and related techniques to allocate main memory in a more dynamic way. We will explore virtual memory in the next chapter.

QUIZ

Choose the correct response to each of the multiple-choice questions. Note that there may be more than one correct response to each question.

1. **What is the simplest memory allocation scheme?**
   A. Relocatable dynamic partitions
   B. Single user
   C. Fixed partitions
   D. Paged

2. **Which of these allocation schemes require that the entire job be loaded into memory before execution can begin?**
   A. Relocatable dynamic partitions
   B. Single user
   C. Dynamic partitions
   D. Paged

3. **What's the advantage of the dynamic partitions scheme over fixed-partition scheme?**
   A. It can reset partitions by rebooting the system.
   B. It eliminates external fragmentation.
   C. It stimulated the development of compaction.
   D. It can reset partitions without rebooting the system.

4. **What's the advantage of first-fit over best-fit allocation?**
   A. It wastes less space.
   B. It wastes more space.
   C. It's faster to implement.
   D. It's slower to implement.

5. **Using best-fit allocation, how does the memory manager find the best partition for a job?**
   A. It subtracts job size from partition size.
   B. It subtracts partition size from job size.
   C. It totals all the available partitions.
   D. It totals all the wasted memory space.

6. **If the size of each page frame and page is 512 bytes and the entire job is 2,970 bytes, how many page frames will the job need?**
   A. 4
   B. 5
   C. 6
   D. 7

7. **What information is listed in the Page Map Table (PMT)?**
   A. The job number and its page numbers
   B. The job's pages and the address of each page
   C. The address of each partition
   D. The page number and page frame number

8. **What information is listed in the Job Table?**
   A. The job number, job size, and address of the PMT
   B. The number of pages, page size, and the address of each page
   C. The job number, partition address, and page frame number
   D. The page number and page frame number

9. **Which of the following are true statements about overhead processing?**
   A. It's good because it allows system maintenance.
   B. It's good because it reduces job processing.
   C. It's often necessary for overall system efficiency.
   D. It's bad because jobs are processed faster.

10. **How is internal fragmentation different from external fragmentation?**
   A. Internal fragmentation is much better than external fragmentation.
   B. Internal fragmentation exists within partitions and page frames.
   C. Internal fragmentation is much worse than external fragmentation.
   D. External fragmentation can't be prevented.

chapter 7

Virtual Memory Management

Here we introduce the memory management allocation schemes that ushered in the age of virtual memory. All of the schemes discussed in these pages differ in one critical respect from those in the previous chapter—each one allows program instructions to begin execution even though only a portion of the job or program is loaded into memory. This development allowed system designers to accommodate enormous, complex programs composed of modules that could be loaded, or not, as they were needed, or not. Because of the flexibility it introduced, virtual memory was a welcome advance in memory management.

CHAPTER OBJECTIVES

In this chapter, you will

- Understand the fundamental concepts of virtual memory
- Be able to describe three competing page replacement schemes
- Appreciate the importance of the working set
- Be able to describe the role of cache memory

Virtual Memory Allocation Schemes

Virtual memory is a technique that makes excellent use of available space on a hard drive, or other secondary storage device such as a flash drive, to temporarily store data that would otherwise require massive amounts of main memory. Then, during program execution, it swaps data from storage to main memory and back again to storage, as necessary, when it's required to be there. By doing so, it keeps the data "within arm's reach" and allows the memory manager to manipulate the data quickly.

Because this technique gives the illusion that the system has much more physical memory than it really does, it was given the name *virtual memory*—that is, it doesn't really exist, but it appears to. In a nutshell, it allows a computer with only 1GB of main memory to allocate more than 2GB of memory space. Sounds impossible, doesn't it?

Because it allows pages to be swapped very quickly on an as-needed basis, virtual memory removed the requirement that every page of a job had to reside in main memory before program execution could begin. Instead, virtual memory allocation schemes *only* load pages that have instructions that are required at that moment. As the program moves through the many possible phases of its processing needs (initialization, data acquisition, data calculations, printing, releasing resources, communicating with the user, and so on), the only pages that actually reside in memory are those that address the current need. The remaining pages stay in an easy-to-access place on a hard drive, flash drive, or other secondary storage device. Pages that are never needed are never loaded.

NOTE *Microsoft Office 2010 installation requirements call for computers to have 3GB of available disk space, but its software can run on computers with only 256MB of RAM (512MB is recommended for graphics features). This is an example of a program that takes advantage of virtual memory.*

Although virtual memory was made possible with the development of paging, discussed in the previous chapter, it required the development of the demand paged scheme, which is described next, to be widely implemented.

Demand Paged Memory Allocation

As one of the first widely used virtual memory implementations, the *demand paged memory allocation scheme* was dramatically different from those described in the previous chapter. As you may recall, those memory allocation schemes didn't take into consideration the immediate usability of the instructions within the job, so that even instructions that would rarely be needed were still loaded into memory before execution was allowed to begin. What's worse, if the entire job didn't fit, none of its pages were loaded and it never had the chance to run. Therefore, if there was only 1GB of main memory available, a program that was larger than that would never be allowed to start its processing.

One might ask how a job might need only some pages, and not others, and still run to completion. The clue to the answer can be found in the development of program modules. The demand paged scheme takes advantage of the fact that certain portions of a program are rarely implemented, whereas other portions are mutually exclusive. That is, many programs contain instructions that address a wide variety of events, but are executed only from time to time. For example, the automatic update feature of an accounting application might be run once a week, or twice a month, but not every hour of every day (except under really unusual circumstances).

Here's a different example. When a print job is just beginning to run, it may not need to send data to the printer for quite some time, so the printer-specific parts of the program may not need to be loaded into memory until printing is requested. Likewise, the user-help sections can often remain unloaded until they are specifically required by the user. Even then, when someone asks for help, it is often topic specific—so, only the pages that address that specific topic are loaded into memory, and they remain there only while they're needed. As soon as the help section is closed, the memory space it occupied is released.

Let's watch how demand paging loads main memory. Let's say that the program being processed needs to retrieve certain data from the disk and these instructions are located on Pages 12, 13, 15, and 17. Figure 7-1 shows that these pages are loaded into Page Frames 9, 5, 16, and 13, respectively.

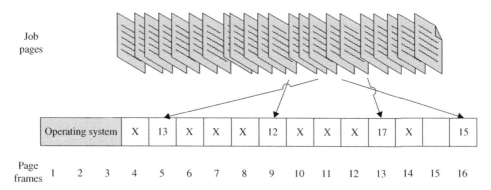

FIGURE 7-1 · Four pages being loaded into four page frames

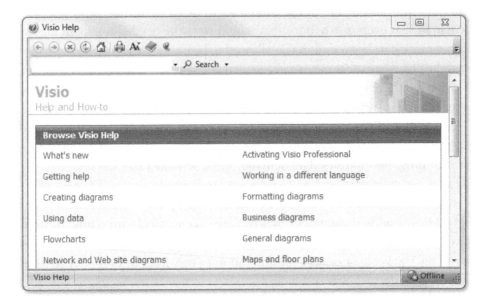

FIGURE 7-2 • Typical main Help screen

As shown in Figure 7-1, five page frames are available, and the four pages that are required are loaded into four of them. Notice, too, that the four pages do not need to be loaded sequentially; each one can be placed anywhere in main memory. Finally, you can see that the portions of the program that are not required *at this moment* are not loaded into memory at this time. They may be moved into main memory at some time in the future, just not now.

The development of virtual memory enabled the development and commercialization of large, complex programs that can run on computers with a relatively small amount of main memory (RAM). (As we noted earlier, Microsoft Office 2010 is an example of such a program because it can run on computers with only 256MB–512MB of RAM.)

When this takes place, you can watch (and sometimes hear) it happen when you open a program installed on your computer's hard drive, such as a sophisticated word processor, and click the program's Help menu the first time. When the main Help menu, as demonstrated in Figure 7-2, begins loading, you may be able to hear the hard drive start up as it begins to retrieve the program instructions from the hard disk or DVD drive. Notice the delay that's usually required to bring up this window. (If your help instructions are loaded dynamically from the Internet or other portion of the "cloud," you'll see the information open in a new browser window. The principle is identical to what we're

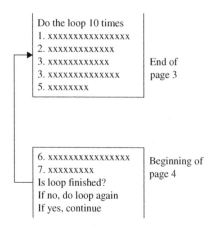

FIGURE 7-3 • Thrashing results if both pages aren't in memory at the same time.

describing here, but instead of the instructions being retrieved from your hard drive, they are being retrieved from a secondary storage device in some other part of the world.)

As you work your way through the Help menus, you may notice additional pauses as the memory manager retrieves each of your requested screens. Finally, as you close the Help section, you may notice more disk activity as the Help code stored in main memory is replaced by data or instructions that are required to carry out your next command.

A severe disadvantage to this scheme is that the program is broken into pages that are the same size as the page frames in memory, without regard for the program's internal structure, and without accounting for awkward page breaks in the middle of an instruction or procedure. For example, if a single instruction is divided awkwardly across two pages, as illustrated in Figure 7-3, then it could cause repeated and inefficient loading and unloading of the two pages if there's room for only one page in memory at a time.

Let's say this instruction, which is called a *loop* (because it cycles repeatedly from the first step to the last step), must be executed in sequence from Steps 1 to 7 ten times (let's say, as the variable *n* is incremented from 1 to 10). Unfortunately, the first five steps are on Page 3 and the last two steps are on Page 4. This is an example of a bad page break.

Let's further assume that there's only one available page frame in memory. Therefore, to begin execution, Page 3 is loaded into the only page frame and Steps 1–5 are performed. Then, that page must be unloaded so Page 4 can be loaded into that page frame and Steps 6–7 can be performed. However, the loop isn't finished and must be repeated—so Page 4 is unloaded and Page 3 reloaded so that Steps 1–5 can be done again (with the next value of *n)*. Once again, at the conclusion of Step 5, the two pages have to be swapped so that Steps 6–7 can be performed. But, yet again, the loop is not finished, so the process is repeated eight more times until the loop is completed.

The overhead time spent moving pages back and forth into memory and back to secondary storage reduces the system's speed and efficiency. (This is called *thrashing* and is discussed in detail later in this chapter.) To address this disadvantage, the next scheme divides programs not into arbitrary pages, but into logical segments.

Segmented Memory Allocation Scheme

The *segmented memory allocation scheme* divides a program according to its internal structure instead of arbitrary pages. And memory is used differently—instead of having page frames, each of uniform size, data is stored in chunks of variable length.

This scheme takes advantage of the natural segments that make up most programs; a *segment* is a group of instructions that performs a related function. For example, one segment may have the instructions to open a file; another segment may have the printing instructions. In particular, this scheme watches for any instructions that might cause thrashing, such as a repeated loop or a nested set of codes. Internal modules known as *procedures* or *subroutines* are natural segment choices.

> *A procedure is a specific sequence of instructions, a module, that performs a specific task, which can be performed repeatedly.*

As you may know, most programs are written using modules. For example, one module can load the instructions required to start up the application, a second can initialize the variables and prepare the app for user input, a third can accept the first user commands, and so forth. When a segmented memory allocation scheme is used, each of these modules can be a segment, and when the segment is active, it is loaded into memory as a unit. When that module's function is no longer required, the segment is swapped out of memory so its space can be allocated to the next module (segment) when it is needed. Only those segments needed are loaded, and they are only loaded when they're

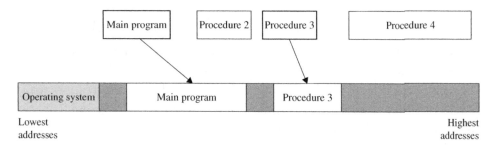

FIGURE 7-4 · The segmented memory scheme reintroduces external fragmentation and does not use page frames.

needed, as shown in Figure 7-4 with only two of the program's four segments loaded.

However, as illustrated in Figure 7-4, by allocating memory to segments of variable length, the problem of *external fragmentation* has returned. You may recall that this is wasted space between segments that becomes increasingly problematic over time as memory is allocated and deallocated over and over again. The problem is exactly the same as the one introduced with dynamic partitions, described in the previous chapter. And the solution is exactly the same—to take time to compact memory so that tiny slivers of unused memory can be combined into larger pieces that can then be allocated to segments that are waiting to come into memory. Thus, memory compaction (not to be confused with file defragmentation) is an overhead process that reduces system efficiency while it is being done.

Another complication of this allocation scheme is that it requires more effort on the part of the memory manager to track (using segment map tables) each segment, its size, its location in memory, and details about its status and recent modifications.

One advantage of segmented memory allocation (one it shares with the demand paged scheme) is that these segments do not need to be loaded in adjacent memory locations. In fact, they don't need to be loaded at all unless, and until, they are needed. Unfortunately, these disadvantages outweighed the advantages, thus opening the door to the next scheme—which combines the strengths of the two we've just discussed.

Segmented/Demand Paged Memory Allocation Scheme

The last virtual memory innovation we'll discuss is the *segmented/demand paged scheme*, which combines the best features of both previous schemes. As with the segmented scheme, incoming programs are divided into logical pieces, with one segment for each program module. But here's where it's different: as with demand paged, each segment is subdivided into pages that are the same size as page frames in memory, and then each page is loaded into a page frame, as shown in Figure 7-5.

Notice that when a segment is loaded into memory, all of its pages are loaded into available page frames, which can be anywhere in main memory. (You might ask, why aren't the three pages of Procedure A shown in Figure 7-4 loaded more closely together? In practice, they can be, but it's not necessary—they don't need to be near one another. They only need to be somewhere, anywhere, in memory.)

However, when a segment is loaded, *the entire segment* must be loaded before it can begin. If there are not enough available page frames to accommodate all its pages, the segment is not loaded until there's sufficient memory for every page.

By combining demand paged and segmented allocation schemes, operating systems designers eliminated the problem of external fragmentation, but they reintroduced the problem of internal fragmentation. Consider the case of a segment that is 600 bytes and divided into two pages. If the page size, and page frame size, is 512 bytes, then the segment's first 512 bytes can be found on the

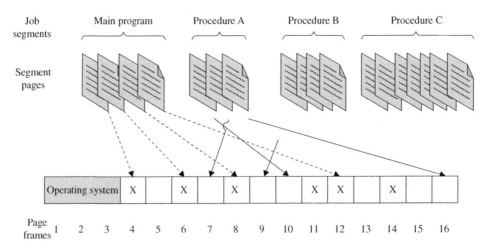

FIGURE 7-5 · Pages of this segment (Procedure A) loaded into three available page frames.

first page and the final 88 bytes are on the second page. When the two pages are loaded into memory, 424 bytes of memory space are wasted within the second page frame. This is internal fragmentation because the wasted space is *within* a page frame, not *between* blocks of occupied memory.

Still Struggling?

The demand paged and segmented schemes are very similar; their differences lie in the way each one divides a long program into smaller pieces. Demand paged is just like a typical chapter in a book, where pages are of equal size without regard for the content of each page. On the other hand, the segmented scheme is similar to a book chapter that is divided into smaller pieces with each subheading beginning its own section.

Virtual Memory Challenges

Virtual memory introduced certain challenges. To explore them, let's take a moment to examine how, when, and why pages are loaded into main memory. The same logic applies to all page frame schemes, including demand paged and segmented/demand paged.

Before a page can be moved into memory, the memory manager must find an available page frame. The exact course of action depends on the circumstances in memory:

- If enough page frames are already vacant, no further decisions are required; the memory manager simply loads the waiting pages into the empty page frames.
- If not enough page frames are available, the memory manager will either wait for the page frames to become available or swap out the contents of some page frames to make way for the incoming pages. (This assumes that the incoming pages have a higher priority than the pages that already reside in memory.)

Whenever a resident page is swapped into memory, it's called a *page fault* or *page interrupt*, and the actual process is managed by the part of the operating system called the *page fault handler* or *page interrupt handler*. Which pages deserve to be interrupted? Which should stay and finish? These are issues addressed by designers of operating systems who must chose an appropriate page removal policy, two of which are First-In First-Out and Least Recently Used.

TIP *You may be able to improve your system's performance by manipulating the size of its virtual memory. In a Windows system, pages moved into virtual memory reside in a file called pagefile.sys located in the root of a partition. How big should it be? A common suggestion is to make it 1.5 times the size of RAM. Therefore, if your computer's main memory is 1GB, the pagefile.sys should be 1.5GB. But there's no single answer for everyone. We recommend that you try several sizes to see what's right for you.*

Exercise 7-1: Change the Size of Virtual Memory on a Windows 7 Computer

You can manage the size of the virtual memory area allocated on your computer using tools available from the operating system. In a default Windows installation, the size of the page file is preset, and the size is determined by the amount of RAM in your computer. The default size—which is 1.5 times the amount of physical RAM if physical RAM is less than 1GB, and equal to the amount of physical RAM plus 300MB if 1GB or more is installed—is generally optimal.

Should you change the default size? If you are short of hard disk space, you might want to set a smaller initial page file size. That's OK. But, should you *enlarge* the page file? Probably not, but if you notice in the Resource Monitor during routine testing that the memory chart is above normal most of the time while you're working (not while the computer is defragmenting files or indexing, for instance), you might consider it. To change the size of the paging file on a Windows 7 computer, follow these steps:

1. Left-click the Windows Start button.
2. Right-click Computer.
3. Left-click Properties.
4. Click Advanced System Settings.
5. Under the Advanced tab, under Performance, click Settings.

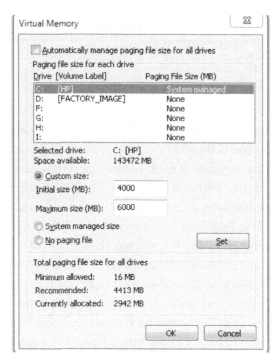

FIGURE 7-6 · Manually configure the size of your computer's paging file.

6. Click the Advanced tab.

7. Under Virtual Memory, click Change.

8. Deselect Automatically Managing Paging File Size for All Drives, if applicable.

9. Select the drive you want to manage, as shown in Figure 7-6.

10. Type in the new custom settings, as desired.

11. Click OK, and continue clicking OK until all dialog boxes are closed.

First-In First-Out Policy

The *First-In First-Out (FIFO)* page replacement policy identifies the pages that have been in memory the longest (those that were loaded first) and swaps them out in order, from those that were loaded first to those loaded most recently. This policy assumes that the pages that have been in memory the longest are the pages that are least likely to be needed again soon. This was one of the first

Operating system	11	12	2	10	4	15	3	7	6	17	14	8	9

Page frames 1   2   3   4   5   6   7   8   9   10   11   12   13   14   15   16

FIGURE 7-7 · Main memory: First-In First-Out page replacement policy

policies. It's fast to implement and, of the two policies discussed here, it results in the least amount of overhead.

Figure 7-7 shows a snapshot of main memory and the order in which its pages were loaded in each page frame from 2 to 17. The page with the lowest number (2) in Page Frame 6 has been in memory the longest, whereas the page with the highest number (17) in Page Frame 13 has been in memory the shortest period of time. Notice that some pages (1, 3, 5, 13, and 16) are not listed here because, presumably, they have already finished their operations and are not in main memory.

Using the FIFO policy (and assuming that each of these pages continues its processing and does not vacate its page frame voluntarily), the next page frame to be targeted would be Page Frame 6, which currently holds Page 2, because it has resided in memory the longest. The next page frame to be vacated would be Page Frame 10, which currently holds Page 3, because it has resided in memory the second-longest. Therefore, to remove all the pages shown in Figure 7-7, the order would be as follows: Page Frame 6, 10, 8, 12, 11, 15, 16, 7, 4, 5, 14, 9, and 13.

Is FIFO effective? Before deciding, let's compare it to an alternative policy.

Least Recently Used Policy

The *Least Recently Used (LRU)* page replacement policy keeps track of how recently each page has been used and gives preference to those that show recent use. The first pages it swaps are those that were used least recently. The concept here is to keep the busiest pages in memory even if they were loaded first and even if they have resided in memory longer than other pages.

Using LRU, before deciding to empty a page frame, the memory manager checks the Page Map Table (often abbreviated *PMT*) to see which page was last referenced. Once that page is identified, the page is swapped in exactly the same way as described for FIFO. The only difference is in choosing which pages will stay and which will go.

Some systems perform better using the LRU policy than the FIFO policy, but LRU requires more overhead than FIFO, and some systems might see improved performance with the simpler FIFO. Because some programs reference a few pages repeatedly whereas others move sequentially through their instructions from beginning to end, there's no general rule that can be used to choose the best policy.

As you'll see next, a program's structure can have a profound effect on the efficiency of the policy that's chosen by the operating system's designers.

FIFO, LRU Comparison

To see how these two policies work in a dynamic environment, where many pages are constantly swapped into and out of memory, imagine that there are five pages (A, B, C, D, E) to be executed using the only two available page frames. Assume that the program instructions will reference its five pages in the following order: A, B, A, C, A, C, D, C, E. Using FIFO, Table 7-1 shows how the pages are swapped in and out of Page Frames 1 and 2 (an asterisk notes which page was loaded first into a page frame). Every time a new page is loaded into a page frame, it's noted in the column titled "Page Fault/Page Interrupt?"

As shown in Table 7-1, using FIFO, the pages loaded first, shown with an asterisk (*), are the first to be swapped out later, and the pages that are loaded last are the last to be swapped out. For example, at Time 3, both Pages A and B are already in memory, so there's no need to remove a page, but at Time 4, when Page C is requested, the page that has been there the longest (Page A in Page Frame 1) is swapped out to make room for Page C. Likewise, at Time 5, when Page A is requested again, the page that has been there longest (Page B in Page Frame 2) is swapped out.

Notice that in order to process this sequence of five pages, the FIFO policy required seven page faults out of nine page references. In other words, the only

TABLE 7-1   First-In First-Out Policy: Pages Loaded First Are Shown with an Asterisk (*)

Time	Contents of Page Frame 1	Contents of Page Frame 2	Page Fault/ Page Interrupt?	Pages Being Referenced
0	\<empty>	\<empty>		A, B, A, C, A, C, D, C, E
1	A*	\<empty>	Yes	A, B, A, C, A, C, D, C, E
2	A*	B	Yes	A, B, A, C, A, C, D, C, E
3	A*	B	No	A, B, A, C, A, C, D, C, E
4	C	B*	Yes	A, B, A, C, A, C, D, C, E
5	C*	A	Yes	A, B, A, C, A, C, D, C, E
6	C*	A	No	A, B, A, C, A, C, D, C, E
7	D	A*	Yes	A, B, A, C, A, C, D, C, E
8	D*	C	Yes	A, B, A, C, A, C, D, C, E
9	E	C*	Yes	A, B, A, C, A, C, D, C, E

TABLE 7-2 Least Recently Used Policy (Pages Used Least Recently Are Shown with an Asterisk (*))			
Time	Contents of Page Frame 1	Contents of Page Frame 2	Page Fault/ Page Interrupt?	Pages Being Referenced
0	<empty>	<empty>		A, B, A, C, A, C, D, C, E
1	A*	<empty>	Yes	A, B, A, C, A, C, D, C, E
2	A*	B	Yes	A, B, A, C, A, C, D, C, E
3	A	B*	No	A, B, A, C, A, C, D, C, E
4	A*	C	Yes	A, B, A, C, A, C, D, C, E
5	A	C*	No	A, B, A, C, A, C, D, C, E
6	A*	C	No	A, B, A, C, A, C, D, C, E
7	D	C*	Yes	A, B, A, C, A, C, D, C, E
8	D*	C	No	A, B, A, C, A, C, D, C, E
9	E	C*	Yes	A, B, A, C, A, C, D, C, E

times when a page *was not swapped out* to make room for an incoming one, was at Times 3 and 6. That's a great deal of swapping, which results in high overhead.

If we use the same page sequence to test the LRU policy, the results are quite different, as shown in Table 7-2. Assume again that the program instructions on its five pages are referenced in the same order as before: A, B, A, C, A, C, D, C, E.

Using LRU, the pages that were referenced least recently (shown in Table 7-2 with an asterisk) are the first to be swapped out, and the pages that were referenced most recently are the last to be swapped out.

In this case, the processing of the same sequence of five pages using the LRU policy required many fewer page faults—only five page faults (compared to seven page faults for FIFO). Does this mean that LRU is superior to FIFO? Not necessarily. If you notice, this example included a bit of repetition, with Page A and Page C being referenced over and over again. This is an example of a structure that favors LRU, as shown in Table 7-3.

TABLE 7-3 Comparison of FIFO and LRU Examples		
Policy	Number of Page Faults	Overhead Required
FIFO	Seven faults of nine page references	Overhead needed to perform numerous swaps
LRU	Five faults of nine page references	Overhead needed to monitor page reference status in the Page Map Table

On the other hand, if a program had little repetition, there might be little or no difference between the number of page faults resulting from the two policies, and when one considers the higher overhead required to run LRU, it might be less efficient than FIFO. The question to be answered is this: is the overhead required to run LRU offset by the savings in page faults that result? If the answer is yes, then LRU is the favorable choice. If not, then FIFO would be the obvious candidate.

Other page replacement policies have been developed to supplement FIFO and LRU. Although we won't detail them here, their goals are the same—to reduce the number of page faults and overhead and increase system efficiency.

Thrashing

Thrashing is a consequence of quickly and repeatedly loading and unloading pages into main memory because too few page frames are available; obviously, it's not a good thing. On the simplest level, this happens if a page in memory is swapped out to make room for a second page to continue processing, but *that* page is then swapped out to make room for the return of the first page, which is quickly swapped out to make room for the second page, and so on.

Figure 7-8 shows a single command that starts on Page 5, continues on Page 6, bounces back to Page 5, then back to Page 6, and so on.

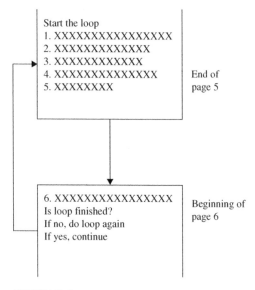

FIGURE 7-8 · This six-step loop can cause thrashing if Pages 5 and 6 can't be in memory at the same time.

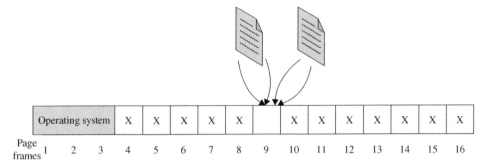

Operating system	X	X	X	X	X		X	X	X	X	X	X	X

Page frames: 1 2 3 4 5 6 7 8 9 10 11 12 13 14 15 16

FIGURE 7-9 · Thrashing occurs as two pages take turns loading into one page frame.

As Page 5 and Page 6 swap into and out of a single page frame, it's clear that a great deal of time is being wasted, thus increasing overhead and producing very little effective work (see Figure 7-9).

The colorful term *thrashing* describes what the read/write head of a hard drive is doing while it's loading and unloading these two pages—it's thrashing from one track to the other and back again. In addition to the obvious wear on the drive, it also slows processing and adds to overhead. In an effort to reduce thrashing, operating system designers try to identify a program's working sets.

Working Sets

A *working set* is a collection of instructions that call on each other repeatedly to accomplish a task during a phase of job execution. There could be one working set to get a process started, another to perform many similar calculations, and yet another to release resources and leave the system. For larger jobs, there are opportunities to create many working sets as processing progresses from start to finish.

For example, watch what happens in Table 7-2 from Times 3–6 when our five pages are called in order: A, B, A, C, A, C, D, C, and E. Beginning with Time 3, the program references instructions repeatedly on Page A and Page C until it calls Page D at Time 7. In this example, these two pages (A and C) represent a very small working set.

System designers generally attempt to identify a program's working set and keep it in memory as a unit until it's no longer needed, so that they can reduce page faults and improve system efficiency. We can glimpse that in Table 7-2, as the number of page faults drops while Pages A and C reside in memory as they are repeatedly referenced.

As a program runs through its execution, it's common for a number of working sets to be identified, usually grouped around standard operations. For example, a program might begin its execution with a set of instructions (Working Set 1) that loads subprograms, one after another, until all the required subprograms are loaded and job execution can begin. Then, the emphasis changes from loading subprograms to executing instructions (Working Set 2) that are very similar, such as looking up data in a collection of tables. Then, before the job concludes, it issues instructions (Working Set 3) to write the results of its calculations to the files stored on the disk. Finally, the exiting instructions (Working Set 4) close each subprogram in turn and release its resources.

Before a program begins, it's not obvious to the system where it can find a working set, but it can identify it by watching as pages are swapped in and out. Whenever the rate of page faults drops dramatically, the working set is in memory.

Before concluding this chapter, let's consider a related innovation—that of cache memory and how it speeds up data retrieval.

Cache Memory

Cache memory is a small portion of memory that's made accessible to a device located close to main memory. Cache memory is not main memory. Rather, it is a separate chip that can be accessed faster than the page frames in main memory.

Cache memory works as a temporary storage area where recently used data is kept. The success of cache memory is based on the assumption that some of the data that will soon be requested is the same data that was recently removed from memory.

NOTE *Although cache memory can be used to speed up hardware devices, we're limiting our discussion to caches that speed up main memory.*

In simplest terms, cache memory works like a rental counter at a tool center. In the back room, all the tools for rent are stored neatly in their places—ready for customers to request them. When the first customer of the day asks to rent a garden tiller, the attendant goes to the back room, retrieves the tiller, and the customer soon leaves to improve the garden. The next customer comes in, rents a chain saw, and soon departs. At noon, the first customer returns the garden tiller.

It's at this point that having a cache, or not, makes a difference. If the attendant is diligent about returning each tool to its proper place in storage (so there is no cache of tools near the counter), then the time required to retrieve each tool is approximately the same.

However, if the attendant chooses to keep a collection of recently rented tools near the front counter (a cache), they would be within reach if someone else asked to rent that same tool later that day. For example, if an afternoon customer wanted to rent the garden tiller, it could be quickly retrieved (from the cache) and the time that would have been required to return it to storage and later retrieve it for the second customer would be saved. Likewise, when the chain saw was returned, it would join the tiller in the cache and could be quickly rented again to a new customer. At the end of the day, before closing shop, all the tools would be returned to their proper places in the back room so a new cache could be created the next day.

If you think about this example, it makes a lot of sense to create a cache because in the spring time, there might be repeated requests for tillers and saws, while in the winter, demand might favor snow blowers and generators.

The tool center with the nearby, recently rented tool collection resembles, in its simplest form, a cache for main memory. A main memory cache holds a copy of data that has been swapped out of main memory recently. When the next page is requested, the memory manager quickly checks cache memory to see if it's "within easy reach." If so, the data is retrieved from the cache. If it's not, a parallel search of secondary storage finds and retrieves it.

The tool center without the nearby collection of recently rented tools is similar to memory management without a cache. Data is retrieved from main memory and (modified) data is rewritten to main memory as necessary.

How effective is cache memory? That depends on the number of times the cache can provide the requested data. For many, including game players and systems administrators trying to speed throughput, it is a valuable asset. Cache management continues to be the subject of exciting research, but it exceeds the scope of this book; we recommend that you explore further on your own.

Why not replace all of main memory with cache memory? Although it's true that cache memory is very fast, it is also very expensive, so it's not a suitable replacement for main memory. But as a tool to speed up access, it's very good indeed.

TIP   *You may be able to use a newer flash memory device to enhance your virtual memory. Windows systems support a feature called ReadyBoost that does so. For more information, check out the feature at www.microsoft.com.*

Summary

In this chapter, we introduced the concept of virtual memory, which gives the illusion that the system has much more physical memory than it really does, and we discussed the allocation schemes that made it popular. Unlike the schemes discussed in the previous chapter, those described in these pages (demand paged, segmented, and segmented/demand paged memory allocation schemes) allow program instructions to begin execution even if the entire job is not loaded into main memory. The management of working sets, critical to the success of virtual memory allocation schemes, allows computers to execute large, complex programs. The development of cache memory further speeds page retrieval.

In the next chapter, we discuss the challenges of device management, how conflicting demands from numerous peripheral devices are resolved, and device management policy options.

QUIZ

Choose the correct response to each of the multiple-choice questions. Note that there may be more than one correct response to each question.

1. **Which allocation scheme was the first to accommodate virtual memory?**
   A. Paged
   B. Demand paged
   C. Segmented
   D. Segmented/demand paged

2. **Which allocation scheme in this chapter causes external fragmentation?**
   A. Paged
   B. Demand paged
   C. Segmented
   D. Segmented/demand paged

3. **Name the advantages of the First-In First-Out page replacement policy.**
   A. Higher overhead
   B. Faster implementation
   C. Lower overhead
   D. Slower implementation

4. **What is a working set?**
   A. A group of pages that call on each other and reduce page faults
   B. A page replacement policy
   C. A group of pages that are thrashing
   D. A group of page faults

5. **What is the page fault hander?**
   A. It is part of the operating system software.
   B. It is used only in conjunction with segmented memory allocation.
   C. It decides when a page can be printed.
   D. It manages the page fault process.

6. **Which of these allocation schemes require the entire program to be loaded before execution can begin?**
   A. Paged
   B. Demand paged
   C. Segmented
   D. Segmented/demand paged

7. **When the last part of a segment occupies only part of a page and that page is loaded into an empty page frame, what is the result?**

   A. Internal fragmentation
   B. External fragmentation
   C. Page fault
   D. Demand paging

8. **Which of these was a major innovation of virtual memory?**

   A. It allowed users to see the size of their main memory space.
   B. It allowed pages to be placed in page frames.
   C. It allowed a program to begin execution without the entire program being required to reside in memory before starting.
   D. It eliminated fragmentation.

9. **Thrashing is the result of what?**

   A. Pages being modified before they're saved to the disk
   B. Using an antiquated page replacement policy
   C. A corrupt working set
   D. Too few available page frames

10. **What is the role of cache memory?**

    A. To speed job throughput
    B. To speed memory retrieval
    C. To enhance graphics and game experiences
    D. To reduce page faults

chapter **8**

Managing System Devices

This chapter is devoted to the responsibilities of the device management portion of the operating system, and how it balances demands from all of the peripheral devices connected to the computing system. In the pages that follow, we'll explore methods of reading and writing data from and to a variety of devices and explore some policy options available to those who design operating systems.

CHAPTER OBJECTIVES

In this chapter, you will

- Appreciate the complexities of managing many diverse devices
- Learn the differences among shared, dedicated, and virtual devices
- Be able to describe examples of sequential and direct access devices
- Be able to discuss fundamentals of magnetic, optical, and solid state media
- Understand the importance of device drivers

Overview

Almost every computer is connected to at least one peripheral device, and often there are several of them to be watched and controlled. Whether it involves a monitor, mouse, keyboard, DVD drive, flash drive, or some combination, every device connected to the system must be rigorously managed to keep things running smoothly. (These devices were once commonly called *I/O devices* for *input/output devices*, though that name is not as widely used today.) A sample listing of items managed by the device manager (accessible from the Windows 7 Control Panel) is shown in Figure 8-1.

The device manager has primary responsibility to allocate each device properly, deallocate it when appropriate, and enforce the policies made by the operating system's designers regarding who gets what device and for how long. That's not always easy, given how quickly new devices appear on the market, while others disappear with similar speed. These devices generally fall into three distinct categories:

- **Shared devices**   These can be used by more than one individual at a time. Examples might include access to a hard drive, USB, or a port to a network, such as the Internet. Administrators of Windows computers often use the

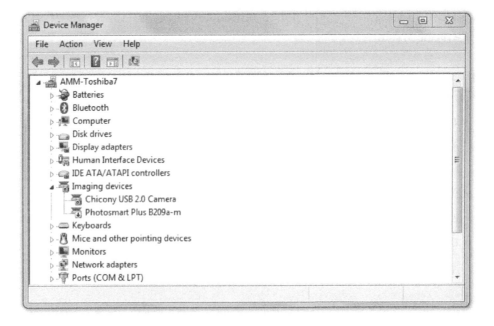

FIGURE 8-1 · Sample list of devices installed on this Windows 7 computer

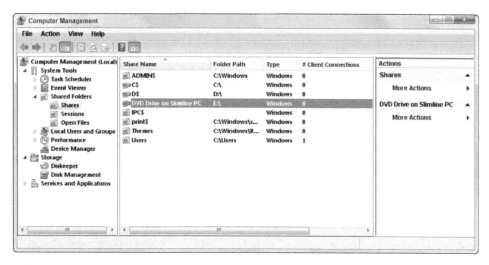

FIGURE 8-2 · Operating systems such as Windows 7 offer tools that enable administrators to manage what's shared.

Administrative Tools Computer Management window to manage sharing on a workgroup computer (as shown in Figure 8-2).

- **Dedicated devices**   These can be allocated to only one process or user at a time. Printers fall into this category because each one is allocated to one user or process at a time.

- **Virtual devices**   These are a combination of dedicated and shared. That is, they're dedicated devices (such as a networked printer) that can appear to be shared. The virtual printer does this by sending all pages to be printed to a secondary storage device (such as a hard drive) until the print job is complete. Only then (and not before) is the entire job sent to printing.

Types of Storage Media

Permanent storage media fall into two categories: those that allow access sequentially and those that can be accessed directly.

Sequential access storage devices include cartridges and reels of magnetic tape (and, long ago, paper cards and paper tape) that record data in sequence, sometimes with records that are of variable length and sometimes fixed length (file formats are discussed in Chapter 9). Sequential access is not only the oldest kind of storage; it's still the perfect media for data that is archival—that is, data not likely be retrieved, such as backup files. That's because the data stored on

| Tape header | Record 1 | Record 2 | Record 3 | Record 4 | Record 5 | Record 6 | Record 7 | Record 8 | etc. |

FIGURE 8-3 · Sequential access media is written (and read) in sequence.

sequential media can only be retrieved by reading it from the beginning, as illustrated in Figure 8-3.

Routine storage on magnetic tape has been replaced by the widespread use of hard disk drives and other direct access media to be discussed next, but there is still a market for sequential media because tape drives can quickly and economically copy data.

Several vendors offer a range of magnetic tape backup systems, and at least one has a capacity of 800GB of storage physical capacity, which can be expanded to 1.6TB if the data is compressed.

A direct access storage device (DASD) can quickly read and/or write directly to all of its storage locations. Examples of these devices include internal and external hard disk drives, USB storage such as flash memory and camera cards, solid state drives, optical disc drives (which read and/or write to CDs, DVDs, and Blu-ray discs), and more. All of these devices store data somewhere on the media and use a table or index to track the location of records (or blocks of records) so they can be accessed directly and very quickly, as shown in Figure 8-4.

Let's compare how these two kinds of devices work. Consider the command to find the address of Joanne Jones in a database where records are stored alphabetically. (In reality, this exact scenario is highly unlikely because databases are normally *stored* in no order at all, though they can be *accessed* in an alphabetical order by using an index.) So, if the database is being searched on a tape, the device manager would find the desired record by starting with the first one (perhaps that of Michael Aaron) and moving through the database, record by record, until reaching that of Joanne Jones, where it would retrieve the needed address. Alternatively, if the file is located on a DASD, the device manager

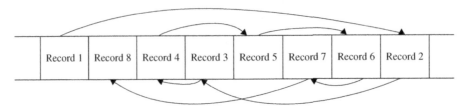

| Record 1 | Record 8 | Record 4 | Record 3 | Record 5 | Record 7 | Record 6 | Record 2 |

FIGURE 8-4 · DASDs can retrieve records even if they're not located adjacently.

would refer to a table or index to find the location of the desired record and go directly there, which is much faster than a sequential search.

Alternatively, look what happens if we need to restore a database from backup tapes to a new hard drive, which could become necessary after another drive dies or develops a fatal error. To do so, we simply copy each record, one after the other, from the tape to the new hard drive. There's no need to pause and review the contents of certain records—we merely copy all the records of all the files, in order, from beginning to end. It's very fast and easy.

NOTE   *Historically,* direct access *was also called* random access *because files could be retrieved in a random (not sequential) order. As you may remember, a synonym for main memory is* random access memory (RAM) *for similar reasons.*

How Direct Access Works

Although devices that fall into the direct access category come in many shapes and sizes, the principles are exactly the same. Let's see how several of them store and retrieve data.

Hard Disk Drives

A hard drive commonly consists of several *disks* (sometimes called platters), each coated in a magnetic material, stacked on a single spindle, and spinning in perfect unison, as shown in Figure 8-5. A stack of disks is also known as a *disk pack*. It doesn't matter if the hard drive has one or many disks; the drive mechanism generally has a single arm that moves all read/write heads in unison and rotates the disks clockwise at a constant speed—they're either stopped or running at full speed.

The surface of each disk is divided into concentric circles called *tracks,* and each circle divided into *sectors*—and this is where data is stored. A group of sectors is called a *cluster,* and although one cluster can be as small as a single

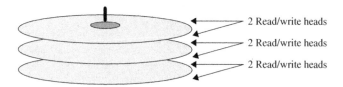

FIGURE 8-5 · A disk pack with three disks and one read/write head for each surface

sector, more often it includes more sectors (always a power of 2, such as 2, 4, 8, 16, and so on), which do not need to be located next to each other. The precise number of sectors in a cluster is chosen by the system's designer to maximize storage efficiency.

There can be more than a thousand tracks, and because the tracks are larger at the edges of the disk than toward the center, the outer sectors located there are larger, as shown in Figure 8-6. However, all sectors contain an equal number of bits—they're just closer together in the smaller sectors and farther apart in the larger ones. Don't forget that magnetic disks spin at a constant speed; therefore, as one sector moves under the read/write head, the bits being retrieved are moving at the same speed regardless of whether they're located near the center or the outer edge. (The twin concepts of constant speed and identical sector size are very different for optical discs, as we'll explain later in this chapter.)

On the top and the bottom of each disk surface is a pair of read/write heads—one to read the bottom of the disk above it, and one to read the top of the one below. All read/write heads are moved by an arm that moves them in unison so that when one head is poised over Track 12, all of the device's heads are positioned over Track 12 of their respective disk surfaces. Likewise, when the arm moves one head over Sector 4 of Track 27, all other read/write heads are also poised over Sector 4 of their respective disk surface.

NOTE *Read/write heads hover over the disk surface—they never touch it. If contact should occur, such as when the device is dropped, a portion of the disk would likely be damaged and its stored data unreadable, and if the read/write head is damaged, the disk may not be repairable.*

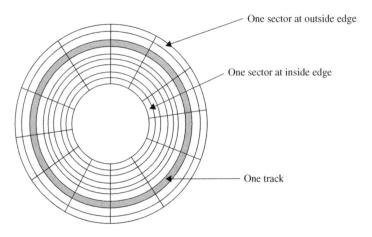

One sector at outside edge

One sector at inside edge

One track

FIGURE 8-6 · Simplified sketch of magnetic disk layout

When all of the read/write heads are positioned over a single track, they form a *virtual cylinder*, thus enabling each read/write head to read and write very quickly to their relative sectors without waiting for the arm to move to another track. Because arm movement is the most time-consuming part of data retrieval, the device manager can read and write to multiple surfaces of the cylinder faster than it would take to fill up each disk one track at a time. In other words, if a 36-sector file is copied to a 12-surface hard drive, it's likely that the file will be written to 3 sectors (let's say Sectors 5, 6, and 7) on all 12 disk surfaces rather than 36 sectors on a single disk. You can see why the concept of the virtual cylinder is so important to hard drive access.

Defragmentation can be a critical aspect of good hard disk management. Because file fragments can be stored and retrieved no matter where they're located on a disk, large files, especially those that are frequently updated, can end up having pieces scattered in numerous places on the disk. It is possible to retrieve these fragments in order, but it takes longer to retrieve a file that's scattered in multiple places. To speed file access, disks should be compacted, or defragmented, regularly.

Exercise 8-1: Defragmenting a Hard Drive

Many computers now defragment hard drives automatically on a schedule set by the operating system. Often this occurs once a week. However, if you want to disable automatic defragmenting, analyze a drive, or verify that the computer is actually defragmenting on a schedule, you can. In Windows Vista and Windows 7, as well as other operating systems that offer a Search feature from the Start menu, you simply type **Defrag** to get started.

Using a Windows 7 computer, follow these steps:

1. Click the Windows Start button, and in the Search Box, type **Defrag**.

2. Choose Disk Defragmenter from the results.

3. To analyze or defragment the disk:

    a. Select the drive if more than one exists.

    b. Click Analyze Disk or Defragment Disk, as shown in Figure 8-7.

4. To configure or verify that the process is scheduled:

    a. Click Configure Schedule.

    b. Set the schedule.

    c. Click OK.

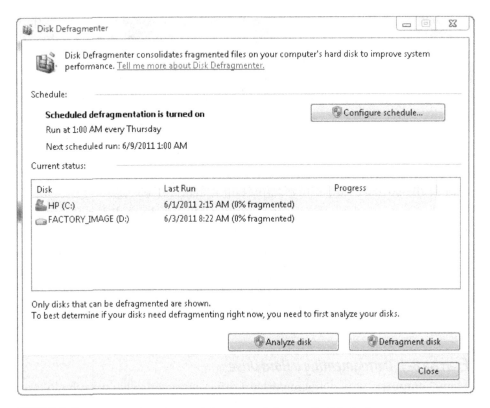

FIGURE 8-7 · You can easily analyze or defragment a disk manually, if desired.

Optical Disc Drives

Optical disc drives read the data stored on plastic-like platters using a laser. They all feature a single spiral track and sectors that are all the same size (unlike those on magnetic disks), as shown in Figure 8-8. This track originates close to the center of the disc and continues uninterrupted to the outer edge.

The disc drive has to change the speed with which the disc rotates so it can read the sectors close to the center as well as those near the outer edge. That's because the sectors near the center of the disc require a slower rotation speed to pass under the laser lens that's reading it. Likewise, sectors near the edge can be read at a faster rotation speed. Sometimes you can hear the drive speed up and slow down as it reads data from different sections of a disc. This concept is called *constant linear velocity*, versus that used for hard drives, which is known as *constant angular velocity*.

In this section, we'll discuss three popular formats: CDs, DVDs, and Blu-ray. All of them use a laser to read the indentations (called *pits)* and blank spaces

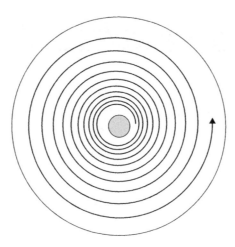

FIGURE 8-8 · An optical disc has one spiral
track and sectors of equal size.

(called *lands)* on a layer of a disc. Because the bottom of a pit is a different
elevation than a land (which is merely the absence of a pit), the laser can detect
the pattern of pits and lands and convert them to zeros and ones. Now that you
know a little bit about how the three technologies are similar, let's see how
they're different.

NOTE *According to industry conventions, magnetic* disks *are spelled with a* k *and*
optical discs *are spelled with a* c.

Compact Discs

CD drives use a red laser to read pits and lands through the disc's polycarbonate layer. CDs are available in formats that include read-only (CD-ROM),
write-once (CD-R), and read-write (CD-RW). It is the job of the operating
system's device manager to know what type of disc drive is being used so it can
successfully receive data from it and, if it's a writable device, send data to be
recorded on the CD.

DVD Discs

DVDs also use a red laser to read the pits and lands through a polycarbonate
layer, but that layer is thinner so the laser can read data that's placed closer
together, thus allowing a DVD to hold substantially more data than a CD.
What's more, it's possible to place data on more than one layer, so that the laser
can effectively look through the top layer to read the bottom one, thus enabling

TABLE 8-1 CD, DVD, and Blu-ray Data Capacity (Source: Blu-ray Disc Association)

Media (Single Sided)	Laser Type	Laser Wavelength	Data Capacity
CD	Red	780 nm	0.7GB
DVD (1 layer)	Red	650 nm	4.7GB
DVD (2 layers)	Red	650 nm	8.5GB
Blu-ray (1 layer)	Blue-violet	405 nm	25GB
Blu-ray (2 layers)	Blue-violet	405 nm	50GB
Blu-ray (20 layers)	Blue-violet	405 nm	500GB

a dual-layer DVD to hold twice as much data as one with a single layer. See Table 8-1 for detailed comparisons of three types of popular optical media.

The category of DVDs includes those that are read-only (DVD), write-once (DVD-R), and rewriteable (DVD-RW). The device manager is responsible for keeping track of the type of disc being used and the mechanics of reading and writing. There are additional types, such as DVD-R, and DVD-R+, but space does not allow us to explore them all here. For more information, we suggest you search reliable sources on the Internet.

Blu-ray™

Unlike CDs and DVDs, Blu-ray discs use a blue-violet laser (which is finer than a red laser) to read pits and lands placed on very thin layers. Blu-ray discs can read data stored even closer together than would be possible on CDs or DVDs, and can be manufactured with multiple layers. Because they can hold so much data, they are used for high-density projects. Blu-ray discs can also be read-only (BD), write-once (BD-R), and rewriteable (BD-RW).

NOTE *The term is properly spelled as Blu-ray. Alternatives such as Blue-ray and Blu-Ray are incorrect. For details, visit the Blu-ray Disc Association (www.blu-raydisc .com), which holds several trademarks associated with this technology.*

In 2008, Pioneer Electronics announced that it developed an experimental disc with 20 layers and capable of holding 500GB. Given that this is a subject of exploding change, be sure to keep tabs on optical storage innovations using online sources.

Solid State Devices

Two popular storage devices are solid state drives and flash memory. Neither has moving parts—electronic controls have replaced the mechanical movement that's required by hard disks and optical discs. These solid state devices are both direct access and nonvolatile, which means that unlike main memory, they do not lose data when they're powered off.

All solid state devices use a phenomenon derived from the concepts of Fowler-Nordheim tunneling; the name "flash" was first applied because this technology erased a large chunk of its memory at one time, unlike previous technology that erased memory one byte at a time. Let's explore flash memory and solid state drives.

Flash Memory

This technology is widely used to store groups of files and/or transfer them easily from one device to another. Flash memory goes by several different names, including thumb drives, camera cards, flash drives, smart media, pen drives, compact flash, and memory sticks. They fall into an official category called *flash electrically erasable programmable read-only memory (flash-EEPROM)* and are commonly found in cameras, cell phones, music players, navigators, and so on. Figure 8-9 shows a typical USB flash drive.

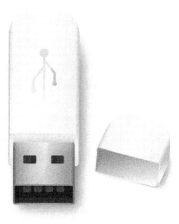

FIGURE 8-9 · Typical USB flash drive

Flash technology is relatively inexpensive, so it's the media of choice for small devices. And as you might expect, the cost of flash memory media is directly proportional to its size, hence the industry's effort to make them smaller and smaller.

NOTE *Flash memory devices degrade with use. Every time a flash is used to erase a block of data, that block loses some of its stability. Therefore, after tens of thousands, or hundreds of thousands of flashes, the device cannot store data reliably.*

Solid State Drives

A solid state drive (SSD) features nonvolatile storage space, has no moving parts, and stores data using the same concepts of flash memory devices but on a much larger scale. An SSD can replace a hard drive if the proper device driver is installed. SSDs offer some terrific advantages over hard drives:

- They can read data substantially faster than traditional hard drives.
- They can be compact enough to fit into handheld devices.
- Because they have no moving parts, they are much more rugged than a hard drive and generate less heat.

However, despite their impressive benefits, SSDs have not been an easy sell, and there are several reasons for this:

- SSDs often cost substantially more than comparably sized hard drives.
- Although reading data is very fast, writing data can be less so.
- Performance degrades over time. Testers have noted varying benchmarks between SSDs that are "new out of the box" and those that are "used."

Compared to hard drives, SSDs are quiet, lighter, and not susceptible to magnetic interference because data is stored on a chip instead of a magnetic surface. SSDs can access data very quickly from anywhere on the device, so defragmentation isn't necessary, which is a plus. As of this writing, they are available up to 2TB, but are more often sold in smaller sizes (less than 120GB) because of their relatively high cost per gigabyte.

Bottom line? For systems that primarily retrieve data (and do not modify it), or those that would benefit from exceptional access speed (such as those that use multimedia applications), SSD technology can offer substantial performance improvements.

Device Communications

For the device manager to perform its assigned tasks, it must be able to control each device's workings, track its free/busy status, know how to accommodate access requests that arrive when the device is busy, and handle the different data transmission speeds when some devices are slower or faster than other parts of the computer system. This last task is particularly tricky when working with the CPU and main memory, which are often much faster than devices such as drives, monitors, and keyboards.

A crucial task is learning when a device has completed its work, thus becoming available to take on the next request. When that happens, the device manager gets an *interrupt* (sometimes abbreviated as *IRQ*) indicating that the device needs attention. Interrupts are managed by an *interrupt handler*, which does the following:

- Balances the ebb and flow of interrupts from all the system's devices
- Monitors which interrupts came from which units
- Tracks the status of every device
- When appropriate, returns control to the process that can continue now that the read and/or write request has been accomplished

Some of the tools necessary to do this are device drivers, buffers, and direct memory access.

TIP   *One of the major challenges when a new major operating system is released is to have drivers available for all devices that customers are likely to want to use. Therefore, the drivers for all current devices are written and tested first. For this reason, new releases might not have drivers for your older devices—the ones you've had for several years. If this happens to you, go to the support website for your operating system and submit a notice about the device you're trying to connect— it's quick and easy. Also, check out the support website by the device manufacturer to see if they have a new driver you can download. Over time, the driver may become available, so keep on trying to find and install it.*

Device Drivers

A *device driver* contains the programming code required to manipulate a device. Therefore, the device driver for your monitor makes it possible for the operating

FIGURE 8-10 · Every device must have a device driver, including this Bluetooth USB controller.

system to send that monitor data, display that data properly, manipulate images that appear on it, and handle interrupts. On a Windows 7 computer, you can check out the status of a device driver from the Control Panel. Choose Device Manager and select the device to reach the display shown in Figure 8-10.

Because device drivers are powerful and can cause headaches for end users and network administrators alike, Microsoft offers manufacturers a path for having their device drivers "signed." For a device driver to be signed, the driver must pass rigorous testing and function in any computer configuration imaginable. You can trust signed drivers; that's the takeaway. However, not all manufacturers get their drivers signed. Thus, you may not be able to find a signed driver for old hardware, and may be forced to install an unsigned driver to get the hardware to work. You may have done this before, and you may be familiar with the warning that informs you when you're about to install an unsigned driver. As you know, you're encouraged not to install these drivers because they can harm the computer. If you install the unsigned driver and have problems, though, Microsoft computers offer various ways to recover from that, including System Restore and Device Driver Rollback.

You can find out whether there are any unsigned drivers on a problematic Windows computer by running the command **sigverif**. On a Windows 7 computer, you can simply type it in the Start Search box. Figure 8-11 shows an example of a computer with one unsigned driver.

Virtual device drivers can be used to manage system devices in an environment where one operating system appears to be running inside another operating system. Although fascinating, this software goes beyond the scope of this book, but we encourage you to search the Internet for more information if you find it of interest.

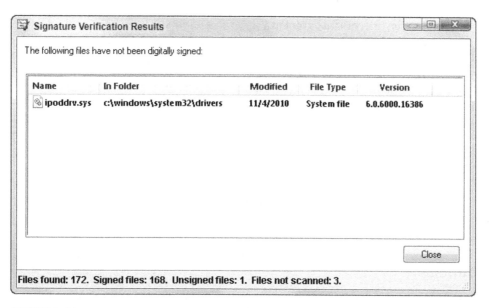

FIGURE 8-11 · The File Signature Verification utility in Windows helps you locate potentially problematic device drivers already installed on the system.

When the Device Is a Port

The physical interface that allows certain devices to transfer data to and from a CPU is called a *port*. Device drivers for ports can be found either in the operating system kernel or as modules that are loaded separately. Three of the most common are detailed here:

- **USB ports**   These allow access to USB devices. As of this writing, USB devices include almost any kind of I/O device and have replaced many uses of the two that predated it: COM and serial ports.

- **COM ports**   These provide access to devices that can manage data sent in parallel, such as printers, zip drivers, and scanners. On new computers, they can be emulated via the creation of a *virtual COM port*. Adapters are available that can connect a legacy printer to a USB port—look for a "USB to parallel" adapter.

- **Serial ports**   Technically known as *RS-232 ports* because they were compliant with an established industry standard, these are used to access devices that can use data that's sent in a series, in a single stream of bits. Serial ports are still used to communicate with some scientific instruments or industrial components, and can be emulated by creating a *virtual serial port*.

> **NOTE**   *A single USB port (with the help of several hubs connected to it) can control data from up to 127 different devices, including combinations of cameras, music players, disc drives, keyboards, mice, and so on. (Although the USB port is capable of handling their data, these devices may need sources of external power to work properly.)*

Buffers

In its most general form, a *buffer* is a storage space where data can stay for a very brief instant of time. Systems generally feature one of several arrangements of buffers to allow a slow I/O device to communicate smoothly with a much faster CPU:

- **Single buffer**   This is the simplest configuration. It is loaded with data slowly, and when it's full, its contents are quickly sent to the much faster device, such as a CPU.

FIGURE 8-12 · The colored portion of the buffer bar, to the button's right, measures data already downloaded.

- **Double buffer** This type of buffer works similarly, but while the contents of one buffer are being sent to the CPU, the other buffer is filling with the next batch of data. Later, as that batch is sent, the first buffer is being filled.

- **Circular buffer** This type of buffer (also known as a *ring buffer*) works continuously as if it has two ends that are connected (though in practice, this is not the case—it's actually a virtual circle). This type of buffer is a favorite for use in multimedia applications.

You can watch your system's buffers in action when you start to watch a video. Notice the progress button at the bottom of the screen—the solid line to the button's left shows how much of the video has already been displayed, and the moving transparent line to the button's right (often of a contrasting color) shows how much of the video's data has already been downloaded to your device. For example, as shown in Figure 8-12, even though this viewer has seen only 36 seconds of the video so far, more than a minute of the upcoming footage has already been downloaded.

Direct Memory Access

As we mentioned in Chapter 6, direct memory access (DMA) allows certain hardware to communicate directly with main memory via special channels, which reduces CPU overhead because it doesn't need to monitor the transfer of each byte. Basically, it's a shortcut designed to make best use of three critical resources: CPU, main memory, and devices. In this way, DMA allows devices such as disk drive controllers, graphics cards, network cards, sound cards, and more to send and receive streams of data at a high rate of speed.

Multicore computers often take full advantage of DMA to facilitate data transfer between each core's local memory and system devices, with minimal attention by the processor. The CPU just starts the transfer and then allows the DMA controller to supervise the transfer of the bytes that follow. Later, when

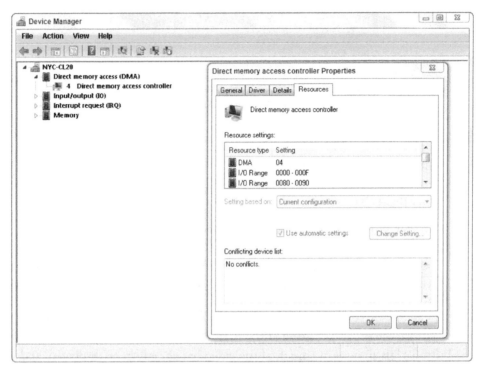

FIGURE 8-13 · The direct access memory controller is a component and therefore can be viewed from Device Manager.

the data stream ends, a signal is sent back to the CPU so that it can retake control and move on to the next phase of data transfer.

Because the direct access memory controller is a component, you can view it in Device Manager on Windows computers. Figure 8-13 shows an example. As expected, there are no conflicts for this controller, and it's working properly.

Managing I/O Requests

The success of the device manager that's retrieving data from a hard drive hinges on the time required to do three things: move the arm holding the read/write heads into the correct position, wait for the disk to rotate to the correct sectors, and transmit the data that's retrieved from those sectors.

Although, for this discussion, we'll concern ourselves with hard drive data retrieval, the concepts are similar for optical discs, but instead of moving an arm with read/write heads, the optical disc drive is moving the reading lens back and forth while adjusting the disc's rotational speed to access the desired sectors on the track.

NOTE   *Data retrieval delay isn't an issue for SSDs because they have no moving parts and every part of the drive can be accessed with equal speed.*

These concepts, called *seek strategies*, dictate the disk pack's arm movement and have been the subject of much research because this is the most time-consuming element of data retrieval. To see why, let's say that the queue of requests to be filled requires the arm to move the read/write heads to the following tracks: 78, 409, 601, 787, 12, 944, 943, 11, and 58.

The operating system designer can choose to have these requests served in one of several ways: the order in which they arrived, their nearness to the previous request, their ease of retrieval, and so on. We'll compare three of them here, though there are several more that you can explore on your own.

First Come, First Served is a strategy that takes each request in chronological order. In this example, it would start at 78 and move to 409, 601, 787, 12, 944, and so on. It's very fair, but not very efficient because the read/write heads can skip over newer requests that are waiting even though they're located "on the way to" the next request. Understandably, this simple strategy is not often adopted.

Shortest Seek Time First looks through the requests that are waiting in the queue and retrieves the next closest sector. In other words, watching our queue (78, 409, 601, 787, 12, 944, 943, 11, 58), when the read/write heads leave track 409, they'll proceed to 601, 787, 943, 944, in that order, and will get around to tracks 12, 11, and 58 some other time. And that's the problem. If there are numerous requests, this strategy will seldom visit any track that is near the inner or outer edge of the disk. It naturally favors sectors that are most easily reached—those in the middle.

The *Scan* strategy evaluates all the waiting requests, puts them in a certain order (either from lowest to highest or highest to lowest), and always moves from one edge to the other so it can pick up every request in the queue along the way. Therefore, if the arm was starting in the center of the disk, it would rearrange the queue to be in this order: 11, 12, 58, 78, 409, 601, 787, 943, and 944. If the arm was moving from the outer to the inner edge, the order would be reversed so that the read/write heads on the arm would move from 944 to 943 to 787, and so on. This strategy offers obvious time-saving benefits, but it sometimes forces the arm with the read/write heads all the way to the edge even if there are no requests there, thus wasting precious time.

Another research area addresses the order in which sectors on a track should be read. If you recall the concept of the virtual cylinder, this research addresses how sectors can be accessed in this cylinder with the greatest efficiency. This is called *rotational ordering* and it addresses such questions as these: Is it faster to access multiple track sectors located next to each other on a single platter? Or is it faster to read all the sectors in the same relative place on multiple tracks, thus reducing arm movement?

Keep in mind that device management is one of the most changeable operating systems topics because it's inevitably tied to the quick development of newer, smaller, faster, more rugged devices that are (hopefully) compatible with your computers. Watch this field closely because it changes often.

Still Struggling?

The basic concepts described in this chapter are the same regardless of the media used to store your files—on magnetic disks, optical discs, or flash memory. Therefore, no matter how, when, or where your data is stored, files must be written accurately and retrieved properly later on when you need them. That's the bottom line.

Summary

The device management portion of the operating system must delicately balance the demands from the many peripheral devices connected to the computer, even if their requests conflict with one another. In this chapter, we compared sequential access to direct access and we described how data is retrieved and stored on a variety of media (including disk packs, optical discs, and solid state). We also covered some policy options available to those who design operating systems, as well as introduced a few elements of device communications, including the roles played by device drivers, buffers, and direct memory access.

In the next chapter, we'll explore the management of the system files, utilities, databases, applications, and all other files on the system, as well as how that task affects overall system efficiency.

QUIZ

Choose the correct response to each of the multiple-choice questions. Note that there may be more than one correct response to each question.

1. **Which of the following has been classified as direct access storage media?**
   A. Flash memory
   B. Tape cartridge
   C. DVD
   D. Paper punch cards

2. **Which of the following is likely to be considered a dedicated device?**
   A. Monitor
   B. Port with access to the Internet
   C. Mouse
   D. Networked printer

3. **Without making use of the virtual cylinder concept, how would a file of 50 sectors be written to a hard drive with a stack of five disks, each with two read/write surfaces?**
   A. On the same sector of all 10 surfaces
   B. On every surface of all 10 surfaces of the five disks
   C. On a single surface of two of the five disks
   D. On a single surface of a single disk

4. **Identify how the pits on a DVD are different from those on a Blu-ray disc.**
   A. They're closer together.
   B. They're farther apart.
   C. They're smaller.
   D. They're larger.

5. **What are the biggest differences between magnetic and optical media?**
   A. Track size
   B. Data transfer speed
   C. Sector size
   D. Spin speed

6. **Why is disk defragmentation important?**
   A. It's not important.
   B. It makes file deletion easier.
   C. It combines pieces of spread-out files.
   D. It reveals which files are missing.

7. **Which of the following are excellent uses for a buffer?**
   A. To send data from a slow I/O device to a fast CPU
   B. To send data from a fast CPU to a slow I/O device
   C. To send backup data from a fast hard drive to an archival tape
   D. To send an e-mail

8. **What is flash memory?**
   A. A device that cannot wear out
   B. An example of secondary storage
   C. A device that works with only one operating system
   D. An essential element of main memory

9. **Why might a device driver need to be updated?**
   A. It never needs to be updated.
   B. The device stopped responding correctly.
   C. The computer has been rebooted.
   D. The driver's software needs to be fixed.

10. **Which seek strategy moves methodically from one edge of the disk to the other edge?**
    A. Shortest Seek Time First
    B. Scan
    C. First Come, First Served
    D. None of the above

Part IV

File System Management

chapter 9

File System Management

This chapter describes the way that the operating system manages every file on the system. The management of utilities, databases, applications, and all other files is an essential part of overall system efficiency. If not done well, it can lead to corrupted files and doubts about the integrity of every file. In these pages, we'll explore how files are stored, retrieved, modified, and deleted, as well as the methods used to restrict access to these files (hopefully) to those with authority to do so. And we'll conclude with a look at some future challenges for file managers of every system.

CHAPTER OBJECTIVES

In this chapter, you will

- Understand the importance of file structures
- Learn the requirements for naming files and folders
- Be able to discuss file hierarchies and path structures
- Gain an understanding of some fundamental file organization systems

What Is File Management?

The file manager controls each file on the computer system and maintains its organization and storage requirements as well as the structure of the records that make up that file. To do so, the file manager must have the capability to uniquely identify every file, make sure each one is allocated to an appropriate place in secondary storage (as described in Chapter 8), know the exact address where every file is stored, allow users or applications to access the correct file when appropriate (and deny access when it's not), remove access when the user or program no longer needs the file, and more. It's a tall order—let's start with how the operating system puts files in a hierarchical order, and how it uses that hierarchy to track every file on the system.

> In its most fundamental form, a file is a collection of records, and each record is a collection of fields. In computer systems, files are software entities that can be manipulated by the user, the operating system, and other applications. In many operating systems, files can be grouped into entities that are called folders or directories.

Think of a file structure as an upside-down tree, with the trunk at the top and the leaves at the bottom. The most important item (the master file directory) is at the top and the individual files are at the bottom, as shown in Figure 9-1.

This figure shows a simplified example of a three-directory-level file system. Although we are relying on this example to explain how file systems work in general, please remember that to manage the many thousands of files on a typical system, an actual hierarchy would be much more complex.

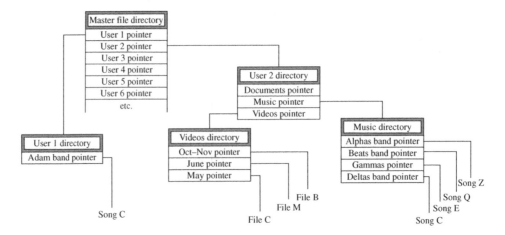

FIGURE 9-1 · Simplified view of a file structure

In the example shown in Figure 9-1, file requests start at the top and then work their way down the file tree:

- The top level is the master file directory, which lists all the system users who are using files. A pointer in this space tells the file manager where each user's file directory (on the next lower level) is located.

- The next level down has a directory for each user that lists all of that user's subdirectories (if they have them, as User 2 does) or pointers to files (if they have no subdirectories, like User 1).

- In most operating systems, there can generally be many levels of subdirectories, some of which will point to lower-level subdirectories or directly to files.

- At the bottom level are the files themselves.

Therefore, to get to "Song Z" in the "Music" directory for User 2, the file manager must follow these steps in this order:

1. Start with the master directory and move through it until reaching the entry for User 2; then follow the pointer to get to…

2. … the file directory for User 2, and then move through that directory until reaching the entry for the music directory; then follow the pointer to…

3. … the music directory, and then go through that directory until reaching the entry for the band called the Alphas; then follow the pointer to…

4. … the song that's stored as Song Z.

TIP *Because the file manager is following pointers to go from directory to directory to directory to file, there is no need for the files or directories to be stored near each other on the hard drive or optical disc. If they happen to be nearby, access might be slightly faster, but it's not necessary.*

We've just uncovered two key concepts of file retrieval: the differences between a *relative file name* (such as Song Z) and an *absolute file name*, which includes the entire path and lists every directory name along the way from the top of the tree to the bottom. This is called the *file path* and it's critical when locating each file on the system, whether it's stored on a disk, device, or network. Each absolute file name *must be unique*. Because the path name is essential to locating each file, it allows two files to exist on the same system with the same *relative file name* (such as Song C, which is the name given to two different files—for two different users, as shown at the bottom of Figure 9-1), as long as they're in different directories and thus have different *path names* and, hence, unique *absolute file names*.

TIP *Although a file name can be quite long, sometimes up to 255 characters, you should remember that this limit includes not only the name of the file, but the name of the path leading to that file. Check your system for exact limitations.*

There are many ways to view the path name for a directory. Figure 9-2 shows a path listing in the Command Prompt display (accessible from the Accessories menu on many Windows systems) using the TREE command. Notice that the root directory (C:) is at the top of the window, followed by directories and then subdirectories, all listed down the upside-down tree. (This TREE command does not include files in the listing.)

You can see similar information using standard folder views on Windows systems, as shown in Figure 9-3 (we used Windows Explorer to create this display). The tree structure is graphically illustrated in an indented format on the left, and the files are listed on the right with their key statistics (name, type, size, date taken, and dimensions). File listings for other directories may include different key statistics.

In Figure 9-3, the first file listed has a relative file name of IMG_0003.JPG, whereas its absolute file name includes the entire path: Ann's iPhone/Internal Storage/DCIM/800AAAAA/IMG_0003.JPG. Notice that this name begins with the name of the device (Ann's iPhone), then lists each directory in turn

FIGURE 9-2 • Sample results from the TREE command listing directories and subdirectories

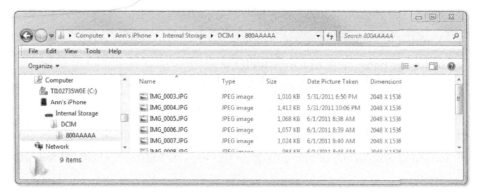

FIGURE 9-3 · Viewing the paths for a file using Windows 7

(Internal Storage, DCIM, 800AAAAA), and then lists the photo file's relative file name (IMG_0003.JPG).

NOTE *In this limited space, we can give only a very brief explanation of path names. When a file or directory name is created that is long or includes special characters (such as spaces), the file manager may give it a nickname that's still unique but shorter and easier to handle. Refer to your system's technical specifications for precise details.*

Exercise 9-1: Explore the File System on Your Computer

No matter what kind of computer you use, you'll have a file structure to explore. As you've learned, you'll have various top-level folders, subfolders, and (in Windows 7) even libraries. By exploring your own folder structure, you can easily see how and why folders and subfolders are configured hierarchically. It maintains order for you, any additional users, and the computer's file manager, of course.

On a Windows computer, follow these steps to explore the file system:

1. Right-click the Windows Start button.

2. Left-click Open Windows Explorer (or something similar, depending on your system).

3. Scroll down the leftmost pane to find the folder called Computer and then double-click its folder for the primary hard drive (generally C:).

4. Double-click the folder called Users.

5. Double-click your user folder.

6. Open each subfolder, clicking the Back button as necessary. Note which folders you've created and which ones are available by default.

Here are the steps to follow on a Mac computer:

1. Double-click Finder.

2. In the left pane, click Macintosh HD.

3. Note the folders and then open Users.

4. Open your personal folder (the one with the icon of a house).

5. Notice the default subfolders as well as any you've created.

6. Continue exploring, clicking to open the various folders and subfolders, as desired.

7. In any folder, click File | Get Info to see more information.

8. Notice the path name, which lets you see where in the hierarchy the folder is located, as shown in Figure 9-4.

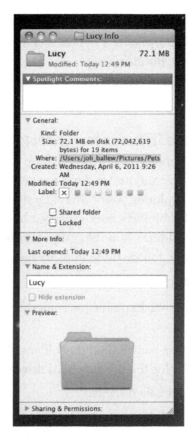

FIGURE 9-4 · The path name is highlighted.

Naming Files and Folders/Directories

Each file in a folder (also called a *directory)* must have a unique name so that the file manager can identify it and retrieve it when necessary. Likewise, each subfolder (in each folder) has to have its own unique name. That doesn't mean that two files or two folders can't have identical names—they can—but those two files or folders can't be in the same place, because no two items inside a single folder can have the same name. For example, you can create a subfolder called "archive" in each of your photo folders to hold the unused versions of your favorite photos. But you cannot have two subfolders that are both named "archive" in a single folder.

If you move a file into a folder that already has another file with the same name, the file manager will either replace the original version with the new one, or append a number to the second version, so "Song Z" and "Song Z(1)" can coexist in the same folder.

Every operating system has its own rules that dictate what is, and is not, a legal name for a directory or file:

- Some only allow names that are a single word (without spaces)—others allow hundreds of characters.
- Some allow special characters—others don't.
- Some differentiate between letters that are in capital letters and those that are lowercase (these are called *case sensitive)*. Some don't.
- Some need a file extension to dictate which application the operating system will use to open the file—others don't.

Table 9-1 shows an overview of some of the differences between three different operating systems, but this is only a quick look. A complete list would

TABLE 9-1 Typical Comparison of Legal File Names (Verify Exact Requirements for Your System)

Operating System	Maximum Character Length	Special Characters Disallowed/Discouraged	Case Sensitive	Extension Required
Linux	256	*, ?, $, &, [,] , / , \	Yes	No
Mac OS X	255	: (colon)	Yes	No
Windows 7	255/256	Most special characters	No	Yes

be very long, so be sure to verify the file and folder name requirements for your system.

The varying requirements between different operating systems can be the source of huge headaches if your network manages computers with two or more operating systems. For example, if Macintosh users need to back up their files to a Windows platform, any files that have names with special characters (which happen to be allowed on the Mac, but not on Windows) might encounter problems during archiving, and the backup application can terminate prematurely. When in doubt, we recommend that you avoid any tricky special characters so that the file you're naming will be more likely to run successfully on multiple systems.

NOTE   *Early Windows systems and MS-DOS required that all file names be only eight characters long plus a mandatory three-letter extension, separated by a dot. Examples of legal names might include TRAFFIC.EXE, INVENTRY.DOC, and SAMPLE10.TXT. This is called the 8.3 filename convention. (Other extensions are listed in Table 9-5, later in this chapter.)*

Files such as WeekEnd12, weekend12, and weekEND12 can coexist in the same folder when using a system that's case-sensitive. Systems that are not case-sensitive would not recognize the differences in the three file names and could overwrite these files until there was only one.

Directories and File Attributes

It's up to the file manager to track each user's authorization to access files on the system, and it does so with *file attributes*, which are codes signifying the ability of every system user to manipulate that file. For most operating systems, these attributes can be viewed in directory or folder listings. There are several standard actions that users can be granted, depending on the operating system.

Linux, Mac OS X (which is built on a UNIX platform), and other UNIX systems assign directory, read, write, and execute access to files, commonly abbreviated as follows:

- **d**   Directory (a file is indicated with a dash).
- **r**   Read access allows a user to view the file but not to make any changes to it.

```
amm@ubuntu: ~
File  Edit  View  Search  Terminal  Help
amm@ubuntu:~$ ls -l
total 36
drwxr-xr-x 2 amm amm 4096 2011-06-13 17:22 Desktop
drwxr-xr-x 2 amm amm 4096 2011-06-13 16:46 Documents
drwxr-xr-x 2 amm amm 4096 2011-06-13 17:01 Downloads
-rw-r--r-- 1 amm amm  179 2011-06-13 12:32 examples.desktop
drwxr-xr-x 2 amm amm 4096 2011-06-13 16:46 Music
drwxr-xr-x 2 amm amm 4096 2011-06-13 17:24 Pictures
drwxr-xr-x 2 amm amm 4096 2011-06-13 16:46 Public
drwxr-xr-x 2 amm amm 4096 2011-06-13 16:46 Templates
drwxr-xr-x 2 amm amm 4096 2011-06-13 16:46 Videos
amm@ubuntu:~$ 
```

FIGURE 9-5 • Typical directory listing in Ubuntu Linux from the Terminal screen showing attributes on the left.

- **w**   Write access allows a user to modify the contents of the file.
- **x**   Execute access allows the user to run the file, assuming that it has code that can be executed.

If you display a directory on Linux in terminal mode using the command `ls -l`, you receive a listing similar to the one shown in Figure 9-5. Notice that the attributes of each file are listed in the leftmost column.

In Figure 9-5, you can see a variety of directories and files (files are items in the list without a *d* in the leftmost position) as well as many combinations of access codes for the user and the members of his or her group and world. Figure 9-6 illustrates the meaning of the code for the first item shown in Figure 9-5.

Here's how to read the code: *d* indicates that this is a directory (if it was a file, the *d* would be replaced with a dash, as is the case in the fourth item shown in Figure 9-5); the following *rwx* indicates that the *file's owner* is allowed to read-write-execute the file; the following *r-x* indicates that others in the *user's group* are only allowed to read-execute the file (they are denied access to write to or modify the file because the *w* is missing); the final *r-x* indicates that anyone

FIGURE 9-6 • Notice how the position of each attribute describes file access.

outside the user's group is only allowed to read-execute (but not modify) the file. This final group is often called *world*.

NOTE *Operating systems typically have several additional attributes that we, as users, do not see. To keep this explanation simple, we're limiting this discussion to only the most commonly seen attributes.*

Windows systems work in a similar way and use attributes that are abbreviated as follows:

- **D** Directory
- **R** Read-only file access
- **S** System file that can be executed
- **H** Hidden file that will not be included in directory listings unless specifically requested by the user
- **A** Archived file

If you turn on the file attribute listing by right-clicking the heading bar (say, next to the word Name), choosing More, and clicking the box next to Attributes, you can see some of the attributes assigned to each file, demonstrated on the right side of Figure 9-7.

You can change the attributes for a file by opening the Properties dialog box and clicking the Hidden or Read-Only check box, as shown in Figure 9-8. To archive a file, click the Advanced button. Likewise, you can change access for the owner, group, or others in Linux, as shown in Figure 9-9.

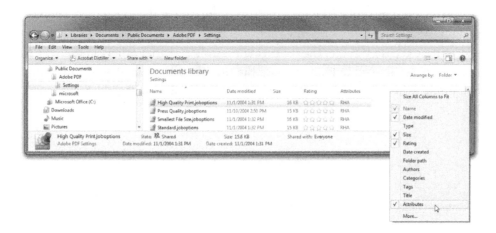

FIGURE 9-7 • Viewing Windows 7 file attributes (RHA)

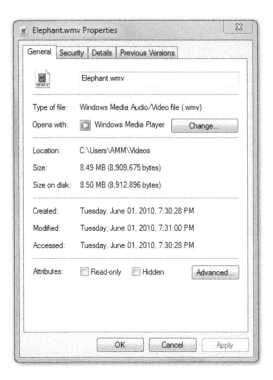

FIGURE 9-8 · In Windows, click Read-Only or Hidden to change file attributes.

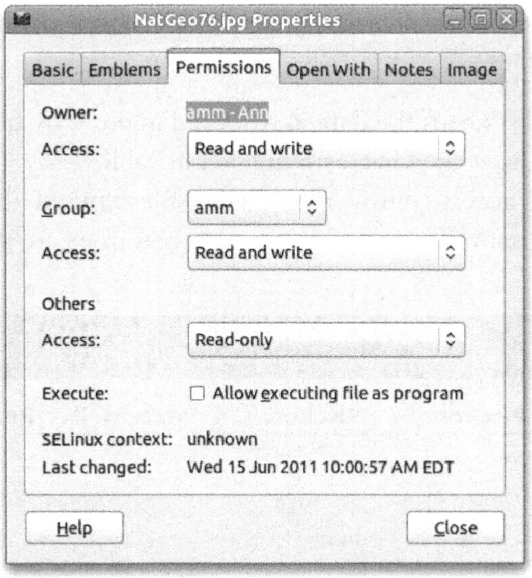

FIGURE 9-9 · In Ubuntu Linux, file access for Owner, Group, and Others is adjustable.

Access Control

How are these attributes stored and maintained on the system? Three popular methods of controlling user access in a file system are an access control matrix, access control list, and capability list. To keep our explanations consistent in these examples, we use four attributes, RWED, for read, write, execute, delete, respectively. If access is restricted, that's indicated with a dash, so a code reading --E- would indicate that the user can only execute the file, but cannot read, write, or delete it. Likewise, four dashes (----) would indicate that no access is allowed.

Access Control Matrix

An access control matrix is a flat file that lists every user along one dimension and every file along the other, as simulated in Table 9-2.

Notice that the matrix format is fast and easy for the file manager to read, but it can become a huge file because of its many duplications. For example, several users have no access to numerous files, but that lack of access is nevertheless shown with four dashes (----) in every case. This duplication is a waste of space. What's more, the matrix itself can become unmanageably large for networked systems, making it an unpopular access control method for any large system. Just look at our small example—it became very large even though it lists only four files and six users.

Access Control List

An access control list keeps the data in rows and in order by file, thus shortening the size of the list somewhat, as simulated in Table 9-3.

Notice that this access control method doesn't explicitly list anyone with zero access to a certain file. Instead these no-access users are put into a group

TABLE 9-2 Sample Contents of an Access Control Matrix for a System with Four Files

	Person_A	Person_B	Person_C	Person_D	Person_E	Person_F
File 1	RWE-	----	----	R-E-	----	----
File 2	----	RWED	----	----	--E-	RWED
File 3	R-E-	----	RWED	----	--E-	----
File 4	----	R-E-	----	RWED	--E-	----

TABLE 9-3	Access Control List with Same Data as Shown in Table 9-2
File 1	PERSON_A(RWE-), PERSON_D(R-E-), WORLD(----)
File 2	PERSON_B(RWED), PERSON_E(--E-), PERSON_F(RWED), WORLD(----)
File 3	PERSON_A(R-E-), PERSON_C(RWED), PERSON_E(--E-), WORLD(----)
File 4	PERSON_B(R-E-), PERSON_D(RWED), PERSON_E(--E-), WORLD(----)

called WORLD. As was the case with the access control matrix, "no access" is shown as four dashes (----). As you can see, this is a smaller listing and is therefore beneficial for systems with many files.

Capability List

A capability list is similar to an access control list, but this one is ordered by the individual user, instead of by file, as shown in Table 9-4.

Notice that a capability list doesn't bother listing any file that the indicated person is not allowed to access. Like the access control list, the capability list is smaller than the access control matrix.

As of this writing, designers of many common operating systems have chosen the access control list to manage file authorization.

We've kept these examples simple to demonstrate the most basic concepts of access control. But in a networked environment that holds critical data that must be kept secure or contains certain devices that need to be allocated to only certain users, additional levels of access control can be extended to control which actions users (who already have full access) may be allowed to perform.

TABLE 9-4	Capability List Organizes the Same Access Data Shown in Tables 9-2 and 9-3
Person_A	File1(RWE-), File2(R-E-), File3(R-E-)
Person_B	File2(RWED), File4(R-E-)
Person_C	File3(RWED)
Person_D	File1(R-E-), File4(RWED)
Person_E	File2(--E-), File3(--E-), File4(--E-)
Person_F	File2(RWED)

Still Struggling?

Access control lists and capability lists work almost the same way, and they both create tables that are smaller than that created by an access control matrix. Their chief difference is that an access control list puts its table in order by file showing who can manipulate it, and a capability list orders its table by user showing the capability granted to each individual.

Elements of File Storage

Files are collections of records, and the way files are stored physically on a secondary storage medium depends in large part on how its records will be accessed and how often. What's more, these records can be *blocked* (stored in groups or blocks to reduce access time) or *unblocked.*

TIP   *Did you know that when a file is retrieved, it is merely copied to main memory while the original version remains where it is on the hard drive? That makes things easier if the file is later closed with no changes because the file does not need to be sent to secondary storage (because the version that resides in storage is still correct). Therefore, the file manager rewrites the file to the hard drive only if the file has been modified.*

File Organization

Let's examine several key factors about the files that are likely to be stored on the system as well as three common types of organization. The three primary categories of file organization are sequential, direct, and indexed, but before making a choice, the designer has to know important aspects, such as the following, about the files that the system is expected to use:

- Typical file size
- Likely required response time
- Anticipated file activity
- Data volatility

For example, some files may be retrieved in very large chunks, such as archival files that are being used to restore a corrupted disk. Alternatively, there may be a large database with records that will be accessed individually in an unordered, random fashion.

Sequential record organization is the technique of choice for records that are typically processed in their entirety and that can be stored on a sequential access or direct access device. For example, if you're storing archival files on a tape, you might want to load those records one after the other, with identifying codes between them so the controller can find records that need to be retrieved. This organization allows many records to be written the first time very fast, although retrieving individual records can be slow and modifying records can be troublesome.

Direct record organization was developed with the evolution of direct access storage devices—it allows a file's records to be retrieved directly. For example, if you want to play the sixth tune that's stored on a CD, the controller quickly gets the address of the music you want, and moves directly there without needing to check the locations of the first five tunes. (If, on the other hand, you are only interested in the third stanza of a song, you might need to start at the beginning and listen to the first two stanzas before reaching the section you really want.) A huge advantage of direct organization is that there's no need to store the records in any order—as long as they're somewhere on the disk, they can be retrieved and modified very quickly. Music CDs and movie DVDs use direct access because the location of the desired tracks or movie scenes is listed in a table on the optical disc.

Indexed record organization relies on an index with key values (unique identifiers used to locate each record) to reveal the first location where the desired record is stored so that the system can begin retrieving records. In essence, this is an index that uses a pointer to go to the beginning of the first record. If the entire record is located in this one place, retrieval is quickly finished and the file manager can move on to the next retrieval request. If the record is housed in multiple locations, a series of pointers directs the file manager from this location to the beginning of the next segment, and then to the next, until the entire file is located and retrieved. An indexed organization plan is very handy when there are modifications to the file, because extra records can be written anywhere on the device and simply linked from one location to the next using this same index and pointer methodology.

File Types Explored

How many types of files does a file manager need to manipulate? Table 9-5 shows a few that have become common. For every file, the operating system needs to know how to open, execute, and close it gracefully. Windows operating systems use the file extension to indicate the application associated with it, but Mac, Linux, and several other operating systems do not require an extension and instead use other information stored with the file to do the same thing. For example, if a file is called EXAMPLE.CAD, a Windows system uses the extension CAD to select a drawing application to open that file.

If extensions are used (as they are on Windows), they are often three letters, but not always. We've only listed a few examples in Table 9-5 because a complete list would run for many pages. You can easily find more examples on the Internet, if you're interested.

TABLE 9-5	Extensions for a Few File Types
ASP	Active Server Pages
BAK	Backup File
BAT	Batch File
DLL	Dynamic Link Library
DOC	Document (usually word processing)
CAD	Drawing
EXE	Executable File
JPEG	Graphics File
MP3	Video File
PDF	Portable Document Format
PS	PostScript File
TXT	Text File

Exercise 9-2: Show Extensions for File Types on a Windows Computer

You may want to always view the extensions for files you view. By default on Windows computers, extensions for known file types are hidden. You can change this using Folder Options from the Control Panel. Here are the steps to follow:

1. On a Windows computer, click the Windows Start button.

2. Click Control Panel.

3. Click Folder Options.

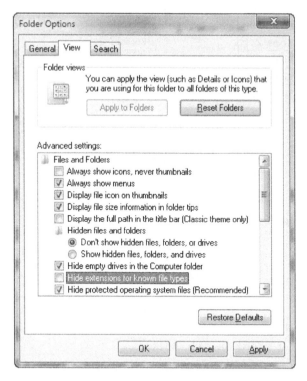

FIGURE 9-10 · Deselecting the Hide Extensions For Known File Types setting

4. Click the View tab.

5. Uncheck Hide Extensions For Known File Types, shown in Figure 9-10.

6. Click OK.

Blocking

At first glance, it might seem efficient to store each record individually so it can be maneuvered without disrupting any other records. But because a single file often contains very many records, records are generally assembled into chunks and moved as units. This is called *blocking* and it can speed up data retrieval (although it might not accelerate rewriting these same records after modifications have been made). The simplified illustration, Figure 9-11, shows how a block can be constructed with multiple records (remember, though, that in real life, blocks are often much bigger than five records).

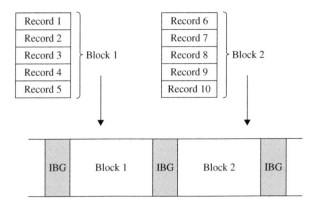

FIGURE 9-11 · Blocking records can accelerate data retrieval.

The actual process is more complex, but here we show you how it works in its simplest form:

1. A standard number of records are grouped into blocks. In Figure 9-11, there are five records in each block.

2. When it's time to store a block, an interblock gap (IBG) is recorded with it containing details about the block and the records it contains.

3. The IBG and block are stored together on the secondary storage device.

4. When it's time to retrieve a record, its entire block is copied from the disk, disc, or tape and moved into main memory, where the record is read from the block.

5. When the task is finished, if no modifications are made to the record, the main memory space is released so it can be allocated to another block. If modifications are made, the new block is assembled and written to secondary storage. (It might replace the previous version, or it might be written to a new place on the media. Regardless, the block is handled as a whole, and records are not handled individually.)

Although our example describes blocks of equal sizes that contain records that are of fixed length, blocks can be constructed that combine records of variable sizes (in which case the IBG holds additional details, such as the length of each record). Nevertheless, the process is similar to the one described here.

Future Performance and Efficiency

The proliferation of files on every computer is a huge problem for system administrators who struggle to accommodate daily storage. Even for individuals who manage their own computers, consider these trends:

- Digital cameras give us the ability to snap hundreds or thousands of photos at a time, and very few of us erase the shots we don't want.
- Audio files litter many computers, from handheld to very large systems.
- Videos can run to many megabytes, and it's common to keep most of them.
- The move to high-definition media means files are becoming even larger.
- Users are recording TV shows on their computers and storing hundreds of hours of video and, too often, users are unaware how quickly their hard drives are filling up. (By default, Windows Media Center records all instances of a TV show, including reruns, unless the user specifies otherwise.)

But the problem is not limited to individuals. Organizations of all sizes face similar problems:

- Datacenters need to manage uncounted numbers of documents (including e-mails, customer chats, technical specifications, images, and audio and video files).
- Databases only grow larger and are updated continuously.
- Legal requirements dictate that certain data must be retained for months, years, or longer.
- Many people are unwilling to discard anything that's stored electronically.

In addition to all these issues, file managers see a consistent need to back up more and more critical files to protect datacenters from catastrophe (and in the process, they may be making duplicate copies of larger and larger stores of files). The result? There's increasing pressure to aggressively manage file systems of every size.

TIP *An often-quoted statistic estimates that 80 percent of the data that's stored on file servers is rarely accessed and never modified after it has been stored for 90 days. Yet all of these files are managed and maintained as if they held critical, current data.*

As file management problems grow in complexity, watch for industry solutions that may include moving more files to the cloud, developing more efficient file compaction techniques so that files can be converted to take less storage space, and more aggressively removing unneeded data files. Because this is such a pressing issue, file management is sure to be a fast-changing topic in the years to come.

Summary

The management of all files (system files, utilities, databases, applications, and more) is an essential part of the operating system. To do that efficiently, the file manager must be able to uniquely identify every file, make sure each one is allocated to an appropriate place in secondary storage, always know the exact storage address for each file, authorize access to the correct users, and deny access to all others. In this chapter, we described the advantages and disadvantages of three access control systems and briefly looked at the future challenges for file managers as the quantity and size of files continue to grow.

In the next chapter, we'll explore how networks allow computers and their users to share resources and data in a way that appears to be seamless.

QUIZ

Choose the correct response to each of the multiple-choice questions. Note that there may be more than one correct response to each question.

1. **Which of the following is the starting place for the file manager when it's fulfilling a request from the device manager?**
   A. File name
   B. Subfolder name
   C. User's directory
   D. Master file directory

2. **Why is it important if the file manager is case sensitive?**
   A. It allows users to type in all lowercase.
   B. It distinguishes between file names with caps and those in all lowercase.
   C. It's not important.
   D. It's only important in a Windows system.

3. **Which of these are legal names for a file in Windows 7?**
   A. reality.doc
   B. music/alphas 7.mp3
   C. Storage/DCIM/800AAAAA/IMG_0007.jpg
   D. land+scape/ohio_valley.mp3

4. **What is the difference between an absolute file name and a relative file name?**
   A. The absolute file name includes the path.
   B. The absolute file name is shorter than the relative file name.
   C. The relative file name includes the path.
   D. The relative file name is shorter than the absolute file name.

5. **How long can a file name legally be?**
   A. 8.3 characters plus a four-letter extension.
   B. 265 characters regardless of the path name.
   C. 265 characters including the path name.
   D. It depends on the operating system.

6. **What is a file attribute?**
   A. A code that tells the operating system how big the file is
   B. A code for each file that tells the operating system what a user can do with it
   C. A code that users may be able to change
   D. A code that deletes a file

7. **If a Linux listing, similar to Figure 9-5, has attributes of -r-xr-xr-x, is this a file or a directory?**

   A. File
   B. Directory
   C. Both
   D. Neither

8. **If a Windows listing has an attribute that includes H, what does this signify?**

   A. Hybrid
   B. Hidden
   C. Holding
   D. Host

9. **What are key disadvantages of an access control matrix?**

   A. It gets too small.
   B. It can't control access well enough.
   C. It gets too big.
   D. It has a great deal of duplicated data.

10. **Which of these are viable record storage techniques?**

   A. Sequential record organization
   B. Consequential record organization
   C. Indexed record organization
   D. Indirect record organization

Part V

Network Participation

10

Introduction to Networking

In order to comprehend the role computer operating systems play in transmitting data to other computers and receiving data from them, you need to understand how general networks function. In this chapter, you'll learn this and more. You'll learn how networks can be physically and logically connected and positioned, and what hardware is necessary to facilitate data transfer. Once you understand the physical and logical network, you'll learn how computers locate each other on their own network and remote ones. As you might expect, each computer or resource (on any network) must have a unique "address" so that data can be sent to it (just as a house must have a unique address to receive postal mail and deliveries). Of course, what you learn in a book, textbook, or classroom and what happens in the real world are often two different things, so throughout this chapter we'll describe the networks you're likely to encounter in real life. With this knowledge, you can then move forward to more complex topics, including routing strategies, connection models, conflict resolution, and networking protocols.

CHAPTER OBJECTIVES

In this chapter, you will

- Learn basic networking terms, types, and configurations
- Understand the role hardware plays in a network

- Explore real-world networks
- Understand how computers locate other computers

Introduction to Networks

Networks enable computers and computer users to share and access resources. Sometimes those resources are physical, such as printers and physical storage devices, and other times the resources are less tangible, such as company data, contact information, and digital media. Because networks are now an integral part of (dare we say) almost every home and business that incorporates multiple computers and contain resources that must be shared, computer operating systems must be able to send and receive data, share resources, and make these resources easily available to the end user. There must also be built-in solutions to handle problems that arise in a network, including data collisions, data corruption, and conflict resolution, as well as troubleshooting options to find out why data can't be delivered (often due to hardware or software issues).

NOTE   *Every computer operating system has a "network manager." This manager assumes the role of managing many diverse resources. By directing the actions of each piece of hardware (CPU, devices, monitors, ports) and software (some shared, some not), the network manager must perform an intricate balancing act.*

Beyond the home and business networks you may be familiar with, it's important to remember that the Internet is also a network. Smaller, private networks must be able to access this larger network seamlessly as well, and operating systems help users do just that. Because the protocols on the various networks can differ, hardware and software must be incorporated to connect the networks, and they must be able to translate one network's protocols into another, resolve hardware and software incompatibilities, and perform other tasks.

Basic Networking Terms and Types

A network consists of many parts and can be configured in many ways. You may already be familiar with various types of network hardware and resources, and you may have already set up a network or two. You've likely connected computers to both wired and wireless networks, from a desktop computer, laptop, or mobile device, and you've certainly accessed the Internet. However, it's important to start any topic with the basics, and that's what we'll do here.

The Internet

The Internet is a large, global network that is made up of millions of other smaller, autonomous networks. In fact, it's the largest network there is, and serves billions of people worldwide. The Internet uses a standard Internet Protocol suite to transmit data. This protocol suite lays out the rules for moving data through networked computers and will be discussed in Chapter 11. What you need to know now about Transmission Control Protocol/Internet Protocol (TCP/IP) is that every unique node (computer, printer, server, and so on) on a network must have a unique Internet Protocol (IP) address. This is how computers find each other and transmit data effectively.

The smaller networks that comprise the Internet can be of many types, including but not limited to the following:

- **Private**   Such as the one in your home or in a small business. Larger private networks may have *subnetworks* as well.
- **Public**   Such as the one at the local library, coffee house, hotel, or even a network that serves an entire city.
- **Academic**   Such as one that might serve a large university, small private school, or city-wide school district. Subnetworks might be configured for each of the academic areas, such as science, engineering, and liberal arts.
- **Business**   Such as one that might serve a large company (for example, Microsoft) or a small company in your local neighborhood (for example, a home improvement store). Subnetworks might be configured for each city in which the business has an office.
- **Government**   Such as one that might serve an entire country's government, a small municipality, or a part of these (for example, the CIA or IRS, or a water or electric service and its subentities).

The Internet is not controlled by any central governmental agency. However, ICANN, the Internet Corporation for Assigned Names and Numbers, coordinates domain names, IP addresses, and other required parameters that must be kept in check for the Internet to function properly.

NOTE   *Intranets and extranets are sometimes considered to be a much smaller version of the Internet, and are created by and for organizations to host their own internal and external data servers, print servers, e-mail servers, and the like. They're also used to host their own internal and external websites.*

Wired and Wireless PANs, LANS, MANS, and WANS

Networks other than the Internet include personal area networks (PANs), local area networks (LANs), metropolitan area networks (MANs), and wide area networks (WANs). Each network type serves its own purpose and is chosen to suit the needs of those designing and using it. These networks can be wired or wireless, or a combination of both.

Personal Area Network

A *personal area network*, shown in Figure 10-1, is a newer network type that is suitable for connecting devices in a small physical area, generally about a 10-foot radius. This network may serve only one person, but it can often serve more. Wireless PANs may depend on Bluetooth or infrared to transmit data from, say, a mobile device to a headset, whereas wired PANs may use USB or FireWire to connect computers with digital cameras, scanners, printers, and the like when no other network exists. Cellular data providers are now providing hardware that allows a single person to create a personal hotspot to share a connection to the Internet with others who are near them, thus creating a new definition and use for a PAN.

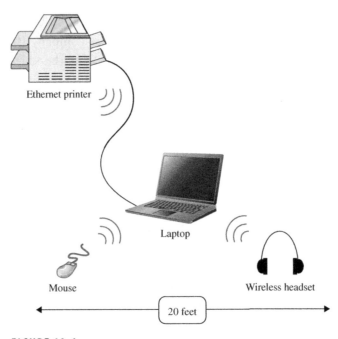

FIGURE 10-1 · Diagram of a PAN

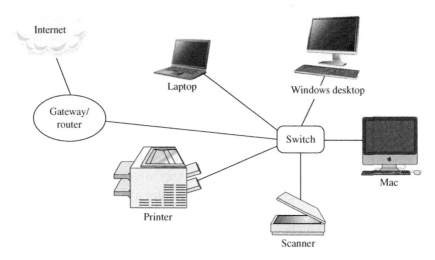

FIGURE 10-2 • Diagram of a LAN

Local Area Network

A *local area network*, shown in Figure 10-2, is used to connect computers and resources in a defined area, such as a home, laboratory, small business, warehouse, campus, school, or similar environment. Most rely on Ethernet and Wi-Fi, although other technologies exist. High-speed Ethernet LANs can have data rates as high as 10 Gbps. Wi-Fi is much slower than this, and depends on how close one is to the wireless access point, but transmission rates can be as high as 100 to 130 Mbps, although 300 Mbps is theoretically possible. A wireless local area network (WLAN) similarly uses wireless technology to connect computers and resources.

Metropolitan Area Network

A *metropolitan area network* is like a LAN, but is used in a larger physical area. A MAN might serve a university campus or an entire city. Seattle, Washington, for example, currently provides free wireless Internet access (Wi-Fi) in the Columbia City and the University District business districts as well as the City Hall lobby area, and the city is likely to expand this to include other areas in the future.

Wide Area Network

A *wide area network* connects different parts of the world and encompasses transmissions over very large areas. WANs use transmission media that include satellites, microwave technology, and hardware owned and operated by telephone and cellular phone companies.

VPNs

A *virtual private network (VPN)* enables a user to connect to a private local area network from a remote location, securely, using insecure infrastructure (the Internet through an unprotected public network, for instance). The VPN offers two layers of protection: it uses authentication methods to keep out unauthorized users and uses encryption to protect the data being transmitted. A VPN can be used to send any kind of data securely, including voice, video, or simple text. As you might imagine, the operating system plays a large role in making this a safe transmission!

Still Struggling?

A network administrator can set up virtual private networking on employees' laptop computers before they leave on business trips. Then, those employees can use the VPN to connect to the company's servers, securely, from anywhere, even a hotel room or coffee house.

When you set up a VPN, you use the tools available from the computer's operating system. Figure 10-3 shows the configuration options in Windows 7 Home Premium. Note that during the configuration of the VPN, you must enter the destination address of the desired host computer.

TIP *Figure 10-3 shows that when creating a VPN, you can enter the domain name, or an IPv4 or an IPv6 address. You'll learn more about these later in this chapter.*

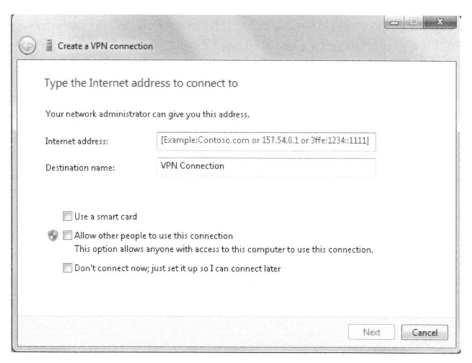

FIGURE 10-3 · Create a VPN using the tools available from the computer's operating system.

Network Hardware and Software

A network must have specific hardware and software to function. Hardware physically transmits the 1's and 0's that comprise the data and directs this data to the proper place. Software enables the user to easily state where the data should go and, for that matter, type an e-mail and click Send. In addition, software enables network administrators to manage all the hardware and to fix problems with the network as they arise.

Ethernet Connections and Cables

Almost every computer you'll encounter these days has an Ethernet port built in, making physical connections simple. Because not all computers include wireless components, Ethernet is almost always made available. Routers as well

as cable, satellite, and DSL modems offer Ethernet ports, as do computer servers. Even printers, new TVs, and DVD and Blu-ray players offer Ethernet connections these days.

> Ethernet is the most widely used LAN technology; it transmits data in packets called
> frames. Each frame contains source and destination addresses, as well as informa-
> tion that is used to check for errors so that damaged data can be detected and
> retransmitted. A cable is used to connect computers to a modem that allows Inter-
> net access. Ethernet is defined by the Institute of Electrical and Electronics Engineers
> (IEEE, pronounced eye-triple-E) as the 802.3 standard.

Although you may see some coaxial cable (also called coax), fiber optic
cable, or even null-modem cables on a network, Ethernet cabling is the most
prevalent. Figure 10-4 shows an Ethernet cable. For larger networks, fiber optic
cables may be used as a "backbone," whereas Ethernet and Wi-Fi are used to
connect computers to the LAN.

> A coaxial cable consists of an electrically conductive wire surrounded by a layer of
> insulating material, a layer of shielding material, and an outer layer of insulating
> material, usually plastic or rubber. The purpose of the shielding layer is to reduce
> external electrical interference.

> A fiber optic cable uses glass (or plastic) threads to transmit large amounts of data
> at the speed of light. Fiber optic cable is relatively expensive to install.

FIGURE 10-4 · Ethernet is a common type of network cable.

Most Ethernet ports support two speeds: 100 Mbps (100Base-T) and 1000 Mbps (1000Base-T), although there are faster options. Ethernet cables that connect these ports to their respective hardware offer a maximum segment length of 100 meters (328 feet), and are often used to configure the "star" type of network commonly found in homes and small businesses, which you'll learn about later in this chapter.

Routers (Wired, Wireless, and Hybrid)

A router has many features and uses. Basically, though, a router is a network device that handles data transfer between two different networks. A router uses lots of information to get data to its destination, including the destination's IP address. This information is in the data itself, in a place called the *data packet header.*

A router acts as a dispatcher of data too, choosing the best path for data to take to get to its destination quickly, using what is known as a *routing table.* Routers move data along the Internet, from their starting point to their destination, very quickly. (You know how quickly you can send an e-mail across the country, for instance, or access a webpage that's hosted in another country entirely. It's fast!)

NOTE   *A router can figure out the most direct and/or safe route to a destination using information it has acquired previously about other routers in the area, and it "learns" the best routes quickly.*

A router can also be used to share a single connection to the Internet on a small LAN as well as facilitate data transfer from the local network to the Internet and back, as needed. Sometimes, data that makes its way to a router doesn't need to leave a network, though, and the router can determine that too using the data's starting and destination IP addresses. If the starting and ending destinations share common IP address information, the router knows the data is destined for the local network. In such cases, it sends the data on its way to the proper destination on the LAN.

Still Struggling?

A router's purpose is to move data from one point to another. On the Internet, data will pass through multiple routers before reaching its destination. On a local area network, the data will only encounter one router—the network's.

Routers often offer both wired and wireless connection options. A router on a small home network might have four Ethernet ports for physically connecting up to four computers, and also offer a local Wi-Fi connection, to be used by laptops, netbooks, iPads, mobile phones, and other wireless devices. Routers in larger enterprises might support more than Ethernet and Wi-Fi; they may offer compatibility with various cellular standards (such as GPRS, EDGE, CDMA, and other technologies), support multiple WAN connections, offer a firewall, provide remote management, and provide failover schemes (backup options in case a component of the system fails), among other things. These larger routers offer ports and access to many users at one time.

NOTE *A router can connect a small local network to the Internet and share that Internet connection with others on the network. It can also connect two different LANs, two WANs, or a LAN to a MAN or other network for the purpose of moving data among them.*

Exercise 10-1: Locate and Follow the Path of an Ethernet Cable

It's highly likely that you can locate an Ethernet cable on the desktop computer nearest you. By locating, touching, and following the physical path of an Ethernet cable, you can get a better sense of how Ethernet is used. Follow these steps to explore your system:

1. Look at the back of a networked desktop computer. Locate the Ethernet cable. It looks like a phone cord and has similar connectors, but it's a bit larger. Ethernet is often blue, but it can also be yellow, tan, or another color.

2. Follow the Ethernet cable from the computer to its end. It may end at a wall outlet or a piece of equipment, such as a router or hub. In a large

network, it may end at an Ethernet repeater (to extend the signal) or an Ethernet "closet," which contains stacks of Ethernet switches.

3. Repeat with other computers to explore other ways Ethernet is used.

Hubs and Switches

Hubs and switches are not as "smart" as routers, but they still move data (in the form of data packets) from one computer to another. Whereas a router looks at a piece of data and determines which network segment and computer to send it to, switches and hubs do not. These devices also can't learn what a router can learn, and they can't keep the data in a routing table for future use either.

A hub is the least sophisticated. It takes a piece of data and transmits it to every other computer on the network. It's up to the computer to determine whether or not that data is meant for it. This creates a lot of network traffic. Hubs don't forward data packets to other networks.

NOTE *Hubs are generally only used in low-traffic, unsophisticated, and uncomplicated networks.*

A switch is more complex than a hub, but less sophisticated than a router. Switches can look at the information in a data packet and determine which computer should get it. This means the switch doesn't simply broadcast data packets as a hub does, and the result is less data traffic. It is not smart enough, though, to forward data packets to another network—you need a router for that.

In the real world, large networks have routers to pass traffic from the local area network to other networks, including the Internet, and use switches in series (called a daisy-chain) as needed to provide every computer on the network with network access. In fact, large networks may have closets full of Ethernet switches (see Figure 10-5).

Gateways

A gateway in your neighborhood is a gate that allows entry and exit into your yard or from one part of your yard to another. When closed, it keeps intruders out and kids and pets in; when open, it lets anyone out or in. Large apartment complexes and large, secure business campuses can also have gateways and require you to swipe a card or type a passcode to enter. Similarly, a gateway on a network is a device that acts as an entrance and exit to a network. As with certain real-life gateways, you get to decide who and what can come in and

FIGURE 10-5 · Large organizations will use very large Ethernet switches to physically connect nodes on the network.

what can go out using firewalls, user names and passwords, and other security software. Much of this protection is offered by the operating system.

On a home network, a router will likely serve as your gateway. A router in this scenario manages the data that flows between the Internet and the local network. It's also possible to turn a computer into a gateway. In this configuration, the computer has two network adapter cards. One is connected to the local network and the other to the Internet (or outside network). In a large business, computer gateways and sophisticated gateway devices are used to connect local network subnetworks, such as an office in, say, Dallas, to an office in, say, New York. A gateway, like other network devices, has a unique IP address, as shown in Figure 10-6.

FIGURE 10-6 · A gateway, like all other networked devices, has an IP address.

A Little about TCP/IP

TCP/IP (Transmission Control Protocol/Internet Protocol) is the protocol suite used to transmit data over the Internet. To do so, each computer on the network needs to have a unique address, called an IP address. There are two addressing schemes: IPv4 addresses (32-bit) that are created using four sets of up to four numbers each, such as 200.158.40.2 or 130.1.58.3, and IPv6 addressing (128-bit), which is newer and consists of four 16-bit blocks, each of which is converted to a four-digit hexadecimal number that's separated by colons.

You may be starting to wonder how TCP/IP is incorporated into the local networks we've been talking about in this chapter. The address may be "static" and never change, or it may be dynamically assigned by a DHCP (Dynamic Host Configuration Protocol) server, or by other network hardware and software. Every router has an IP address, too. Every gateway has one. In fact, every network device has one, even network printers! These addresses are what enable data to be delivered and for computers to distinguish themselves from other computers on the network.

NOTE   *A printer connected to a computer via USB and shared over a small network does not get its own IP address. However, printers on a network that are connected via Wi-Fi or Ethernet do.*

You can see the IP address associated with any Windows-based computer by typing the command **ipconfig /all** at a command prompt. Figure 10-7 shows an example, and Exercise 10-2 shows you how to explore it on your own computer.

Still Struggling?

Every computer (or node) on a network has a unique IP address, just as each house on a typical street has a unique physical address. Without a unique home address, mail could not be effectively delivered and firemen and police could not find you if you needed help. The same is true of a computer network. Without a unique address, a router, for instance, would not know where to deliver data.

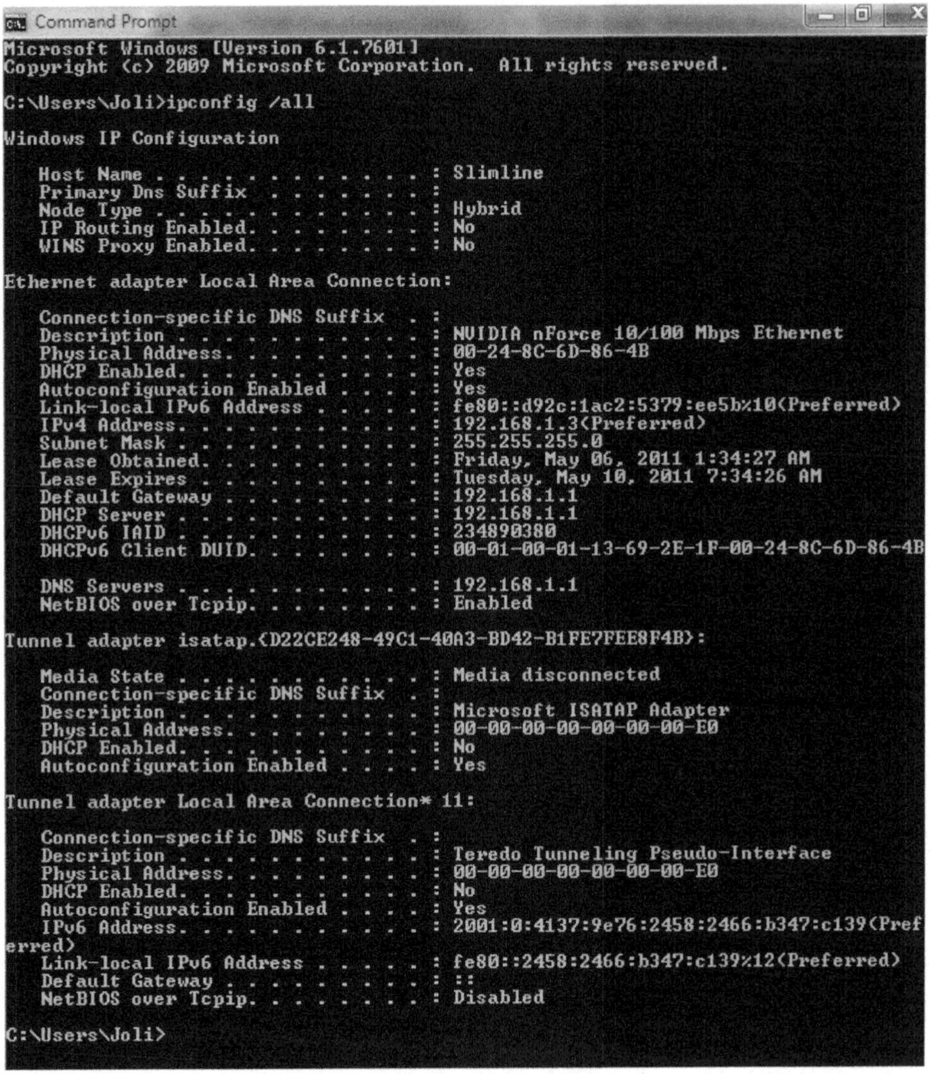

```
Command Prompt                                                    _  □  X

Microsoft Windows [Version 6.1.7601]
Copyright (c) 2009 Microsoft Corporation. All rights reserved.

C:\Users\Joli>ipconfig /all

Windows IP Configuration

    Host Name . . . . . . . . . . . . : Slimline
    Primary Dns Suffix  . . . . . . . :
    Node Type . . . . . . . . . . . . : Hybrid
    IP Routing Enabled. . . . . . . . : No
    WINS Proxy Enabled. . . . . . . . : No

Ethernet adapter Local Area Connection:

    Connection-specific DNS Suffix  . :
    Description . . . . . . . . . . . : NVIDIA nForce 10/100 Mbps Ethernet
    Physical Address. . . . . . . . . : 00-24-8C-6D-86-4B
    DHCP Enabled. . . . . . . . . . . : Yes
    Autoconfiguration Enabled . . . . : Yes
    Link-local IPv6 Address . . . . . : fe80::d92c:1ac2:5379:ee5b%10(Preferred)
    IPv4 Address. . . . . . . . . . . : 192.168.1.3(Preferred)
    Subnet Mask . . . . . . . . . . . : 255.255.255.0
    Lease Obtained. . . . . . . . . . : Friday, May 06, 2011 1:34:27 AM
    Lease Expires . . . . . . . . . . : Tuesday, May 10, 2011 7:34:26 AM
    Default Gateway . . . . . . . . . : 192.168.1.1
    DHCP Server . . . . . . . . . . . : 192.168.1.1
    DHCPv6 IAID . . . . . . . . . . . : 234890380
    DHCPv6 Client DUID. . . . . . . . : 00-01-00-01-13-69-2E-1F-00-24-8C-6D-86-4B

    DNS Servers . . . . . . . . . . . : 192.168.1.1
    NetBIOS over Tcpip. . . . . . . . : Enabled

Tunnel adapter isatap.{D22CE248-49C1-40A3-BD42-B1FE7FEE8F4B}:

    Media State . . . . . . . . . . . : Media disconnected
    Connection-specific DNS Suffix  . :
    Description . . . . . . . . . . . : Microsoft ISATAP Adapter
    Physical Address. . . . . . . . . : 00-00-00-00-00-00-00-E0
    DHCP Enabled. . . . . . . . . . . : No
    Autoconfiguration Enabled . . . . : Yes

Tunnel adapter Local Area Connection* 11:

    Connection-specific DNS Suffix  . :
    Description . . . . . . . . . . . : Teredo Tunneling Pseudo-Interface
    Physical Address. . . . . . . . . : 00-00-00-00-00-00-00-E0
    DHCP Enabled. . . . . . . . . . . : No
    Autoconfiguration Enabled . . . . : Yes
    IPv6 Address. . . . . . . . . . . : 2001:0:4137:9e76:2458:2466:b347:c139(Pref
erred)
    Link-local IPv6 Address . . . . . : fe80::2458:2466:b347:c139%12(Preferred)
    Default Gateway . . . . . . . . . : ::
    NetBIOS over Tcpip. . . . . . . . : Disabled

C:\Users\Joli>
```

FIGURE 10-7 · The command ipconfig /all offers the IP address of your computer, the gateway on the network, and other information.

Exercise 10-2: Find the IP Address of Your Gateway

You know a gateway is a device that lets data travel from your local network to another network. On your own personal home network, the gateway is probably also the router. To find the IP address of your gateway, follow these steps:

1. Open a command prompt. Here's how to do so on a Windows 7 computer:

    a. Click Start.

    b. Type **Command Prompt** or the shortcut, **cmd**.

    c. Click the Command Prompt option in the results (if you see more than one, click the one with the black icon beside it).

2. At the command prompt, type **ipconfig** (you can also type **ipconfig /all** to see more information).

3. Press ENTER.

4. Look through the results to see the IP address of the gateway.

Clients, Hosts, Servers, Sites, and Nodes

The resources on a network that are given names such as "client," "server," or "node" are often hard to decipher. It's much easier to interpret what a more specific term like a "print server" is, or to simply assume something called a "computer" is, well, a computer. In order to understand network terminology in a textbook or on the job, though, you have to know what these commonly used, more generic terms mean.

A client, in the real world, is often a person who wants to buy something, obtain something, or needs a service. A client on a network is similar. A *network client* is often a computer that needs access to company resources such as servers, data, printers, and similar hardware. Clients are generally desktop computers, laptops, mobile devices such as netbooks, and similar hardware used by office or mobile workers.

A host (or server), in the real world, can be a person who creates and manages a party or serves food and drink. A host (server) may make sure there's ample parking and that people are communicating and having fun. A host may even make sure all guests get home safely, should they have too much to drink. A host (server) on a network is similar. A *network host* is a computer that offers information and data, manages data transfer, and otherwise enables other computers and servers to perform the work they need to perform. (They may even revoke access to a client, just as a responsible host might take a person's keys, if it is determined they should not have access to their car at this time.) Hosts can also resolve problems that the clients don't even know about! Hosts are generally computer servers, as you can likely guess by now, including data servers, e-mail servers, print and fax servers, and backup servers.

NOTE   *When configuring a network, a designer takes into account the number of hosts, clients, nodes, and the like, and builds an infrastructure to support them.*

Sites and nodes also have real-world counterparts, but to make a comparison would be a stretch here. Therefore, we'll leave our real-world analogies and stick to networking: a *site* on a network is often an office building, warehouse, or facility. A *node* is most often a computer. Most nodes are clients, but they can also be kiosks or servers, among other things. In general terms, just about anything that has an IP address on a network might be called a node in network-speak.

> *A kiosk is a self-contained, secure, and guest-friendly computer or hardware unit. A kiosk may allow a visitor to log in and/or place themselves in a service queue; upload, crop, and print digital photos; purchase an item without the need for a salesperson or assistant; print an airline boarding pass; learn more about a museum exhibit; or explore the virtues of a product available at the store or elsewhere.*

How Operating Systems Manage Network Connectivity

A network operating system is a special breed of software that oversees every aspect of network connectivity. In broadest terms, it manages a common file system, resource sharing, application sharing, and the ability to manage the network's directory structure, security, and other critical elements. For example, each computer's operating system must be capable of joining the network and successfully transmitting and receiving data. It isn't all hardware, addresses, and the transmissions of 1's and 0's over cables and Wi-Fi. There are several very popular network operating systems, including Microsoft's Windows Server 2003 and 2008, Mac OS X Server, and Novell Netware, to name only a few.

Many popular network operating systems offer the following:

- Secure access to the local network, to the Internet, and to local and remote resources.
- The ability to centrally manage network resources. Those resources can be data, other hardware devices, and programs.
- The ability to access the local network and local resources from outside the network—and to do so securely.
- The ability to easily add clients, servers, and other network resources and hardware.
- A user interface that enables users to back up data to network servers easily and seamlessly.
- Options for monitoring the health of the network and to locate problems and fix them.

- Distributed programs and software updates to computers on the network.

- The efficient use of servers on the network.

Without network operating systems, we would have very inefficient networks!

How Computers Address and Find Each Other

On a network, computers and other resources must be able to "find" each other. You learned a little bit about TCP/IP earlier, and TCP/IP and IP addressing are part of that process. However, many other pieces must fit into place to make a network function and to enable data to flow from one computer to another successfully. One of those pieces is the physical and logical layout of the network. Let's take a look at network topologies.

Topologies

The hardware on a network—including wired and wireless routers, hubs, and switches; Ethernet, coaxial, and other cables; additional gateways; and hosts, clients, nodes, and servers—are all a part of a network's design. Network specialists who create networks use this hardware to create various physical and logical *topologies*. A network may be created out of existing hardware and software, or it may be created on paper first, and the hardware and software purchased later.

To further explain this, in your home network, the hardware and software you own generally determines the kind of network you'll create (or have created). For instance, if you have a cable modem and a single router and do not use a server, you'll often create a simple "star" network. In a larger network that contains multiple servers, hundreds of computers, and lots of office and mobile workers, designers will take a more complex approach to meet those specifications.

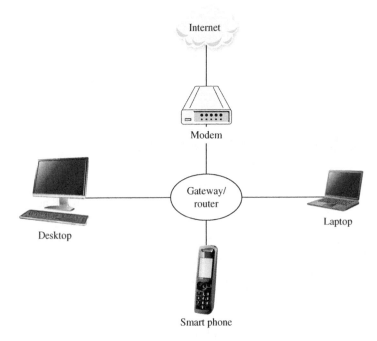

FIGURE 10-8 · A star topology is popular for home networks and small businesses.

 Still Struggling?

For our use here, a *topology* describes the way the nodes (computer terminals and other network resources) are connected to the network.

Star

In a *star topology*, there's generally a single piece of equipment (such as a hub, switch, or router) that directs traffic on the network (see Figure 10-8). Every computer on the network is connected to it, either by Ethernet cable or Wi-Fi, and all data passes through this hardware to reach other computers on the network. Often, in this kind of network, there's also a piece of hardware that enables users on the local area network to access the Internet. This is called a gateway, and may well be the router itself. In this configuration, the router knows the path to all the other sites, nodes, and resources, and can direct traffic to them efficiently. The downside to this is that if the router (or other central unit) fails, so does the network.

NOTE *On an Ethernet network in a star configuration, data is sent along the Ethernet cable to the central unit (often a router or switch), where it is passed again via Ethernet cable to the destination computer. Routers can also produce Wi-Fi signals for mobile network nodes.*

Ring

In a *ring topology*, as you might expect, computers (or nodes) are positioned logically in a closed circle (even though they don't need to be in a physical circle). In this topology, hosts are connected to each other with data flowing in only one direction. Data is passed from node to node, until it finally reaches the destination computer. Data doesn't continually pass around the circle, though, if it doesn't belong to any node on the ring; in that case, it's discarded.

Token Ring is a special kind of ring topology where a token is passed around from node to node, and a computer can only send data when it has possession

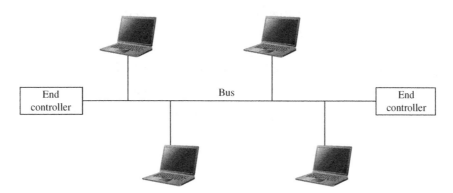

FIGURE 10-9 · In a bus topology, data moves up and down the bus, and nodes are connected to it.

of the token. For ring topologies, a gateway (or a bridge) can connect the local network to another network.

> A bridge is a hardware device that connects two local area networks that use the same protocol, such as two Ethernet or two Token Ring networks.

Bus

In a *bus configuration*, nodes are connected to a single communication line (see Figure 10-9). Data flows in both directions on the shared line. There's one controller at the end of the line and another at the beginning to manage data on the bus that isn't claimed by any computers connected to it. In this configuration, there's no central unit such as a hub, switch, or router. Data simply moves up and down the bus until it's claimed or discarded. You can compare this to a specific bus route, say, that runs from the airport and back, multiple times a day, picking people up and dropping them off.

NOTE *A big problem with an Ethernet bus topology is that it works like the old telephone party lines did. No one can use the line if someone else is using it. And when someone is using the line, everyone else can listen to what's being said, so there's no privacy. Additionally, a person who wants to make a call must wait until the person who is talking disconnects. This often causes problems, especially on a busy network.*

NOTE *Two other configurations are not detailed here, but they're pretty obvious. A tree configuration is a collection of busses. A hybrid configuration is a combination of any other topologies in any order.*

Exercise 10-3: View the Network Topology of a Computer Running Windows 7

Windows 7 comes with a feature called the Network and Sharing Center, which provides the option to view a *network map* that shows the logical topology of your network. Follow these steps to use the Network and Sharing Center:

1. On the taskbar, in the Notification area (the location near the date and time), click the Network icon.
2. Click Open Network And Sharing Center.
3. Click See Full Map.

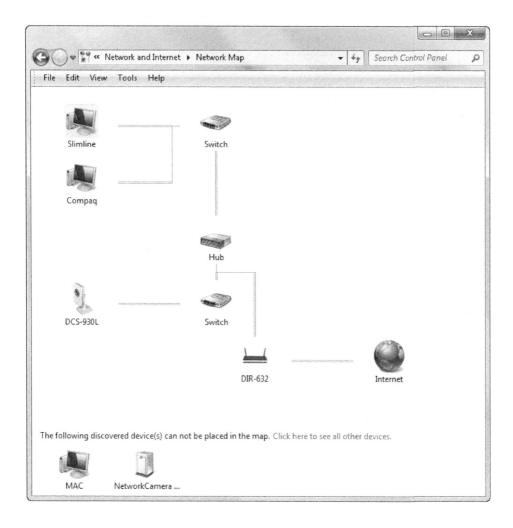

Networks and Subnets, and Local and Remote Resources

A small home or business network may be one physical network housed in a home or office. These small networks are self-contained into one, single network. Management is simple, and often controlled by a single router whose function is virtually invisible to its users. The only other network in play is the Internet.

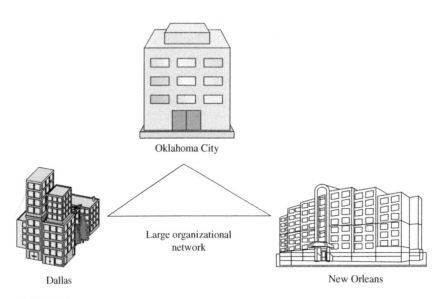

FIGURE 10-10 · A large network can be broken up into subnets to more easily manage the resources on it.

A larger network may be contained in a warehouse or office building, or it may span two or more cities. Although still considered a single organization's "network," it contains subnetworks, or *subnets*, to separate the offices or physical locations. Figure 10-10 shows an example. Here, a single organization's network has an office in Dallas, one in Oklahoma City, and another in New Orleans. Each office is a subnet of the larger network.

> *A subnet is a logical subdivision of a network, and the computers on it are generally in close proximity, such as those in an office building. A network's subnets are connected by routers.*

All nodes on a subnet have IP addresses with the same network prefix as the other nodes. The prefix used is determined by the IP addressing structure of the network. This structure allows routers to know which subnet the data should go to, based on the information in its IP address, or if it is destined to go somewhere outside of the network (or even stay on the local subnet). Additionally, each computer has a *subnet mask* to further identify it.

Furthermore, local and remote resources are associated with the local network and its remote subnets. If a resource is on the network, it's considered local. A user in Dallas might print to a local printer down the hall, for instance. That's a local resource. Alternatively, a user in Dallas might print to a remote printer in the New Orleans office for the purpose of sharing data with a user there or to access a four-color printer that's not available in the local office. That's a remote resource. A Dallas user might also pull data from a remote data server, get e-mail from a remote e-mail server, or back up data to a server at another site and on another subnet.

Employing Static and Dynamic IP Addressing

If you recall, an IP address is like your home address; it defines your location, who you are, and where mail and other items should be delivered. Similarly, each network node must have a unique address. IP addresses can be manually assigned for very small networks. Generally, though, static, manual addressing is only used when devices on the network do not support *dynamic* addressing (detailed next), or when very specific needs must be met, such as assigning, say, a network camera its own, permanent IP address on a network.

There are various ways to reach the IP address box shown in Figure 10-11, and once you're there, it's easy to manually input an address, provided, of course, you understand TCP/IP addressing schemes, which is another book unto itself!

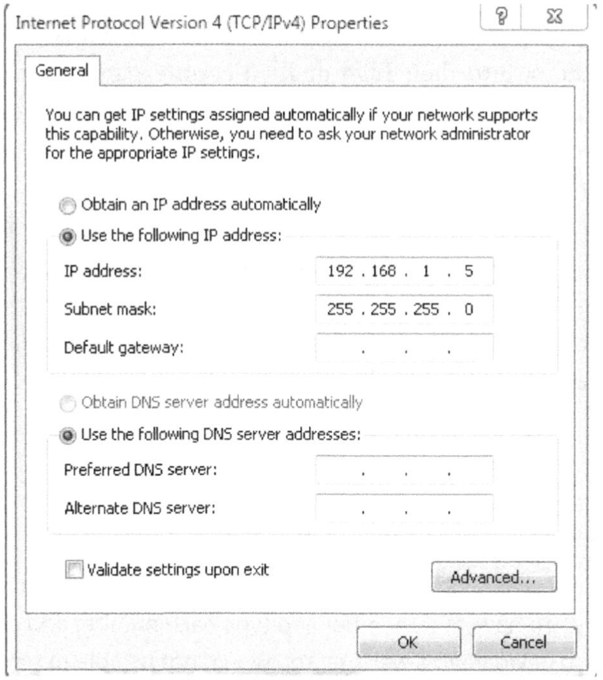

FIGURE 10-11 • You can manually enter an IP address, if you understand TCP/IP addressing schemes.

NOTE   *IPv6 hosts may use* stateless address autoconfiguration *to generate an IP address. If IPv6 stateless address autoconfiguration is unsuitable for any reason, a network may use DHCPv6, or hosts may be configured statically.*

As you can guess, in most cases, it would be inefficient to assign IP addresses individually; this is especially true if there are more than, say, a dozen computers on a network. DHCP provides a way to have IP addresses dynamically assigned to the computers on a network. With DHCP, you don't have to worry about IP addressing.

DHCP not only allows a computer to be configured automatically; it also provides a central database for keeping track of computers that have been connected to the network. This prevents two computers from accidentally being configured with the same IP address. DHCP also provides the IP addresses of local caching DNS (Domain Name System) resolvers. DNS is responsible for translating a domain name (such as www.microsoft.com) to its IP address so that the webpage you're looking for can be found on the Internet.

About DNS

DNS is a tiered naming system for computers, services, or resources connected to the Internet or any private network. DNS translates domain names, such as www.microsoft.com, into their IPv4 or IPv6 counterparts. These IP addresses are what enable resources to communicate, data to be transferred, and people to access resources, as you well know by now.

The most common analogy used to describe DNS is an online phone book. Using an online phone book, you type a name and ask for the person's phone number, and then you use that phone number to call your contact. You don't "dial" the person's name; you dial the person's phone number. Some entity must exist to offer you that number, and in this particular example, it's an online phone book. That's how DNS works, too.

Still Struggling?

Without DNS, you'd have to remember and type each number and character of the IP address to navigate to a website. You would not be able to type the company name, followed by .com or .org, for instance.

Physical (MAC) Addresses

MAC stands for Media Access Control and is another unique identifier. MAC addresses are now being referred to as "physical" addresses; you can see a reference to this in Figure 10-7, earlier in this chapter. Every computer has its own MAC address. Unlike IP addresses, though, which work at various "network" levels, MAC addresses work on the physical level, the bottom-most level for computer-to-computer communications. MAC addresses are assigned to the network interface cards by the manufacturers that create them, and work with various technologies, including Ethernet, 802.11 wireless networks, Bluetooth, Token Ring, most other 802.11 networks, and more. If a computer or other node has multiple network interfaces, it'll have multiple MAC addresses too. Each interface has its own MAC (physical) address.

Still Struggling?

MAC is an older term associated with the physical number stamped on a network interface card. Microsoft no longer refers to these numbers as MAC addresses, though, and now calls them "physical addresses."

Summary

Computers need to connect to networks to transmit and share data. Those networks can be wired or wireless, secured or unsecured. They can include hubs, switches, routers, Ethernet cables and devices, shared printers, and even computer servers. For each computer to communicate effectively and access network resources, it must have a unique address as well. Operating systems incorporate networks by default, and are a big part of what enables us to communicate with others effectively over both long and short distances.

In the next chapter, we'll explore the actual preparation and transmission of data, safeguards that step in when data collides or disappears, and the two most widely used routing protocols: Routing Information Protocol (RIP) and Open Shortest Path First (OSPF).

QUIZ

Choose the correct response to each of the multiple-choice questions. Note that there may be more than one correct response to each question.

1. Which one of these networks is the largest?
   A. WAN
   B. MAN
   C. LAN
   D. PAN

2. What type of connection enables a user to connect to a private local area network from a remote location, securely, using insecure infrastructure?
   A. Wi-Fi
   B. Voice Over IP
   C. Government Dial-up
   D. LAN
   E. Virtual private network

3. Which type of networking cable is the most used in home and office networks?
   A. Coaxial cable
   B. Ethernet cable
   C. Fiber optic cable
   D. Null-modem cable

4. Which two options describe a router's main purpose?
   A. To route data to a specific destination
   B. To broadcast data to any node in its range
   C. To act as a gateway between a LAN and the Internet
   D. To assign IP addresses to nodes on a network

5. How can TCP/IP addresses be obtained by a node on a network?
   A. Dynamically from a DHCP server
   B. Assigned by a hub
   C. Assigned by a router
   D. None of the above

6. A laptop computer on a network is most often an example of what?
   A. A server
   B. A client
   C. A host
   D. A site

7. Which network topology is most often used when there's a cable modem, router, and three nodes on a small home network?

   A. Bus
   B. Token Ring
   C. Star
   D. Tree

8. Which of the following are examples of a remote resource?

   A. A printer on a different network than the user's network
   B. A data server in a branch office in another city
   C. An e-mail server on the user's subnet
   D. A printer connected to a networked computer on the LAN

9. Which one of the following options is the best way to assign IP addresses for a network that contains 1,000 nodes?

   A. DNS
   B. DHCP
   C. Static IP addressing
   D. MAC

10. What makes a computer unique from all the other computers on the network, specifically speaking, at the physical level?

   A. The IP address of the gateway the computer uses to access the Internet
   B. The IP address of the DNS server the computer uses to resolve domain names
   C. The serial number written on the back of the computer
   D. The MAC address of the network interface card

Routing Strategies and Conflict Resolution

In Chapter 10, you learned quite a bit about networks, including how they are physically and logically created, what hardware is used most and why, and a bit about how computers find each other on their local network and on remote ones. In this chapter, we'll dive deeper into the challenges faced by network operating systems, and talk more about the 1's and 0's as well as the actual preparation and transmission of data. As you might guess, there must be built-in safeguards for when data collides on a network, when data is lost in transmission and needs to be resent, and what protocols are used by the systems that send and receive data over local networks and the Internet.

CHAPTER OBJECTIVES

In this chapter, you will

- Understand the strategies used to route data to other networks
- Learn how data finds its way to the proper node on a network
- Understand how conflicts can be avoided on a network
- Learn how problems that occur in data transmissions are resolved
- Gain a general understanding of the OSI reference model and the TCP/IP protocol suite

Routing Strategies

You learned a lot about routers in the previous chapter. You know their main purpose is to send data from one network to another, for the purpose of forwarding it on to its destination. You also know that a router uses a routing table to help it find the way, that most routers simply forward data to the next router in the line, which then forwards it on, until the data reaches its proper network. The router there has the task of forwarding the data to the correct node.

NOTE *At specified intervals, routers broadcast what's in their routing table to all other routers in the vicinity. That is how routers eventually learn where to send data they receive.*

To do its job, to maintain communication with other routers, to broadcast its routing table, and to get data to its destination properly, each router must follow some specific rules. Those rules are called *protocols*. In the real world, following a protocol is equivalent to following the rules of etiquette, or following military procedures. There are rules, and you follow them so that you can function properly and fulfill your purpose in the society or group. The same is true in networks. In this section, we'll look at the two most widely used *routing* protocols: Routing Information Protocol (RIP) and Open Shortest Path First (OSPF).

RIP

The *Routing Information Protocol (RIP)* requires that data get to its destination using the fewest number of "hops." A router is one hop, so if it takes 20 routers to get to a destination, that's 20 hops. RIP is a distance protocol, and the shortest distance, or the route with the fewest number of hops, is always chosen. You might suspect that the shortest distance between two points isn't always the best route, though, and you'd be right.

Here's an example: let's say you want to drive to the airport. The highway is the most direct route, requires few stops, and is the shortest distance to drive. You can also opt to drive the city streets to get to the airport, but it's a longer distance with lots of traffic lights and stop lights. If you're forced to take the highway every time because of a city-wide protocol, you may find yourself late to the gate if there's construction along the way or if there's an accident. In this case, it would be better to take the less travelled route to the airport, even if it does have more stops—you'd still get there faster! This analogy can be used to describe the limitation of RIP. Although RIP is a good protocol for forwarding data, it may not be the best one to follow all the time. In fact, a better protocol might consider all the other open routes, and from them, choose the shortest option.

OSPF

Open Shortest Path First (OSPF) is a viable alternative. Using this protocol, the state of the route is determined beforehand, and if something is found to be wrong along the way (such as a malfunctioning router), a different route is selected. If more than one route exists, the shortest one is chosen.

Still Struggling?

To continue from our previous analogy, if you heard about an accident on the highway prior to pulling out of your driveway, you could opt to take a different route to the airport. If there were multiple available routes, you'd choose the shortest from the options. OSPF works the same way.

Although choosing the shortest open route is effective, it does require more resources than simply barreling through the transmission process using the shortest route (obtained from a routing table). OSPF requires that the router know more than just how to get from point A to point B; when using this protocol, routers must also monitor problems along the routes. This causes additional traffic and data transfer overhead when compared to RIP.

Exercise 11-1: Use Nslookup and Tracert to Find Out How Many Hops It Takes to Get to a Destination Address

On a Windows-based computer, nslookup can give you the IP address of a website. Tracert can determine how many hops it'll take to get from your computer to that destination. Traceroute and traceroute6 can also be used, depending on the circumstances. Linux can use tracepath. Macs can use traceroute. These commands and others can be used to determine where along a path the data transmission failed, if applicable, or to simply determine the number of hops it takes to get there.

```
C:\Users\Joli>nslookup www.yahoo.com
Server:   UnKnown
Address:  192.168.0.1

Non-authoritative answer:
Name:     www.yahoo.com.tx.rr.com
Address:  208.69.32.145
```

FIGURE 11-1 • Use nslookup to get an IP address for a website.

To locate the IP address of another computer and to see how many hops it takes to get there on a Windows Vista or Windows 7 computer, follow these steps:

1. Open a command prompt. (You can use the Start Search window and type **cmd** to find it.)

2. Type **nslookup www.yahoo.com** (see Figure 11-1).

3. Type **tracert** followed by a space, and then type the IP address for Yahoo .com. In our example, that's 208.69.32.145. Some sites have multiple IP addresses, though, so what you see for Yahoo.com may differ. Press ENTER on the keyboard.

4. Note the results, specifically the location of the routers in the list. In Figure 11-2, you can see our results. Each entry is a hop. (You can also type **tracert www.yahoo.com**, but we wanted you to explore nslookup in this exercise.)

```
C:\Users\Joli>tracert 208.69.32.145

Tracing route to 208.69.32.145 over a maximum of 30 hops

  1    <1 ms    <1 ms    <1 ms  192.168.0.1
  2   353 ms   382 ms   421 ms  cpe-76-184-48-1.tx.res.rr.com [76.184.48.1]
  3   530 ms   594 ms   614 ms  24.164.211.177
  4   373 ms    92 ms   128 ms  70.125.216.228
  5   493 ms   487 ms   492 ms  70.125.216.106
  6   345 ms   241 ms   209 ms  te0-8-0-0.dllatx13-cr01.texas.rr.com [72.179.205
.72]
  7   277 ms   293 ms   346 ms  ae-4-0.cr0.dfw10.tbone.rr.com [66.109.6.88]
  8   495 ms   519 ms   522 ms  ae-3-0.pr0.dfw10.tbone.rr.com [66.109.6.209]
  9   529 ms   582 ms   637 ms  xe-11-3-2.edge9.Dallas1.Level3.net [4.59.32.13]
 10   662 ms   673 ms   677 ms  vlan90.csw4.Dallas1.Level3.net [4.69.145.254]
 11   436 ms   237 ms   338 ms  ae-93-93.ebr3.Dallas1.Level3.net [4.69.151.170]
 12   329 ms   359 ms   419 ms  ae-7-7.ebr3.Atlanta2.Level3.net [4.69.134.22]
 13   543 ms   577 ms   595 ms  ae-2-2.ebr1.Washington1.Level3.net [4.69.132.86
 14   641 ms   717 ms   721 ms  ae-91-91.csw4.Washington1.Level3.net [4.69.134.1
42]
 15   726 ms   727 ms   675 ms  ae-43-90.car3.Washington1.Level3.net [4.69.149.1
97]
 16   292 ms   406 ms   322 ms  SPLICE-COMM.car3.Washington1.Level3.net [4.79.16
8.118]
 17   401 ms   447 ms   531 ms  208.69.32.145

Trace complete.
```

FIGURE 11-2 • Tracert lets you calculate the number of hops to an IP address.

Connection Models

When data comes into a network via a router, it must be forwarded to the proper node on the network, and that "node" is often a computer. It doesn't matter to the router or to the network what kind of data it is, though. It could be a simple e-mail or streaming media. Whatever the case, the operating system's network manager will use one of two common connection models to send the data to a node on a network: circuit switching or packet switching.

Circuit Switching

Using *circuit switching*, the network manager sets up a single communication path to send data from one specific node to another specific node in a layout deemed a "circuit." This circuit enables the data to be transmitted continuously both effectively and efficiently (once the connection is made).

If you're familiar with electrical circuits in your home, you understand that a circuit is actually a circular path that must be maintained while it's in use. (It doesn't have to be a real circle though!) As long as the circuit is healthy, the connection is healthy. If that circuit is broken (a mouse chews through a wire in the circuit, say), you're not going to be able to turn on the light using the switch on the wall!

The most recognized example of circuit switching is a landline telephone network. A path must be created from one phone to another for transmission to begin, and that connection is maintained until one phone disconnects (or something happens to cause the connection to fail). In the old days, this was done manually, as shown in Figure 11-3.

NOTE   *Land-based telephone networks use analog signals to transmit data. On the other hand, a computer network uses digital signals.*

Along those same lines, Integrated Services Digital Network (ISDN) is a circuit switched network and is implemented on WANs for data transmissions (not voice). For example, a dial-up modem transmits data through an ISDN network.

Circuit switching isn't often feasible in computer networks, because there isn't usually a cost-effective way to connect two computers directly to each other. However, it is implemented when one node needs a dedicated connection to another for a very specific time and purpose. Figure 11-4 shows how it could be implemented.

FIGURE 11-3 · In the old days, telephone circuits were created manually.

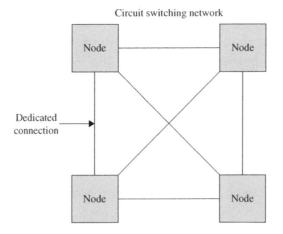

FIGURE 11-4 · In a circuit switching connection, one node is directly connected to the other.

Circuit switching is more reliable than packet switching, which we will detail next, but it is an old technology that is rarely used nowadays.

Packet Switching

Packet switching is nothing like circuit switching because it does not require a dedicated connection between the two computers to transmit data. Rather, it uses routers, switches, and hubs to move the data from point A to point B. Using this connection method, data is divided into small manageable data packets before it is sent, and each of those packets is transmitted individually through the network infrastructure. Once all the data packets have made it to their destination, they are reassembled and offered to the end user or node, as applicable. This enables each of the data packets to take separate paths, at different data transmission rates; none of them sit idle waiting for the proper route to open up. In this way, a large message or data package can be sent successfully. This is a common way to send data over long distances and is very efficient.

But why does it work? What's so great about this packet switching method (other than not requiring a dedicated route)? Consider this scenario: You purchase a play set for your children at the local hardware store. It's big and you can't fit it in your car. It would be costly and ineffective to call and wait for a big truck to arrive to move it to your house. You decide that you can disassemble the play set more quickly than waiting for a large truck, and with the help of your friend, get it to your place using two cars very quickly too. You and your friend can take the same or different routes home, drive at different speeds, and arrive at different times, so there's no arguing over which route is more efficient or who is (or is not) a bad driver! You can easily reassemble the play set once you're home. This is kind of what happens with packet switching. It's just more efficient to break up data and send the packets individually to their destination, especially when it's simply impossible to send it all together (even if you take the same route home and drive the same speed).

Data packets can use two methods to find their way to their destination along a path: datagrams and virtual circuits. Using the first method, *datagrams*, the packet's sequence number and its destination are included with every data packet that's sent. Each data packet can then take different routes to the destination. Once data packets start arriving, the receiving node puts those packets together and then requests any missing packets be resent. Once the packets are all there, they are reassembled and the message is delivered.

In the second method, *virtual circuits*, no destination or sequence information is added, because all data is sent through the same route. It's not a "dedicated" route like the one required for circuit switching networks, but a specific route *is* designated using routers, routing tables, and other network information; however, every data packet takes the same route.

Still Struggling?

Consider a simple e-mail message. Perhaps you have some body text, a picture, and an attached document. In the packet switching scenario (and this example is simply provided for the purpose of offering an analogy, and does, by no means, suggest that this is what actually happens), one packet could contain the e-mail's body text, another packet could hold the picture, and the third packet could hold the text file. Once the three packets have arrived at their destination, the message would be reassembled and delivered to the recipient.

As you would guess, each of these models has advantages and disadvantages. In the datagram method, more data must be sent because more data is attached to it, but the route is fault-tolerant because packets take a separate route and lost data can be resent easily. In the virtual circuits method, less data must be sent because nothing extra is added to it, but if a router becomes disabled after transmission starts, the route fails and the entire message must be resent.

Conflict Resolution

So far we've discussed how data can be sent through routers to a destination and the two most common routing protocols (RIP and OSPF). We've also discussed circuit switching and packet switching. Because some networks encounter problems when data is sent at the same time other data is sent, protocols, network topologies, and technologies have been created to limit these data transmission problems, often referred to as *conflicts*.

It's similar to the "conflict" that arises in a telephone-based circuit switching network. A person in one room of a house (Jack) wants to use a land line to make a call, but upon picking up the phone to dial the number, finds that some-one else in the house (Jill) is already using the phone. A conflict arises on the network and something has to give before Jack can make a call—namely, Jill must get off the line! This type of conflict, as well as others, can occur on a computer network too (when data is already on the line and other data needs to use the line to transmit). Protocols must exist to minimize the number of conflicts to a minimum and to resolve them when problems arise.

Access Control Options

Data transmission conflicts can be controlled by limiting a node's ability to send data, but not all networks incorporate transmission limitations. There are vari-ous strategies and techniques. Consider the following:

- With *contention* techniques, nodes can send data whenever they want to. This is a good option for small networks with very little data traffic, but conflicts can occur that will cause data delivery problems—namely, data collisions. Contention-based technologies (CSMA, CSMA/CD, and CSMA/CA) will be discussed a little later in this chapter.

- With a *round robin* technique, each node on the network has a window for transmitting data. Once the window has passed, nodes have to wait for their turn to come around again. This is a solution used when there are lots of nodes with lots of data to send, and it severely limits data collisions and transmission conflicts.

- Using *reservations*, a node can reserve a time slot for sending data. Time slots are often of a fixed length. This is a good method if there is a lot of data traffic, and like round robin, it limits or does away with transmission conflicts.

- Using *token passing*, or *token-passing networks*, an electronic token is passed around the network (using a bus or a ring topology). The computer that has the token can send data; others can't until they possess the token.

There are no data collisions because only one node transmits at any given time.

- Using the *Distributed-Queue, Dual-Bus protocol,* a network that contains two busses is configured so that each bus transmits data in only one direction. Data is transmitted in slots, and data is placed in these slots for transfer. Slots can be free or contain data. This protocol is often used in MANs that manage very large data files among many users.

Still Struggling?

Most busy intersections have access controls to keep cars from running into each other. Some controls are: stop signs, where everyone stops, waits their turn if applicable, and then continues; and traffic lights, which are often on a timer—cars move only when it's their turn. These controls ideally keep cars from running into each other. Similarly, successful network access controls keep data from running into each other, and, in both instances, fewer collisions mean faster transmissions.

More about Contention Technologies

Carrier Sense Multiple Access, or CSMA, is a contention-based data transmission technology. This means that data can collide. In this protocol, a node listens for traffic on a network prior to sending it, and if there's nothing there, it sends its data. However, if another node also listens and decides to send data at the exact same moment, the data can collide. This collision usually goes unnoticed by the end users, because very little time passes before damaged messages are removed and the original data is resent by both nodes. However, these collisions are a problem and can cause a busy network to bog down.

NOTE   *Ethernet is a CSMA/CD protocol.*

In a newer CSMA algorithm, "/CD" is added to indicate *collision detection.* By detecting collisions proactively, it helps reduce both the time it takes to resolve a collision and the time that must pass before a node can resend its message. When a collision occurs with CSMA/CD, a signal is immediately sent to both nodes to tell them to stop sending data. Then, at two different times, the two nodes resend their data.

An alternative algorithm, CSMA/CA, includes *collision avoidance*. Using this method, collisions are avoided because, prior to sending data, the node sends out a very small packet to every node on the network telling all the others to stay off the line until the data has been successfully sent. (Despite this, if two nodes send these small packets at the same instant, they can still collide!)

To sum up, using CSMA/CD, collisions are handled as they occur, but on a busy network, collisions can occur so often that performance suffers noticeably. Ideally, network traffic must be less than 40 percent of the bus capacity for the network to operate effectively. When you add long distances to the mix, time lags that inevitably ensue cause their own problems—namely, even more collisions (due to the lag). Regarding CSMA/CA, although collisions are avoided because each node signals its intent to transmit before actually doing so, the overhead associated with the technology is high. This method, although effective, isn't very popular because of this overhead. Thus, the network administrator has many factors to consider and must weigh the pros and cons of each technology before making decisions about the traffic, status, and setting of the network.

Transport Protocols

Computer systems and networks are made up of devices created by many manufacturers. These devices must all be able to communicate with one another. A device by a computer manufacturer such as Apple, for instance, must be able to send data through the Internet to a computer manufactured by Microsoft, and the transmission must be seamless to the end user. Additionally, a local area network that uses a DLink router and a Motorola cable modem must be able to communicate that data to a network that uses a Cisco router and a satellite modem from Dish Network. Finally, a network interface card from Novell (at a sending computer) must be able to configure outgoing data so that a network interface card from Intel (at the receiving computer) can decipher it. Of course, the hardware that transmits the data must understand and be able to communicate with all this hardware, too, including Ethernet cables, coax cables, and other media.

To make sure that the devices created by all these completely different device manufacturers can communicate with all other devices, certain protocols were created. These protocols enable data to be sent among different networks, using various network hardware devices, routers, switches, network cards, and more. Without universal protocols, these devices could not communicate, the Internet would not exist, and only systems that consisted of hardware by a single manufacturer could communicate data to each other. Two structures in place today spell out these rules and protocols: OSI and TCP/IP.

OSI

The International Organization for Standardization, popularly known as the International Standards Organization (ISO), published the OSI reference model in 1984; the latest standard can be found at www.ios.org. OSI stands for Open Systems Interconnection. If you think about both of these titles for a moment, you can glean that an *international* organization created a set of rules to enable systems to *interconnect*. That was a necessary step that now enables seamless communication among international users. As long as everyone follows the rules, interconnection between open systems is possible.

The OSI model breaks down communications between computers and other network nodes into seven "layers" and each layer can communicate only to the layer that is immediately before or after it. The bottommost layer, the Physical Layer, lays out the rules for the actual transmitting of 1's and 0's "over the wire," so to speak. This means that manufacturers of Ethernet cables, network adapter cards, modems, hubs, and similar hardware must follow the protocols described for their hardware to be used on ordinary networks. The other layers have their own sets of rules for various data transmission tasks. These layers are the Data Link Layer, Network Layer, Transport Layer, Session Layer, Presentation Layer, and Application Layer. The highest layer, the Application Layer, is the end user's layer. It's where the user creates an e-mail or opts to send (or receive) a file using a protocol such as FTP. The next section shows how the layers "stack up."

OSI at the Sending Computer

At the sending computer, data is prepared and sent, and the OSI model is applied as follows:

The Application Layer adds a header to the data, after a user creates an e-mail or otherwise prepares data to send and opts to send it. This layer offers a user interface. The data, with the new header, is passed to the next layer.

↓

The Presentation Layer adds a new header to the data and controls formatting, compression, encryption, syntax conversion, and other data manipulation tasks. The data, with the new header, is passed to the next layer.

↓

The Session Layer adds a new header to the data and controls the flow of the data. This layer provides a user interface, establishes a connection between the applications or processes necessary to transmit it, and resets the connection if it fails. The data, with the new header, is passed to the next layer.

↓

The Transport Layer adds a new header to the data, maintains a reliable data transmission between end users, and regulates the flow of data. TCP (Transmission Control Protocol) is a Transport Layer protocol. The data, with the new header, is passed to the next layer.

↓

The Network Layer adds a new header to the data and provides addressing and routing services. This is where routing tables are accessed and smaller data packets are created. The data, with the new header, is passed to the next layer.

↓

The Data Link Layer adds a new header to the data and establishes and controls the physical path the data will take to its destination. It also readies the data for transmission. The data, with the new header, is passed to the next layer.

↓

The Physical Layer adds a new header to the data and controls the mechanical, electrical, and other physical tasks associated with transmitting data bits (1's and 0's). This layer is only concerned with hardware. All other layers are software related. The data is now physically sent via Ethernet lines, Wi-Fi, coax cable, telephone lines, or any other accepted medium.

OSI at the Receiving Computer

At the receiving computer, data is received and "unpacked" so that the user can ultimately access it, and the OSI model is applied as follows:

> The Physical Layer controls the data as it is received at the computer (or network node). This layer is only concerned with hardware. All other layers are software related. The data is physically received into the computer via Ethernet lines, Wi-Fi, coax cable, telephone lines, or any other accepted medium. The Physical Layer header is removed and the data is passed to the next layer.

↓

> The Data Link Layer establishes and controls the physical path the data has taken from its destination. It also prepares the data to be received at the network node. The Data Link Layer header is removed and the data is passed to the next layer.

↓

> The Network Layer provides addressing and routing services. This is where routing tables are accessed and data packets are beginning to be reassembled. The Network Layer header is removed and the data is passed to the next layer.

↓

> The Transport Layer maintains a reliable data transmission between nodes and regulates the flow of data. TCP (Transmission Control Protocol) is a Transport Layer protocol. The Transport Layer header is removed and the data is passed to the next layer.

↓

> The Session Layer continues to control the flow of the data. This layer provides a user interface, establishes a connection between the applications or processes necessary to receive it, and resets the connection if it fails. The Session Layer header is removed, and the data is passed to the next layer.

↓

> The Presentation Layer controls formatting, compression, encryption, syntax conversion, and other data manipulation tasks. The Presentation Layer header is removed, and the data is passed to the next layer.

↓

> The Application Layer enables the user to access and read the data. This layer offers a user interface. The Application Layer header is removed and the data is ready to be accessed at its destination.

NOTE *You may already be familiar with some of the Application Layer technologies that can use the OSI model. These include DNS, FTP, HTTP, SMTP, Telnet, and DHCP.*

TCP/IP

The *TCP/IP* (which stands for Transmission Control Protocol/Internet Protocol) protocol suite was approved in 1983, a year before the OSI model, and did not make clear distinctions between services, interfaces, and protocols. Because of this limitation, TCP/IP has four layers (compared to the OSI model's seven layers). Sometimes the layers in TCP/IP are named Network Access, Internet, Host-Host, and Process/Application. Sometimes the layers are referred to as Link, Internet, Transport, and Application. And at other times, the layers are referred to as Network Interface, Internet, Transport, and Application. When you're studying and learning about TCP/IP, make sure to keep this in mind. As with the OSI model, TCP/IP layers each have specific functions to perform.

Network Access Layer

This layer is equivalent to the Physical, Data Link, and part of the Network Layer of the OSI model detailed earlier. If you understand what those layers do for that model, you'll have an idea of what they do here. For the most part, this layer provides access to a network, controls the flow of data, deals with errors that occur during transmissions, and otherwise manages data transfer.

Internet Layer

This layer is equivalent to the part of the Network Layer of the OSI model not already covered by the Network Access Layer. For the most part, its job is to route data, most often through gateways and other network hosts.

Host-Host Layer

This layer is equivalent to the Transport and Session Layers of the OSI model. For the most part, this layer manages data that is transferred between two computers, and is also concerned with error-checking, data flow, and other connection control tasks.

Process/Application Layer

This layer is equivalent to the Presentation and Application Layers of the OSI model. Specific protocols include FTP, SMTP, and Telnet. FTP is the File Transfer Protocol, which is used to transmit large files over the Internet (or long distances). SMTP is the Simple Mail Transfer Protocol, which is used to transmit e-mail over the Internet, and Telnet is a networking protocol that is used with virtual terminal connections.

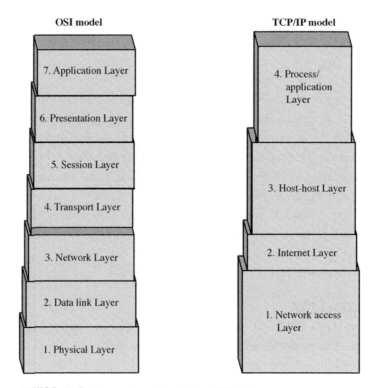

FIGURE 11-5 · Comparison of the OSI and TCP/IP layers

Figure 11-5 compares OSI and TCP/IP layers and shows how they match up with each other.

The subject of network protocols changes all the time. In these pages, we haven't the space to do more than summarize this complex subject. For more details, check out the latest research on the Web.

Summary

Before the operating system's network manager can transmit data, it must be prepared for transmission over the available, physical hardware. Once the data is prepared and transmitted, collisions and other problems can occur. There are built-in safeguards that step in when data collides on a network, and when data is lost in the transmission and needs to be resent. The OSI reference model and TCP/IP protocol suite define how data is sent and received over local networks and the Internet.

In the next chapter, we explore ways that the operating system secures the entire computer system from both intentional and accidental manipulations that threaten its data, software, and hardware.

QUIZ

Choose the correct response to each of the multiple-choice questions. Note that there may be more than one correct response to each question.

1. What routing protocol uses the shortest path to get data from point A to point B when data is sent over long distances?
   A. OSPF
   B. Tracert
   C. RIP
   D. Tracepath

2. What two Windows command-line tools enable you to find out how many hops it takes to get from point A to point B when data is sent over long distances over the Internet?
   A. Traceroute
   B. Ping
   C. Tracerouter
   D. Tracert

3. Which two models are "connection" models?
   A. Circuit switching
   B. Packet switching
   C. OSI
   D. TCP/IP

4. Which connection model is used for landline telephone networks?
   A. Circuit switching
   B. Packet switching
   C. OSI
   D. TCP/IP

5. Which connection model is used over the Internet?
   A. Circuit switching
   B. Packet switching
   C. OSI
   D. TCP/IP

6. Which access control option does not limit when a network node can send data over the network?
   A. Token Ring
   B. Round Robin
   C. Reservations
   D. Distributed-Queue, Dual-Bus
   E. Contention

7. Which contention option severely limits data collisions by having nodes send out a very small data packet to everyone on the network before they send the actual data, thus letting the other nodes know they're about to send some data?

   A. CSMA
   B. CSMA/CD
   C. CSMA/CA
   D. CSMA/CD/CA

8. Which layer of the OSI model is the only one to deal with protocols related to hardware?

   A. Physical
   B. Network
   C. Data Link
   D. Application

9. Which layer of the OSI model deals with protocols related to routing data over the Internet?

   A. Physical
   B. Network
   C. Data Link
   D. Session

10. In TCP/IP, what's another common term used for the Network Access Layer?

    A. Host-to-Host Layer
    B. Internet Layer
    C. Network Interface Layer
    D. Process/Application Layer

Part VI

Protection and Security

chapter 12

System Protection and Security

To keep computers safe from unwanted intrusions, data loss, and unauthorized access to personal data, as well as other security breaches, it's important to have various and sometimes redundant security features in place on every computer, the network and its hardware, and on network servers. This protection may include firewalls; software to keep out viruses, malware, and worms; authentication technologies to validate users (including smart cards and password policies); backup strategies; and more. Some of these security features are built right into the operating system.

CHAPTER OBJECTIVES

In this chapter, you will

- Understand the nature of threats and how to avoid them
- Learn about authentication technologies and password management
- Understand the importance of backups
- Explore the fundamental role that the operating system plays in security

Understanding Internet Threats and How to Avoid Them

You well know that threats that come via the Internet to your computer abound. There are intentional attacks by hackers, viruses and worms, adware-laden downloads, phishing websites, and intentional attacks on networks using various methods, such as denial-of-service attacks. To avoid these threats, you must first understand how they occur and then learn what can be done to avoid them.

Intentional Attacks by Hackers

Did you know that a hacker can stand outside your home office window with a "packet sniffer" and read the data packets you send over your own personal Wi-Fi network? They can! This is a concern for small, medium, and large businesses too, and they do what they can to protect their data from these kinds of attacks and others. Beyond malicious, intentional attacks, though, it's also possible that you (or your clients) will get into trouble by falling for a phishing e-mail, letting a Facebook app have your password so that it can then post unwanted status updates to your Facebook page, or allowing someone to figure out or learn your password and gain access to your computer using it. Whatever the case, you have to protect your information assets by staying informed, and remembering that hackers are always a threat.

> Phishing is a technique used in spam e-mails and on unscrupulous websites to trick e-mail recipients and website visitors into inputting or otherwise giving away personal information such as user names, passwords, and bank account numbers. The bad guys put out the bait (often an official-looking e-mail or web page) and try to "phish" for information.

For the most part, the bad guys, often called *black hat hackers*, are conducting their unethical behavior for malicious reasons. Sometimes they want credit card numbers, bank account numbers, and other personal data, or they want to access corporate data stored on a company's data servers. Sometimes they are agents working on behalf of another government. Or, they may want to exploit a vulnerability for the purpose of showing off their skills to other hackers, perhaps by defacing a home page on a large company's website. You can employ numerous security techniques—including antivirus, anti-malware, and anti-adware software; firewalls; strong authentication techniques; password-protected networks; and other options—to avoid being "hacked."

NOTE *Other types of intentional intrusions include wiretapping and listening on open networks to gain access to the data being sent on them.*

Viruses, Worms, Trojans, and More

A computer virus is a small program that spreads from one computer to another without the permission of the computer user. Viruses are self-executing and self-replicating. This means that they can attach themselves to other programs and data (such as e-mail) and replicate themselves once they are executed (perhaps when a user opens an e-mail attachment the virus is attached to). Viruses can attack data files, boot files, master boot records, and other areas of the computer and are often difficult to get rid of. You can see the current state of virus threats by visiting the site of an antivirus software provider, such as http://us.norton.com/security_response/index.jsp.

Still Struggling?

You know how a cold virus spreads from one person to another in the real world: Uninfected people come into contact with someone who has a virus and then they get infected themselves with the virus germs (if there's no protection in place to prevent it, such as wearing a mask or keeping a safe distance). That's how viruses spread among computers too. Code from a computer with a virus somehow comes into contact with another computer, and the virus is propagated.

A *worm* is a threat that resides in a computer's memory and copies itself from one system to the next without attaching itself to any program, by using the computer network the computer is attached to. Worms generally slow computers down by making problems for memory and processors, although they may be used to create "zombie" computers that unknowingly send out spam e-mail for their creators. Worms are becoming increasing complex, though, and are now morphing into even larger and scarier threats. Future worms may "lie in wait" until millions of computers are infected and then "explode" to infect many computers at once, perhaps bringing down a large group of computers worldwide, simultaneously.

A *Trojan* is another destructive program that masks itself as a valid and benign application. For example, a Trojan may look like a login screen and prompt users to enter their user names and passwords (in order to steal them). Trojans don't replicate themselves like viruses do, though. Trojans are most often created to gain access to computer systems so the creator can access the infected computer remotely. Once in, they can steal data, log keystrokes to gain information about passwords and user names, and even crash the computer.

Of course, there are many other types of threats, including spyware, adware, and various kinds of malware, often created for the purpose of gaining information about users or spamming them with unwanted e-mail. Software exists to catch such problems and get rid of them, but it's necessary for these precautions to be put in place ahead of time. Figure 12-1 shows one option for protecting a home computer from Internet threats such as malware, adware, and the like—Microsoft Security Essentials. It's free and is a good solution for the cash-strapped home user. In the example shown here, the program has been successful in repelling incoming threats, and no threats have been found or quarantined.

FIGURE 12-1 • Typically, anti-malware, anti-spyware, and anti-adware software has a tab that enables you to view any quarantined threats that have been caught and controlled.

Incorporating Software Protection

Figure 12-1 shows one option for protecting a computer system from Internet threats, but many other programs are available. In fact, the Windows Vista and Windows 7 operating systems come with Windows Defender already installed. Although Defender doesn't protect against viruses, it does protect the computer from pop-ups, spyware, and similar threats. Figure 12-2 shows Windows Defender.

TIP *You can download Windows Defender for free if it's not included by default, and as you know, Microsoft Security Essentials is a free download, too.*

Of course, third-party manufacturers offer all kinds of protection software that you can buy. These manufacturers include Norton and McAfee, among others. Whatever you decide to use—and you must use something—make sure that the program is configured to get updates against threats daily and that your

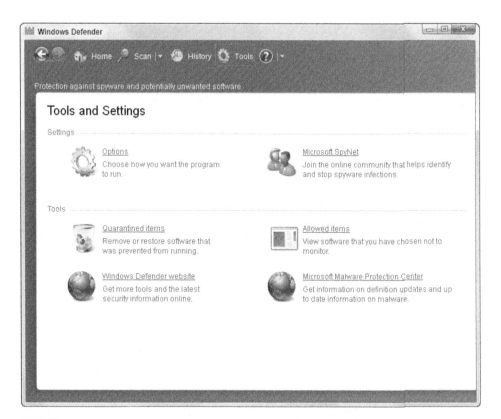

FIGURE 12-2 • With Windows Defender, you can run scans, view quarantined items, and more.

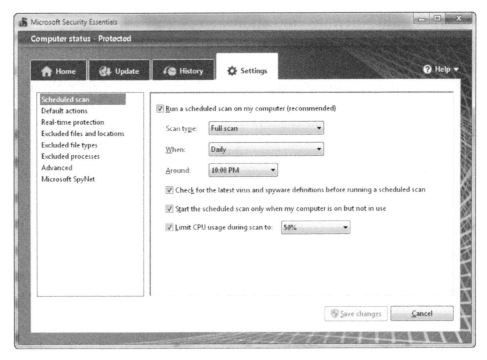

FIGURE 12-3 · Protection software should be updated daily and scans should take place regularly.

computer is scanned regularly. Remember that old software will only find old viruses. Frequent updates are essential. You'll find options in the various settings pages of the program you choose. See Figure 12-3 for an example.

Using Firewalls

Firewalls offer another bit of protection against security threats. Firewalls look at what kind of data is coming into the computer (or gateway, server, or other hardware) and what kind is going out, and if it's an approved data type (and for servers, sometimes source/recipient), the data passes through the firewall. If it's not approved, it is stopped in its tracks. Windows computers come with a built-in firewall, and so do Macs. Router firewalls also exist to help protect a network from unwanted network traffic. Network and computer administrators can configure the firewall to allow and disallow data, as desired. Figure 12-4 shows an example from a Windows 7 computer.

NOTE *If you, as an administrator, disallow something from passing through a firewall and a user tries to invoke the program and transmit data using it, that user*

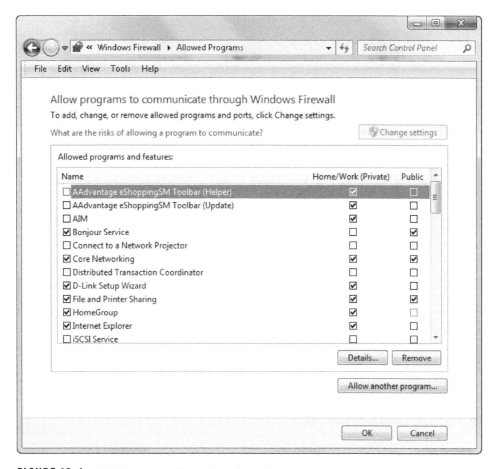

FIGURE 12-4 · Administrators configure firewalls to allow and disallow data.

will be prompted to enable the data to pass through the firewall. Generally, users can only make this change if they enter an administrator user name and password.

Exercise 12-1: Explore the Mac Firewall

Macs come with firewalls, too, and like the Windows firewall, you can control what data passes through and what doesn't. Here are the steps to follow:

1. Open Settings.

2. Open Security.

3. Click the Firewall tab.

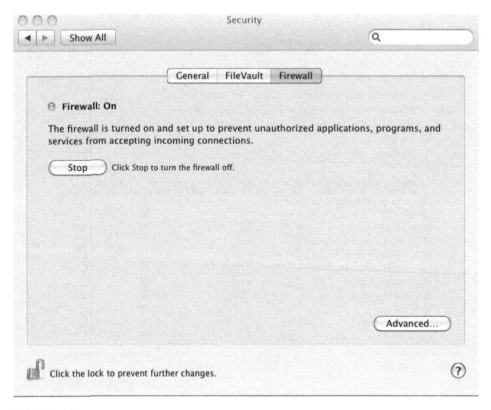

FIGURE 12-5 · Controlling the firewall on a Mac

4. Note the lock to make changes as well as the option to start and stop the firewall, shown in Figure 12-5.

5. Click the Advanced button.

6. Note the options to add and remove incoming connections.

7. Click OK to apply any changes.

Teaching End Users

Even with security options in place, unless you inform your end users about the types of threats they may encounter, you'll still leave yourself open to problems. For instance, a user may bypass the security features you have and download and install an adware-laden software package, or they may input their user ID or Social Security number into a phishing website (often accessed from a phishing e-mail). Likewise, they may simply print and then tape their user name and password to the underside of their keyboard (where most unwanted intruders are likely to look for the information) or share their password with others. Therefore, part of your security plan should include teaching your end users about the threats they'll encounter, and how to stay safe while online and while away from their computer.

Here are some things you may want to suggest:

- Do not download anything, and this includes fonts, screen savers, applications, registry-editing programs, games, and virus checkers, among others. Be wary of attachments too, and don't open any attachments you aren't expecting.

- Never give your password to anyone, whether in the office, at home, or on the Internet. This includes Facebook applications. If you must write down your password, keep it in a safe place, preferably a lock box of some sort, and away from prying eyes and hackers.

- If an e-mail is from someone you don't know, even if appears to be from a bank, mortgage company, or other well-known entity, consider it spam or a scam. The problem is that the e-mail may be from a hacker imitating the real entity, going so far as to create a passable imitation of the official entity's web page. *Never* respond, click, or supply bank account numbers or personal information, and never purchase anything from an unsolicited e-mail link. If in doubt, call the company on the phone or visit their website by typing in their web address (don't click any link in the e-mail to get there).

- Don't disable antivirus software or firewalls because you think they are slowing down your computer. Even if they are, it's best to let them run, or at least reconfigure them so your computer gets updates and run scans at night or after business hours.

- If the web browser states that the website you're trying to access has been reported as a phishing website, click the Back button.

- If you receive a message claiming to be a warning about a security issue, don't click it. It could be executable code that spreads malware. If applicable, run a virus scan or verify the message using other validated tools.

- When in doubt, call a network administrator, research the message on the Internet (for example, snopes.com), or ask someone who knows a lot about computers before doing something dangerous, such as clicking an error message, opting into a Facebook application, or opening an attachment.

User Accounts and Password Management

Not all threats come from the Internet. That's why many operating systems give you the option to manage user accounts, one for each user, which can be a good way to prevent unauthorized intruders from accessing a computer or the data on it. This can be a pretty easy way to protect a few computers on a local area network, such as the ones you'll find in homes and home offices (with regard to configuring user accounts, at least). You simply configure each computer with a standard user account for each person who needs access to the resources on it, apply passwords to those accounts, and set up who wants to share what with whom. Managing larger networks is much more complex, though. Although protecting this kind of network still involves creating standard user accounts, applying passwords, and sharing data, there's much more at stake, there are many more options for configuration, and there's much more to manage.

User Accounts Versus User Account Controls

When you create standard and administrator accounts when setting up a computer or a network, it's likely your main goal is to require users to input a user name and password to gain access to the computer and the resources on it. User names and passwords also protect a user's personal data when data on the computer is shared with others. Additionally, user names and passwords help administrators protect what's on domain controllers, data servers, e-mail servers, and the like. However, creating user names and applying passwords also help the User Account Control (UAC) feature (in Windows) and similar controls on a Mac or Linux-based system to protect the computer from other threats. When user names and passwords are applied, and when a program needs administrator access to make changes to the computer, administrator credentials must be input. This protection from UAC helps keep malware and other threats from gaining a foothold, even if the prompts for administrator credentials seem annoying to the user or administrator. We'll continue our discussion of user account controls in more detail later in this chapter.

Using Standard Accounts

No matter what type of computer you're trying to secure or what type of network it's connected to, all operating systems offer the ability to create users. The most powerful of these users are administrators, with access to everything the computer has to offer (including hidden system files, the ability to create more user accounts, and the rights to disable the firewall and install programs, for instance). You can also create users who have far fewer rights. Administrators can manage these *standard* users, and they can require users to employ passwords and change them often, state how strong passwords have to be, determine what resources those users can access, and prevent users from just about anything imaginable—from installing programs to changing the time. User accounts are the first line of defense against unwanted intrusions and unintentional damage, and they are a built-in feature of the operating system. Figure 12-6 shows the User Account window on a Windows 7 computer, when logged on with an Administrator account.

TIP   *In Figure 12-6, note the option called Change User Account Control (UAC) Settings. You can click this option to change how UAC works on a Windows computer. In fact, you can disable UAC completely, although we certainly don't recommend it.*

Macs offer the ability to create user accounts, too (as do Linux computers). On a Mac running OS X, most of the time you'll open System Preferences and Accounts to get started. In OS X Lion, it's Users & Groups. When you opt to add a user account, by default, it's a standard user. You can type the new user's

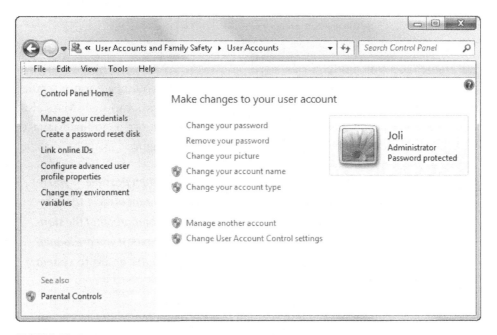

FIGURE 12-6 · Administrators can create new accounts, apply passwords to accounts, and change User Account Control settings, among other things.

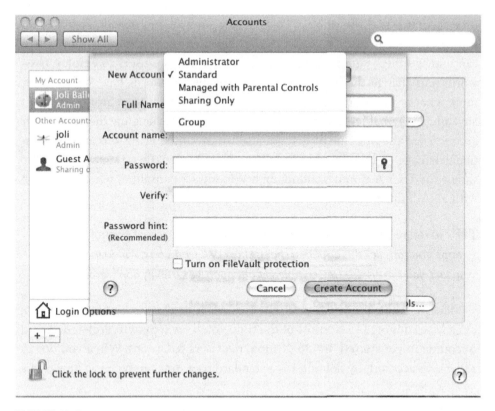

FIGURE 12-7 · Macs offer the ability to create various kinds of secure user accounts.

full name, account name, a password, and even a password hint. Standard accounts are the default on a Mac because standard accounts are more secure than administrator accounts, just as they are on Windows computers. Macs also offer additional accounts beyond standard and administrator, including Manage with Parental Controls, Sharing Only, and Guest (see Figure 12-7).

TIP *It's best to always log on with a "standard" account when possible. If you're logged on as a standard user, and a rogue virus or other threat attacks the computer, generally, the attacker can only access areas of the computer that the standard user can access, and all unauthorized areas are off-limits. If you are logged on as an administrator instead, that intruder has far greater access to system resources and computer data.*

TIP *You can often enable a "guest" account to allow a user temporary access to a computer they don't use often. But make sure that the default password for your* *guest account is changed regularly. Historically, system intruders have tried the guest account with the default password to gain quick-and-easy access to numerous networks.*

Requiring Strong Passwords

Once standard user accounts are configured, a computer administrator in a workgroup or a network administrator in a domain can require that users create "strong" passwords, provided that the operating system edition supports this feature. Passwords can be required to contain letters and numbers, a minimum number of characters, and can be made to include symbols, such as an exclamation point or similar character. Although making it a requirement for the user to create and use a strong password (and possibly change it every 30 days) seems like a good idea, it is often self-defeating. Users will almost always write down their password and keep it handy, often underneath a keyboard, taped to the bottom of a desk, or in a file. Intruders know where to look and will generally check these hiding places. If you ever become the person whose job it is to configure password policies for an organization, try to find a happy medium between what the user wants and what you'd like to require regarding password creation.

NOTE   *Alternative access technologies include smart cards, iris recognition scanners, fingerprint readers, and more. As time passes, these will become more popular and will likely replace the familiar user name/password combination for access to a computer or network. They'll also be more secure, because one user will likely have a hard time, say, obtaining the fingerprint of another.*

Here are some examples of weak versus strong passwords:

- **Fluffy vs. Fluffy87Dog$**   This strong password contains more than a pet's name; it also contains numbers, a symbol, and capital letters.
- **08051962 vs. AugustFifth19X62F#**   The strong password here contains more than the user's date of birth; it contains a license plate number, upper- and lowercase letters, and a symbol.
- **Password vs. P@S$W0rdd5541!**   This strong password is more than the very common "password" and contains letters, numbers, and symbols.
- **MyDogHasFleas vs. MyD0GHazzFleeze!$**   As with the other examples, the strong password here has pizzazz and would be more difficult to discover.

Applying Access Policies

Administrators can configure which users can access which resources, and can place limits on what the user can do if they do have access. As an example, a user may be able to print to a network printer, but not rearrange the print jobs in the queue to place his or hers at the top of the list. In another scenario, a user may be able to read documents stored in a folder on the Human Resources computer server, but not make or save changes to those documents.

NOTE *How access polices are configured is different for a workgroup and a domain, and is beyond the scope of this chapter and book. However, the idea is the same for both: You can protect unwanted access to resources by applying access controls and putting access policies in place.*

Figure 12-8 shows a folder that's shared. This is a Windows 7 computer in a workgroup. Jennifer has been given "read" access to a folder. This means Jennifer can view, open, and read what's there, but she cannot write any data to the files and save them there.

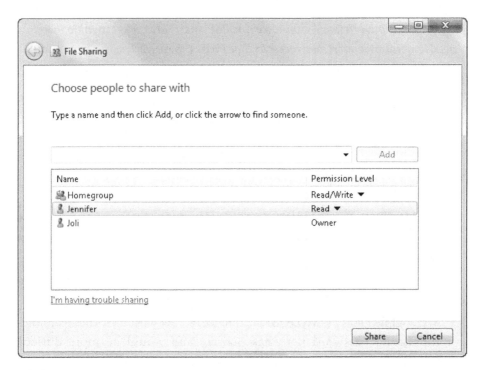

FIGURE 12-8 · Operating systems come with options for sharing folders, among other things.

Applying permissions to shared folders is only one way to offer and control access to resources. Access control can be applied to resources on a network, too. For instance, in a workgroup, a user account can be created on a computer to allow more than one person to access it. With that done, the user can access resources on the computer from another computer on the network, or by logging on to the computer while sitting in front of it.

In a domain, network administrators often create complex groups of users as well as apply rights and permissions to those groups. Administrators can thus manage large groups of users efficiently. As an example, an administrator might create a group called Sales, put all the salespeople in it, and then assign specific rights and permissions to that group, thus limiting its members to only the areas of the network that the administrator deems necessary. The administrator might then create a second group, perhaps called Accounting, assign rights and permissions to the members there, and allow the accountants access to only the parts of the network that they need access to. By creating groups, adding users, and applying permissions, administrators can keep resources safe (by limiting who has access to what) and simplify management. (Can you imagine managing 1,000 people in a large organization one at a time?)

NOTE *For the most part, administrators try to give only the access necessary for one to do one's job, and no more.*

Exercise 12-2: Create a Group on a Mac and Add Users to It

Administrators can create a group on a Mac and then add users to it. The administrator can then manage that group collectively, by sharing data with the group instead of sharing data for each individual. This might be a good idea for a parent who has four children, or a small business owner with one Mac and five part-time employees. Here are the steps to follow on a Mac OS X pre-Lion computer:

1. Open System Preferences | Accounts and then click the lock to make changes.
2. Click the + sign.
3. Click the down arrow next to New and then click Group.
4. Type a name for the group.

FIGURE 12-9 · Create groups to manage multiple users who need similar access to resources.

    5. Click Create Group. See Figure 12-9 for an example.

    6. Select the users to be part of the group.

    7. Click the lock to prevent further changes.

Understanding Kerberos

One of several user authentication tools is Kerberos, which is freely available (under copyright permissions) from MIT (web.mit.edu/Kerberos) where it was developed, or it can be purchased from many commercial sources. The purpose of the authentication process is to verify that the user who is trying to access network resources is really someone you want to allow access to, and once users are logged in, you want them to access only certain resources. There are several ways to authenticate system users, but Kerberos is one of the most popular. It is built into many operating systems and is used primarily in domains that use the client/server network model.

    Kerberos features a very strong cryptography protocol that allows one computer (the sender or receiver) to prove its identity to another computer across a network connection, even if it's an insecure network. Then, once their respective identities are verified using Kerberos, both computers can communicate at will, over this insecure network, by encrypting all transmissions that pass between them, thus assuring that all data remains private and secure throughout the session. Once a session ends, the two computers need to authenticate themselves again before they will be allowed to send or receive more data. Any users that fail authentication are not allowed access to the protected system.

NOTE *When data is encrypted, it is encoded. When network transmissions are encrypted, first the data to be sent is encrypted, then transmitted, then received,*

*then unencrypted, and finally processed by the receiving computer. Encryption
requires the use of an encryption key to lock and unlock the data.*

Understanding the Importance of Backups

It's important to prepare for the worst. You have to have a plan in place if a user
opens an attachment that contains a virus, the computer gets a worm or adware,
or the computer is hacked by a disgruntled employee or outsider. You can often
recover from these things with the software you've used previously to try to
keep out these types of threats. However, recovery isn't always possible and
other threats abound. A computer's hard drive can fail, the user can spill coffee
on a laptop (or lose the laptop), or a desktop computer can be destroyed in a
fire or flood. In these cases, data must be recovered via backups; "recovery"
using system tools isn't possible.

Almost every operating system offers some kind of automated backup option.
You should know what these options are and how to use them. Although learning
how to use Windows Backup and Restore or Apple's Time Machine is beyond the
scope of this chapter, they are introduced in the sections that follow because it's
important to know that these options exist for the home and small office user.

Single-Computer Backup Options

Although the data on a single computer may seem less crucial than that on a larger
computer, to the person who put it there, its significance may be enormous. It
doesn't take much to knock out one computer—whether it's water, fire, tornado,
power surge, or technical failure. For the most part, computer users in homes and
small offices will use one or more of the following to back up their data:

- Users may set up and run the backup program that comes with their
  operating system, either manually or on a schedule. Some operating systems offer the ability to create a system image and other items. Figure 12-10
  shows a few of the options for a Windows 7 Home Premium computer.

FIGURE 12-10 • Operating
systems almost always offer
some kind of backup option.

FIGURE 12-11 · Apple offers Time Machine, where data can be backed up data every day, without user interaction.

- Users may configure a backup program that comes with their operating system to back up data to a backup disk that is available on a network. Figure 12-11 shows Apple's Time Machine.

- Users may drag and drop files to an external drive or a networked computer. External drives include computers, DVDs, USB thumb drives, SD cards, and even mobile devices.

- Users may opt to store data "in the cloud," using paid and free backup services.

- Users may install a backup computer, such as Windows Home Server, and configure it to back up all data on the network regularly.

- Users may install an external hard drive that contains its own backup software and configure it to back up all data on the computer or network regularly.

Creating a Backup Schedule on a Single Computer

It's important to encourage users or systems administrators to incorporate a program that performs backups on a regular schedule. The schedule should be configured to run when the computer is turned on, when the backup device is available, and when the computer is idle. Although that seems like a tall order, as you can see in Figure 12-12, Sunday at 7 P.M. is a pretty good option for most users.

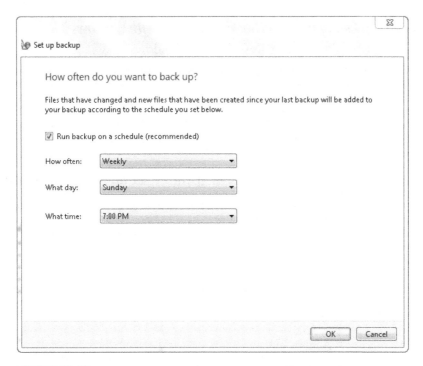

FIGURE 12-12 · Make sure you're performing a scheduled backup at least once a week.

TIP   *If you've set up a weekly backup schedule, consider performing daily backups to protect data you've created between regular backups. You may be able to use a USB drive for this.*

One way to set up a reliable and secure backup—on a Windows computer at least—is to use the built-in backup program. Depending on the edition of Windows you are dealing with, you may have one of several emanations of the supplied program. On a Windows 7 computer, you'll find Windows Backup and Restore. To use it, you'll need to connect an external hard drive, large USB key, or recordable DVD device, and if you have Windows Professional, Enterprise, or Ultimate, you can choose an available, shared drive on the network. You have the option to schedule these backups too, even on Windows 7 Home Premium. For Vista, you'll encounter similar limitations, depending on the operating system version.

Exercise 12-3: Configuring and Backing Up Data with Windows 7 Backup and Restore

To use Windows Backup and Restore on a Windows 7 PC and back up to an external hard drive (the best option, generally), follow these steps:

1. Connect the external hard drive.

2. Click Start (the Windows button in the bottom-left corner), and in the Start Search window, type **Backup**. Click Backup and Restore in the results.

3. If applicable, click Set Up Backup. If you've set up a backup before, you can click Options or another choice.

4. Follow the steps in the wizard. You'll be prompted to choose a backup device first. It's best to select Let Me Choose when prompted.

5. Select the files to back up. A sample is shown in Figure 12-13.

6. Click Save Settings and Run Backup. You can watch the backup process, if desired, as shown in Figure 12-14.

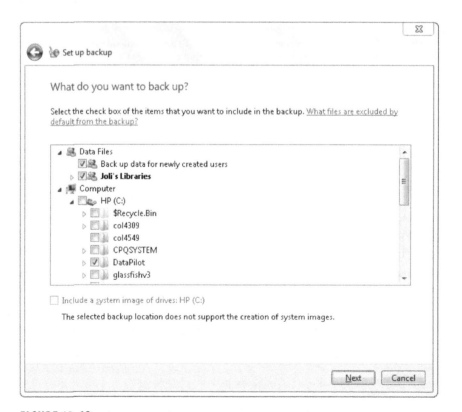

FIGURE 12-13 · Always opt to choose what to back up yourself.

Back up or restore your files

Backup in progress...

View Details

Backup

FIGURE 12-14 · A graphic shows you a backup is in progress.

Workgroup Backup Options

In a network with only a handful of computers, you can manage backups of those computers individually, although it might become more time consuming as you add more computers to the mix. The more you add, the more difficult management of those computers becomes. One solution for securing data on a small workgroup is a "home server."

In small home office or small business networks where backups need to be monitored by an administrator and are often performed nightly, a workgroup computer may be configured and connected (such as Windows Home Server or Apple's Lion Server) to serve as a backup device. This is a good way to ensure that backups are reliably performed, although they do add overhead to the management and cost of backups. This type of configuration works well for small workgroups, though, and is a good option for small companies with valuable and irreplaceable data.

TIP   *You can't trust end users to create and manage their own backups. You're asking for trouble if you do!*

Data Servers, Backups, and Domains

Computers that are part of a larger network, such as those in an enterprise, on a college campus, in a hospital, or similar area, are generally not configured to run backups independently once a week like stand-alone computers or computers in a home network. One reason is that data needs to be backed up more often than that. Another is that backups need to be monitored, tested, and verified, to ensure that the backup is actually taking place and is usable. Often, the data isn't even stored on a user's computer; it's stored on a data server, so backing up a user's computer would be futile (more on this next). Finally, larger corporations generally integrate the computers in a network (often called a domain). Domain servers are available for managing users, computers, and their data, and should be utilized. In these types of scenarios, backups are performed automatically by data servers, tape drives, or other hardware, which is configured and managed by network administrators. The users are not responsible for creating their own backups.

There are many advantages to incorporating a domain and having users save data to a domain control versus their own computers. When data is saved to a data server instead of the users' own individual computers, performing backups is much easier for network administrators than when each computer is configured to run and maintain its own backup. Consider it for a moment. If you had to configure, manage, run, and verify backups for 1,000 computers on a network, you'd be pretty busy all the time, running from computer to computer, making sure everything was running smoothly. Each computer would also need some place to store those backups, preferably not an external hard drive that sits on top of the computer tower! However, if you configure those computers to save data to one of three data servers on the network, you'd really only have to manage the backups for three data servers, and you would not need to manage backups for 1,000 computers. This is one of the reasons administrators configure groups of computers to save data to a central location, often in a different building, city, or state. (They can also manage access to those servers too.)

NOTE *Sometimes in small to midsize enterprises, data is saved to a user's computer and backups are run nightly. In these scenarios, data is backed up to data servers instead of saved there by default.*

To sum up, no matter how and where data is saved, it's important to understand that just about every operating system you'll run across has built-in tools for backing up data. Those tools include the ability to restore data too, if the need ever arises. Additionally, some operating systems allow for the creation of computer "images," where the entire operating system and all its programs are cloned. In this strategy, a computer can be restored fairly quickly from the backup, even if the entire hard drive is destroyed.

TIP *Whatever route you take, put at least one backup strategy in place. If you can, create redundant backups too, just in case something happens to the first backup (such as fire, flood, theft, or data corruption).*

The Operating System's Role in Security

You learned in this chapter that operating systems provide administrators the ability to create user accounts and passwords to protect data, schedule and perform automated backups, and protect against many threats, including worms, pop-ups, and adware, using built-in features such as Windows Defender and Apple's Firewall. However, operating systems provide much more than that to help keep a computer secure. Operating systems can, for the most part, be configured to check for and obtain security updates from the company that created them, be configured to encrypt personal and sensitive data, offer protection for the computer using features such as Window's User Account Control, provide behind-the-scenes protection for the web browser, offer updates (when available) for device drivers and software, and help users resolve problems they encounter through wizards. Although there's a lot more to discover, these next few sections offer a good start for any home user or network administrator, and bring home the point that *security is incorporated into popular operating systems and should be enabled, configured, and utilized.*

Security Updates

Both Apple and Microsoft push out updates on a regular basis to address security problems, fix bugs, and resolve similar issues with their operating systems. These updates help protect the computer from recently uncovered security holes, malware and adware, and other threats. The users can decide whether they want to download and install those updates. For most home users, it's best to install updates as they are offered; in larger enterprises, network administrators generally test updates on a handful of computers first, to verify there are no problems before pushing them out to every computer on the network.

TIP   *If you ever install an update that causes problems on a Windows home computer, simply run System Restore. Windows always creates a restore point prior to installing any update. On a Mac, consider Time Machine.*

Exercise 12-4: Configure Windows Update on a Windows Computer

To see how updates can be configured on a computer, explore Windows Update on a Windows computer. Windows XP, Windows Vista, Windows ME, Windows 7, and others offer Windows Update. Here are the steps to follow:

1. Click Start (the Windows button in the bottom-left corner).
2. Click All Programs (or Programs).
3. Click Windows Update.

FIGURE 12-15 • Windows computers offer Windows Update, a place where updates can be acquired and installed. The default settings can be configured by the computer administrator.

4. Click Change Settings.

5. Note the options and change them as desired (see Figure 12-15).

6. Click OK.

TIP *You may find that in step 3, updates are available. You can review and install those updates, as desired.*

Encryption Options

As you know, encryption is a way to encode data so that only the person who encrypted it can unencrypt it. Encryption is not configured by default, and must be applied manually. Only specific editions of operating systems offer file and folder encryption, though. Windows 7 Home Premium does not, whereas Windows 7 Professional, Ultimate and Enterprise do. Figure 12-16 shows encryption options on a Windows 7 Professional computer; Figure 12-17 shows FileVault on a Mac OS X computer.

NOTE *BitLocker is another encryption option available in Windows 7 Ultimate and Enterprise editions and in Windows Server 2008 and 2008 R2 editions. It allows you to encrypt entire hard drives! You can also incorporate BitLocker to encrypt portable disks, such as USB thumb drives.*

FIGURE 12-16 · Windows 7 Professional, Ultimate and Enterprise offer file and folder encryption options.

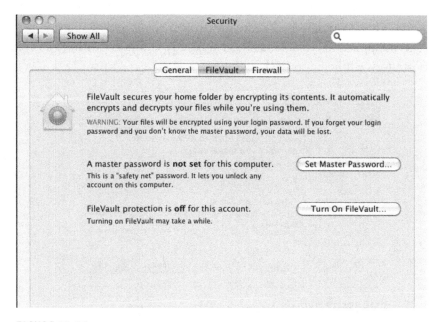

FIGURE 12-17 · Macs offer FileVault, where users can enable encryption by setting a master password and enabling the feature.

> **NOTE** *To access Windows 7 encryption options, right-click the file or folder to encrypt and click Properties. From the General tab, click Advanced.*

User Account Controls

As we mentioned earlier in this chapter, you can create user accounts and passwords to manage access to computers and resources by *people*. These user accounts help control who has access, as well as what they have access to. Operating systems have their own user account controls to keep the computer secure from other threats and other types of unwanted access. This protection incorporates the user accounts and passwords you've configured, but in a different way. User account controls are invoked when a software program tries to perform administrative tasks or make system-wide changes (among other things). Figure 12-18 shows a user account control on a Mac OS X computer; Windows computers have a similar feature.

The User Account Control feature in Windows Vista and Windows 7 protects in many ways:

- It limits application software to standard user privileges and requires an administrator name and password to increase privilege elevation. This keeps applications from making changes to a computer without an administrator's explicit approval.

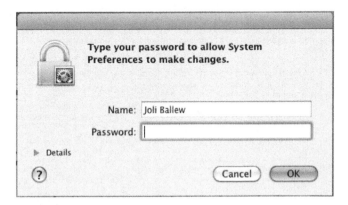

FIGURE 12-18 · User Account Controls insist that users input administrator credentials to make system-wide changes to the computer.

- Malware is kept at bay because an administrator must approve an application to make changes to a computer. If permission is not given, the malware can't take hold.

- In many cases, an administrator can remain logged in with a standard account and still perform many administrator tasks by inputting a user name and password.

Here are a few of the many reasons why you might be prompted to input a user name and password while working with a computer:

- Installing device drivers
- Installing or uninstalling programs
- Changing firewall settings
- Changing system-wide settings
- Configuring parental controls
- Running a task scheduler
- Running a disk defragmenting program
- Restoring data from a backup
- Changing User Account Control settings
- Adding or removing user accounts
- Changing a user account's type
- Configuring Windows Update

Built-in Web Browser Security

Because many security problems arise via the web browser, browsers come with their own security features. Most offer protection against phishing websites, block pop-ups, offer a "protected" mode, and keep third-party cookies off the computer, among other things. Because Windows computers and Apple computers come with a web browser (Internet Explorer and Safari, respectively), it's important to review those programs during any assessment of operating system security features.

You can access Safari's security features from the Safari menu: click Preferences, and from the Preferences window, click Security. In Internet Explorer,

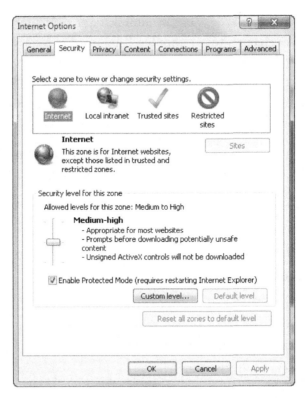

FIGURE 12-19 · Internet Explorer, included with Windows operating systems, offers its own security options.

select Tools | Internet Options, and view the options on the Security tab (shown in Figure 12-19) as well as the Privacy tab's options, and explore the options under the Safety menu. There are many security variables; we won't go into more detail here, but be sure to set aside some time to explore all the options.

The Windows 7 Action Center

The Windows 7 operating system offers a new feature called the Action Center to help keep the computer secure and running at optimal performance. Here, users can check for solutions to problems they've encountered; those solutions may include third-party software updates and improved device driver support. You should check the Action Center regularly and encourage your users to as well. You can access the Action Center by searching for it, or by clicking the

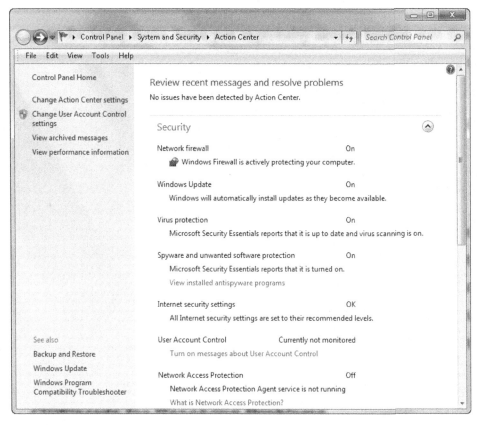

FIGURE 12-20 · The Action Center's Security section helps you determine quickly whether security settings are configured optimally.

flag icon in the taskbar's notification area. As you can see in Figure 12-20, the Action Center can also be used to review security settings, so that users can verify that their security settings are optimal.

Wizards for Resolving Problems

Operating systems may also offer troubleshooting wizards for resolving issues. Figure 12-21 shows the wizards listed for System and Security on a Windows 7 computer. These wizards can help users detect problems and fix them as well as resolve problems with Windows Update, among other things. By enabling users to resolve system and security issues easily, the operating system is better able to protect itself from threats and security holes.

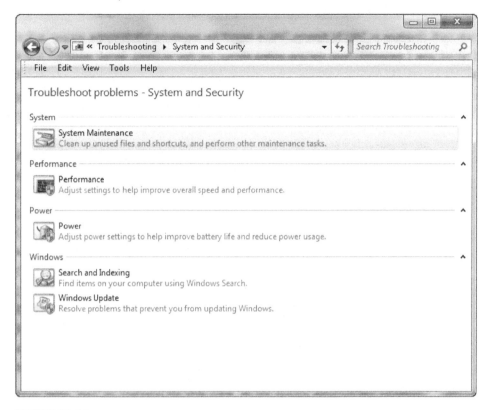

FIGURE 12-21 • Wizards help users resolve security problems on their own.

Summary

In these pages, we've touched on many aspects of operating systems, yet we haven't had the chance to delve into any topic in detail. What's more, this is a subject that changes every day. Therefore, we encourage you to join us in watching as this subject evolves over the coming years. Keep your eyes open for new technologies for logging onto systems, for example, including fingerprint and iris technologies, among others. It's going to be very exciting!

QUIZ

Choose the correct response to each of the multiple-choice questions. Note that there may be more than one correct response to each question.

1. **What is a computer virus?**
   A. A memory-resident program that spreads via a computer network
   B. A self-replicating and self-executing program that often comes into a computer or network via an e-mail attachment
   C. A fake interface, often a login screen, used to trick someone into entering a user name and password for the purpose of stealing that information
   D. An e-mail that tries to get a user to click a link to go to a website for the purpose of obtaining one's bank account numbers, Social Security numbers, and other data

2. **Which of the following can viruses attack?**
   A. Data files
   B. Boot files
   C. Master boot records
   D. All of the above

3. **What are firewalls used for?**
   A. To look at what kind of data is coming into the computer (or gateway, server, or other hardware) and what kind is going out. If it's an approved data type, the data is allowed to pass.
   B. To scan the computer for adware and malware on a regular basis and remove those threats as they are found.
   C. To prevent users from giving out their password to spammers and hackers.
   D. To prevent users from downloading screensavers, fonts, applications, and games.

4. **To create a secure, secondary user account on any workgroup computer, you should create a(n) _____ account and require a _____.**
   A. administrator; password
   B. standard; strong password
   C. guest; password
   D. domain; strong password

5. **Which of the following best represents a "strong" password?**
   A. BobsComputerPassword
   B. Password
   C. Fluffy87$45K
   D. MyComputer51

6. **Which of the following terms is the name of an authentication technology?**
    A. Kerberos
    B. Encryption
    C. User Account Control
    D. Access control

7. **When configuring a backup strategy for a user, you should:**
    A. Create the backup to occur automatically and on a schedule.
    B. Inform the user how to back up data, when desired, to a USB drive.
    C. Propose and configure redundant backups.
    D. Inform the user of network data storage and "in the cloud" backup options.
    E. All of the above.

8. **You want to enable encryption on a Windows 7 Home Premium workgroup computer, but the option to encrypt is grayed out and can't be accessed. Why?**
    A. You are trying to encrypt a system folder, which can't be encrypted.
    B. You are trying to encrypt a public folder, which can't be encrypted.
    C. Encryption isn't available on Windows 7 Home Premium editions.
    D. You must log on as an administrator to encrypt a folder.
    E. You can only encrypt data on a domain, not when connected to a workgroup.

9. **Which of the following are likely to trigger a User Account Control prompt?**
    A. Installing a device driver
    B. Accessing a phishing website
    C. Adding or removing user accounts
    D. Reviewing solutions in the Action Center (Windows 7)

10. **From the available choices, select each item the Action Center offers.**
    A. Updates to device drivers, when they are available
    B. Troubleshooting wizards for resolving problems with the system and security
    C. The ability to share resources with others on the network
    D. An option to review security settings, including whether or not the firewall is enabled

Final Exam

Choose the correct response to each of the multiple-choice questions. Note that there may be more than one correct response to each question.

1. **An operating system manages:**

   A. Memory

   B. CPU

   C. Storage

   D. Data, applications, and programs

2. **How many operating systems have been written?**

   A. Five

   B. Less than 100

   C. Between 100 and 500

   D. More than a thousand

3. **What type of operating system is used in handheld games, barcode scanners, and navigation units?**

   A. Embedded

   B. Real time

   C. Distributed

   D. Single user

4. One gigabyte = _____.

   A. 1,024KB

   B. 1,024MB

   C. 1,024 bytes

   D. 1,024EB

5. Which of the following lets you boot a computer into Safe Mode?

   A. Pressing F8 on a Windows computer during the boot process

   B. Pressing the SHIFT key on a Mac computer during the boot process

   C. Pressing the OPTION key on a Mac computer during the boot process

   D. Pressing F12 on a Windows computer during the boot process

6. The _____ manager tracks the status of each process (task) in an operating system.

   A. virtual memory

   B. device

   C. process

   D. file

   E. network

7. Which of the following are primary types of operating system interfaces?

   A. Boot driven

   B. Network driven

   C. Menu driven

   D. Command driven

8. Which of the following operating systems are primarily command driven?

   A. Windows

   B. Ubuntu Linux

   C. Mac OS X

   D. BSD UNIX

9. **When does the boot process start; end?**

    A. When you press the power button; just before the welcome screen appears.

    B. When you press the power button; after the first beep sounds.

    C. When the first beep sounds; just before the welcome screen appears.

    D. When you press the power button; after the user logs in to the computer.

10. **How can you interrupt the boot process on a Windows computer?**

    A. By entering Safe Mode

    B. By pressing F8 during boot up

    C. By pressing F5 to refresh the boot process

    D. By pressing F2 or a similar key to enter the BIOS

11. **Which of the following are services?**

    A. Event logging

    B. Error reporting

    C. BIOS

    D. Plug and Play

12. **What is the first thing that happens in the boot process?**

    A. ROM is read.

    B. RAM is loaded with instructions.

    C. The power supply starts up.

    D. BIOS is enabled.

13. **Firmware is _____.**

    A. often stored on ROM chips

    B. often stored in CMOS

    C. a set of instructions that changes often

    D. a set of instructions that is fixed

14. What chip keeps the system time and date as well as information about the hardware installed in the computer? Hint: It also holds other information that is dependent on the computer and its manufacturer.

A. ROM

B. RAM

C. CMOS

D. CPU

15. _____ tell(s) the CPU what the user or hardware wants, and pass(es) the word on to the operating system.

A. Registers

B. Firmware

C. EFI

D. Interrupt handlers

16. In which part of the boot process is the computer scanned for a working keyboard, random access memory (RAM), disk drives, partitions, and other required hardware?

A. POST

B. BIOS

C. The reading of the data on ROM

D. When the operating system is loaded and finalized

17. _____ is what enables data to be transferred from main memory to a device without passing through the CPU.

A. IRQ

B. DMA

C. The kernel

D. BootX

E. The kernel loader

18. **Which of the following are true regarding a CPU?**

    A. It's often called the processor.

    B. It interprets and executes program instructions.

    C. CPU scheduling generally becomes more complex as traffic and users increase.

    D. All of the above.

19. **Processes are small pieces of code that can include what?**

    A. Jobs

    B. Threads

    C. System calls

    D. Other processes

20. **Which of these is a "processing state"?**

    A. Ready State

    B. Running State

    C. Caching State

    D. Waiting State

    E. Finished State

    F. Listening State

21. **What happens to a process that has to wait an inordinate amount of time for something to happen (perhaps a printer to become available, for instance)?**

    A. The process will try to access the printer for 30 minutes, and if nothing happens, the waiting process will be automatically killed by the CPU Manager.

    B. The CPU Manager might inform the user via an error message that there's a problem, and ask if they'd like to continue waiting or halt (kill) the process.

    C. The CPU Manager might ask the user for help via an error message (for instance, to turn on the printer or insert paper).

    D. The process will be resent to the CPU and then killed if there's no response from the desired printer on the second try.

22. **What kind of processing system has several CPUs that can work together simultaneously?**

    A. Serial

    B. Parallel

    C. Distributed

    D. Integrated

23. **What is the purpose of a system call?**

    A. To convey instructions from the operating system to the kernel and back again

    B. To convey instructions from the operating system to the CPU (or to multiple CPUs) and back again

    C. To convey instructions from a device to the operating system and back again

    D. To manage process control blocks and thread control blocks

24. **Which of the following are correct regarding the order of operations?**

    A. Exponents and square roots are always performed before any other mathematical operation.

    B. Multiplication and division are always performed from left to right and are calculated last.

    C. All calculations in parentheses are calculated first.

    D. All calculations involving addition and subtraction are calculated last.

25. **A(n) _____ is a collection of processes. In a computing environment that supports threads, a *process* is a collection of _____.**

    A. thread; jobs

    B. system call; simple lines of code

    C. job; threads

    D. operating system; jobs

26. **Which allocation scheme offers the system designer the most flexibility, and is thus the one that's used by many present-day operating systems?**

    A. First Come, First Served

    B. Shortest Job Next

    C. Priority Scheduling

D. Shortest Remaining Time

E. Round Robin

F. Multiple Level Queues

27. **What CPU scheduling algorithm is the fairest, even if it is not the most efficient?**

    A. First Come, First Served

    B. Shortest Job Next

    C. Priority Scheduling

    D. Shortest Remaining Time

    E. Round Robin

    F. Multiple Level Queues

28. **What's the main problem with the First Come, First Served scheduling algorithm?**

    A. This allocation scheme assigns a priority level to each process in the Ready queue, depending on its importance, which causes too much overhead for the CPU.

    B. It requires that the system know in advance how much CPU time will be required by each process.

    C. Throughput can drop dramatically when long processes monopolize the CPU.

    D. There is no problem; it's always best to process the jobs as they arrive at the CPU. It's fair and equitable, and there is no overhead.

29. **How many instructions can a five-core system execute at once?**

    A. 2.5

    B. 5

    C. 10

    D. 25

30. **Which of the following allocation schemes are preemptive?**

    A. First Come, First Served

    B. Shortest Remaining Time

    C. Shortest Job Next

    D. Round Robin

31. What's the simplest and most common way to recover a deadlocked system to make it usable again (assuming the system is not a critical one)? (Pick one answer.)

    A. Reboot the system.

    B. Locate and uninstall the program that caused the deadlock.

    C. Wait until the deadlocked processes work it out among themselves.

    D. Wait and respond to the error message that will appear within a few minutes.

32. Which are indications an end user might see that would indicate a deadlocked system?

    A. Blue Screen of Death

    B. Unresponsive keyboard or mouse

    C. Frozen windows or applications

    D. Inability to reboot the machine normally

33. What kind of problem arises when two processes vie for the same resource, and neither request is stopped and neither request is ever granted?

    A. Deadlock

    B. Livelock

    C. Starvation

    D. Abduction

34. When there's a deadlock, which of the following conditions are evident?

    A. Mutual exclusion

    B. Process holding

    C. No preemption

    D. Round Robin wait

35. Can an operating system be created that's "deadlock proof"?

    A. Yes

    B. No

36. **Where there is a deadlock, what do most recovery solutions require first?**

    A. That at least one process be halted and restarted

    B. That all processes be halted and restarted

    C. That all processes be halted and none restarted

    D. That no process be halted or restarted

37. **Main memory, or RAM, can be which of the following?**

    A. A USB stick

    B. A memory chip that is inserted into the motherboard of the computer

    C. A hard drive

    D. An optical drive

38. **Which of the following is stored in main memory?**

    A. Documents you've written and want to store long term

    B. The instructions required for the operating system and open applications to run

    C. Temporary data required to send a print job to the printer

    D. User names and passwords you've told your web browser to remember

    E. Data you've deleted

39. **Memory is separated into two sections. The first is reserved for _____; the second for _____.**

    A. the operating system; incoming processes

    B. waiting processes; the operating system

    C. the operating system; deadlocked and waiting processes only

    D. computer code waiting to be run; computer code that is finalizing

40. **Which type of memory allocation scheme loads an entire job into main memory and rejects any job larger than the size of the main memory?**

    A. Paged memory

    B. Single user

    C. Relocatable dynamic partitions

    D. All of the above

41. To allow several jobs to occupy main memory at the same time, memory space can be divided into _____. (Choose one.)

    A. fragments

    B. allocations

    C. jobs

    D. partitions

42. Of first-fit and best-fit, which scheme is faster to execute, but causes more memory to be wasted?

    A. First-fit

    B. Best-fit

43. Which of the following incorporates compaction to reduce the fragmentation that occurs in main memory?

    A. Paged memory

    B. Single user

    C. Relocatable dynamic partitions

    D. Fixed partitions

44. Which of the following memory allocation schemes allows a job to be divided into equal sections and then loads those job sections anywhere in main memory?

    A. Relocatable dynamic partitions

    B. Paged memory

    C. Single user

    D. None of the above

45. If a job is divided into pages and allocated to page frames that are created in main memory, but the last page frame isn't completely filled, what term is used to describe the unused space in the unfilled page frame?

    A. External fragmentation

    B. Page frame fragmentation

    C. Internal fragmentation

    D. Adjacent fragmentation

46. When jobs are scattered throughout main memory and are not delegated to fixed partitions, how does the memory manager keep track of each process?

   A. It uses a Page Frame Table.

   B. It uses a Page Map Table.

   C. It uses a single Job Table.

   D. It uses a Job Map Table.

47. If you currently have two 500MB sticks of RAM installed in your computer and you install two more that are exactly the same, you now have _____ of installed memory.

   A. 1TB

   B. 2GB

   C. 4GB

   D. 2,048MB

48. What is it that allows some hardware to communicate directly with memory versus going through a memory manager?

   A. DMA

   B. IRQ

   C. Plug and Play

   D. A second-generation device driver

49. Which of the following makes use of available space on a hard drive (or other secondary storage device, such as a flash drive) to temporarily store data that would otherwise require massive amounts of main memory, and then swaps it back when it's needed?

   A. RAM

   B. Log files

   C. Overflow memory

   D. Virtual memory

50. Virtual memory removed the requirement that every _____ of a _____ had to reside in main memory before program execution could begin.

    A. page; job

    B. program; process

    C. thread; process

    D. process; thread

51. Which memory allocation scheme divides a program into logical segments (and not arbitrarily) to limit thrashing, but in return reintroduces external fragmentation?

    A. Demand/segmented paged scheme

    B. Segmented/demand paged scheme

    C. Demand paged allocation scheme

    D. Segmented memory allocation scheme

52. When a page is swapped into main memory, it's called a page fault. What manages these page faults and ultimately decides what pages should be interrupted and what pages should stay and finish?

    A. The Memory Manager

    B. The Page Fault Handler

    C. The Interrupt Handler

    D. The CPU Manager

53. Which page replacement policy (or policies) assumes that the pages that have been in memory the longest are the pages that are least likely to be needed again soon, and opts to swap them before others that have been there for less time?

    A. First-In, First-Out

    B. Least Recently Used

    C. Single user

    D. First-fit

54. Which page replacement policy wants to keep the busiest pages in memory even if they were loaded first and even if they have resided in memory longer than other pages?

A. First-In, First-Out

B. Least Recently Used

C. Best-fit

D. None of the above

55. _____ happens when pages must be quickly and repeatedly loaded and unloaded into main memory because too few page frames are available.

A. Bouncing

B. Fragmenting

C. Thrashing

D. Lashing

56. Which of the following statements are true regarding cache memory?

A. It's a temporary storage area where recently used data is kept.

B. It's a small portion of memory that's made accessible to a device located nearby or main memory.

C. It's main memory, or RAM.

D. It can be a separate chip that can be accessed faster than a hard disk drive.

57. What are the three basic categories of devices?

A. Shared

B. Cached

C. Dedicated

D. Fixed

E. Virtual

58. Storage media is used to store data long term, including backups of data. Which of these is the oldest type of storage and still in use today?

A. Sequential access storage, such as magnetic tape drives

B. Direct access storage, such as external hard drives

C. Solid state drives

D. Direct access drives

59. Regarding the typical hard disk drive: The surface of each disk is divided into concentric circles called _____, and each circle is divided into _____, and a group of those is called a _____.

    A. sectors; tracks; cluster

    B. clusters; tracks; sector

    C. tracks; clusters; sector

    D. tracks; sectors; cluster

60. _____ occurs when data is written to a hard disk, deleted, new data is written and subsequently deleted, programs are installed and uninstalled, and data is otherwise written to and deleted from various areas of the disk.

    A. Compaction

    B. Defragmentation

    C. Fragmentation

    D. Spiraling

61. Which of the following use a laser to read the indentations (called *pits*) and blank spaces (called *lands*) on a layer of the disc?

    A. Optical drives

    B. CDs and DVDs

    C. Blu-ray discs

    D. Solid state drives

62. A CD can hold _____ of data; a common single-layer DVD _____, and a 20-layer Blu-ray disc _____.

    A. 0.7GB; 4.7GB; 500GB

    B. 0.7GB; 8.5GB; 25GB

    C. 4.7GB; 25GB; 500GB

    D. 8.5GB; 50GB; 300GB

63. How do the pits on a Blu-ray disk differ from those on a DVD disc?

    A. They're closer together.

    B. They're farther apart.

    C. They're smaller.

    D. They're larger.

64. **Which of the following can be used to store data long term but have no moving parts?**

    A. A typical hard drive

    B. A solid state hard drive

    C. A thumbnail or flash drive

    D. A magnetic tape drive

65. **What does the interrupt handler do?**

    A. Balances the ebb and flow of interrupts from all system devices

    B. Knows what devices sent which interrupts

    C. Tracks the status of each device

    D. All of the above

66. **A(n) _____ contains the programming code required to manipulate a device (and for the device to communicate with the system).**

    A. interrupt

    B. device manager

    C. device driver

    D. interrupt handler

    E. memory manager

67. **What is the Windows command that lets you see which installed device drivers are unsigned and thus can't be completely trusted to function properly and without issue?**

    A. msconfig

    B. msinfo

    C. sigverif

    D. nslookup

68. **What kind of port is used to manage data sent in parallel, such as printers, zip drivers, and scanners?**

    A. USB

    B. FireWire

    C. Serial

    D. COM

69. To allow a slow I/O device to communicate smoothly with a much faster CPU, the operating system employs which of the following?

    A. A single, double, or circular buffer

    B. An interrupt handler

    C. Direct memory access

    D. A device driver

70. Where does the file manager look first to fulfill a request from the device manager?

    A. File name

    B. Subfolder name

    C. User's directory

    D. Master file directory

71. Which of these is a relative file name?

    A. DSCN0901.jpg

    B. C:\Users\Joli\My Documents\Taxes.doc

    C. Cookies.txt

    D. C:\Windows\Boot

72. Which of these is an absolute file name?

    A. DSCN0901.jpg

    B. C:\Users\Joli\My Documents\Taxes.doc

    C. Cookies.txt

    D. C:\Windows\Boot

73. What's another name for a folder, such as the one located in C:\Users\Joli\My Documents?

    A. Structure

    B. Directory

    C. Library

    D. Archive

74. **Which of the following would not be a good file name for many operating systems?**

    A. Anything longer than 255 characters

    B. Cat\Picture/Favorite

    C. WeddingPhotoJenniferANDAndrew.

    D. TaXes$

75. **Which file attribute(s) could you apply to a file in Windows to allow a user to access the file and view it, but not make any changes to it or run it (if it's an executable file)?**

    A. R

    B. W

    C. X

    D. H

76. **What are the three most popular methods of controlling user access in a file system?**

    A. An access control matrix

    B. An access control list

    C. A capability list

    D. A blocking list

77. **Which type of file organization is best suited for files that are typically processed in their entirety from beginning to end?**

    A. Direct record organization

    B. Sequential record organization

    C. Indexed record organization

    D. None of the above

78. **Which type of file organization is best suited for files that are housed in multiple locations, such as files that have lots of modifications?**

    A. Direct record organization

    B. Sequential record organization

    C. Indexed record organization

    D. None of the above

79. Records are generally assembled into chunks and moved in batches. This is called _____.

    A. blocking

    B. indexing

    C. batching

    D. compressing

    E. zipping

80. A network in a home or small business is most often classified as a _____.

    A. MAN

    B. WAN

    C. LAN

    D. PAN

81. What type of network enables a user to connect to a private local area network from a remote location (such as a hotel), securely, using insecure infrastructure (such as the Internet).

    A. MAN

    B. WAN

    C. VPN

    D. LAN

82. _____ is a technology that's used to connect computers to a cable modem, router, hub, or similar networking device and uses the 802.3 standard.

    A. Ethernet

    B. Fiber optic

    C. Wi-Fi

    D. Coaxial cable

83. Which of the following is true regarding routers?

    A. They always protect the computers on the network from Internet threats such as viruses and worms.

    B. They can be used to share an Internet connection among multiple computers.

C. They can use a routing table to find the shortest path to another router quickly.

D. They can handle data transfer between two dissimilar networks.

84. _____ takes a piece of data and transmits that data to every other computer on the network. It's up to the computer to determine whether or not that data is meant for it. This creates a lot of network traffic and is not ideal.

A. A switch

B. A hub

C. A router

D. A gateway

85. If you are given these—200.158.40.2 and 130.1.58.3—identify what they can be.

A. The IP address of a network gateway

B. The IP address of an Ethernet printer on a local network

C. The IP address of a computer on a local network

D. The IP address of a computer on a remote network

86. If the IP address of the router is 10.10.0.2, what is a viable IP address for the gateway used on that network to move data in and out of it to a dissimilar network?

A. 10.10.0.5

B. 255.255.0.0

C. 10.10.10.10

D. 127.0.0.1

87. Which network configuration and IP addressing scheme is most often seen in small businesses?

A. Bus

B. Star

C. Ring

D. DHCP addressing

E. Static IP addressing

88. Which routing information protocol requires that the data get to its destination in the fewest number of hops?

    A. OSPF

    B. RIP

    C. Circuit switching

    D. Packet switching

89. If you do not have a dedicated connection between two computers, which connection model would you use?

    A. Circuit switching

    B. Packet switching

    C. ISDN

    D. None of the above

90. Data transmission conflicts can be prevented and resolved in various ways. Which of the following data transmission access control options is best when there are lots of nodes with lots of data to send and you need to severely limit data collisions and transmission conflicts? (Pick one.)

    A. Contention

    B. Round Robin

    C. Reservations

    D. Token passing

    E. Distributed Queue, Dual-Bus protocol

91. Ethernet is a _____ protocol.

    A. CSMA

    B. CSMA/CA

    C. CSMA/CD

    D. CSMA/ET

92. What layer of the OSI model provides addressing and routing services? This is where routing tables are accessed and smaller data packets are created too.

    A. Application

    B. Presentation

    C. Session

D. Transport

E. Network

F. Data Link

G. Physical

93. **What layer of TCP/IP (Internet Protocol Suite) routes data, most often through gateways and other network hosts?**

A. Network Access

B. Internet

C. Host-Host

D. Process/Application

94. **Which of the following is true of viruses?**

A. They are small programs that spread from one computer to another without the permission of the computer user.

B. They are not self-executing or self-replicating.

C. They can attack data files, boot files, master boot records, and other areas of the computer and are often difficult to get rid of.

D. They often appear as login boxes and trick some people into inputting user names and passwords so they can be copied.

95. **Which computer threats often slow computers down by making problems for memory and processors and can create "zombie" computers that unknowingly send out spam e-mail for their creators? (Pick only one.)**

A. Viruses

B. Worms

C. Trojans

D. Adware

96. **_____ look(s) at what kind of data is coming into the computer (or gateway, server, or other hardware) and what kind is going out, and if it's an approved data type, let(s) the data through and on to its destination.**

A. Hardware routers

B. Windows Defender

C. Cable, satellite, and DSL modems

D. Firewalls

97. **How does UAC protect a computer from harm?**

    A. It requires that an administrator's user account name and password be input before system-wide changes can be made.

    B. It causes all users to configure and use strong passwords.

    C. It places limits on which users can access which files and folders.

    D. It requires all users to save their data to a network drive.

98. **Although it's easy for home users and small businesses to perform weekly backups using inexpensive software, larger businesses require more attention. What do large companies generally employ for backing up data? (Pick two.)**

    A. They put an external drive next to each computer and tell users to back up their data nightly.

    B. Users' computers are configured to save data to network drives automatically, which are, in turn, backed up regularly.

    C. They configure a backup program to run on each individual computer, and that backup is saved to a network drive.

    D. Domain servers are made available for managing users, computers, and their data.

99. **What helps protect the computer from recently uncovered security holes, malware and adware, and other threats and is offered by the manufacturer of the operating system?**

    A. Encryption

    B. Security updates

    C. User account controls

    D. Optional updates

100. **Which of the following are likely to trigger a user account control prompt?**

    A. Installing a device driver

    B. Accessing a phishing website

    C. Adding or removing user accounts

    D. Reviewing solutions in the Action Center (when using Windows 7)

Answers to Quizzes and Final Exam

Chapter 1	Chapter 2	Chapter 3	Chapter 4
1. D	1. A	1. B	1. B
2. B	2. D	2. A	2. C
3. B	3. B, C	3. A	3. D
4. A, C	4. B	4. D	4. B
5. A, B, C, D	5. B	5. C, D	5. B
6. A	6. A, B, D	6. A, C	6. C
7. C	7. C	7. B, D	7. A
8. B	8. C	8. C	8. C
9. C	9. B	9. C, D	9. C
10. A, D	10. A	10. C	10. D

Chapter 5	Chapter 6	Chapter 7	Chapter 8
1. B, C	1. B	1. B	1. A, C
2. C	2. A, B, C, D	2. C	2. A, C
3. D	3. D	3. B, C	3. D
4. A	4. C	4. A	4. B, D
5. A	5. A	5. A, D	5. A, C, D
6. D	6. C	6. A	6. C
7. A, B, C, D	7. D	7. A	7. A
8. B, D	8. A	8. C	8. B
9. A, B	9. A, C	9. D	9. B, D
10. D	10. B	10. A, B, C	10. B

Chapter 9	Chapter 10	Chapter 11	Chapter 12
1. D	1. A	1. C	1. B
2. B	2. D	2. A, D	2. D
3. A, B, C	3. B	3. A, B	3. A
4. B	4. A, C	4. A	4. B
5. D	5. A	5. B	5. C
6. B, C	6. B	6. E	6. A
7. A	7. C	7. C	7. E
8. B	8. A, B	8. A	8. C
9. C, D	9. B	9. B	9. A, C
10. A, B	10. D	10. C	10. A, B, D

Final Exam

1. A, B, C, D	11. A, B, D	21. B, C
2. D	12. C	22. B
3. A	13. A, D	23. A
4. B	14. C	24. C, D
5. A, B	15. D	25. C
6. C	16. A	26. F
7. C, D	17. B	27. A
8. D	18. D	28. C
9. A	19. B	29. B
10. A, B, D	20. A, B, D, E	30. B, D

31. A
32. A, B, D, C
33. B
34. A, C
35. B
36. A
37. B
38. B, C
39. A
40. B
41. D
42. A
43. C
44. B
45. C
46. B
47. B, D
48. A
49. D
50. A
51. D
52. B
53. A
54. B

55. C
56. A, B, D
57. A, C, E
58. A
59. D
60. C
61. B, C
62. A
63. A, C
64. B, C
65. D
66. C
67. C
68. D
69. A
70. D
71. A, C
72. B, D
73. B
74. A, B, D
75. A
76. A, B, C
77. B
78. C

79. A
80. C
81. C
82. A
83. E
84. B
85. A, B, C, D
86. A
87. B, D
88. B
89. B
90. B
91. C
92. E
93. B
94. A, C
95. B
96. D
97. A
98. B, D, E
99. B
100. A, C

Index

Curriculum Guide

Operating Systems

Beginning

- Introduction to Operating Systems
- Introduction to Computer Science
- Information Science Concepts
- Information Technology Management
- Computer Systems and Peripherals
- Fundamentals of Information Technology
- Computer Applications
- Information Architecture
- Computer Literacy

Intermediate

- Operating Systems Concepts
- Computer Science and Information Technology
- Systems Administration
- Management of Information Systems
- Information System Applications
- Information Technology
- Library Systems and Services
- Business Information Systems
- Communication Technology

Advanced

- Advanced Operating Systems
- Operating System Design Principles
- Designing Business Intelligence Systems
- Systems Analysis
- System Architecture
- Computer Organization and Architecture

CompTIA Certifications

- CompTIA A+
- CompTIA Network+
- CompTIA Security+
- CompTIA Server+

Microsoft Certifications

- MCTS - Microsoft Certified Technology Specialist
- MCITP - Microsoft Certified IT Professional
- MCDST - Microsoft Certified Desktop Support Technician
- MTA - Microsoft Technology Associate

Made in the USA
Middletown, DE
04 November 2021